COUNT OUT CHOLESTEROL COOKBOOK

Frontispiece (Clockwise, starting at upper left):
Carrot Ginger Muffins (Page 86)
Minted Citrus Salad (Page 102)
Cajun Fries (Page 201)
5-Ounce Filet Mignon Steak with Port Wine Sauce (Page 20)

COUNT OUT CHOLESTEROL COOKBOOK

 American Medical Association
Campaign Against Cholesterol

ART ULENE, MD

RECIPES BY

MARY WARD

WITH ADDITIONAL RECIPES FROM *EAT WELL, EAT RIGHT THE ITALIAN WAY* BY EDWARD GIOBBI AND RICHARD WOLFF, MD

Feeling Fine
1989

Barney Taxel, *Photographer*
Donna Jean Morris, *Photo Design/Art Director*
Mary Ward, *Chef/Food Stylist*
Wendy Ward, *Assistant Stylist*

CONTENTS

A Message from the American Medical Association

Since the American Medical Association was founded in 1847, we have been working to promote the health and welfare of all our citizens. This *Count Out Cholesterol Cookbook* embodies the commitment of our members to take an active role in helping their patients achieve healthier lifestyles. We hope the book helps you to attain that goal for yourself and your loved ones. We wish you good health always.

FOREWORD

For more than 30 years we have known that high blood cholesterol increases the risk of coronary heart disease. But only recently were researchers able to prove conclusively that lowering blood cholesterol levels could actually decrease the risk, and—in some cases—even reverse the atherosclerotic process that blocks coronary arteries. If you have high blood cholesterol, for each 1 percent you lower it—up to a point—you can reduce your risk of coronary heart disease by about 2 percent.

There is no single approach that all of us can use to deal with the problem of high blood cholesterol, because we are all different. However, most people can achieve medically significant and personally satisfying reductions in blood cholesterol levels through dietary changes. The most important changes involve reducing the amount of fat you eat (especially saturated fat), decreasing your intake of cholesterol, and increasing the amount of soluble fiber you consume.

All of the recipes in this book have been designed to help you accomplish those goals—without sacrificing the pleasure that comes from eating tasty and attractive food. You will also learn some general principles you can use to modify and adapt your other favorite recipes so they, too, will help you achieve lower cholesterol levels. As you'll see by making and serving these dishes, it is possible to reduce your cholesterol level without boring menus, rigid diets, or forbidden foods.

This cookbook was designed to be used with its companion volume, *Count Out Cholesterol*, which is the official book of the American Medical Association's Campaign Against Cholesterol. That book describes in detail the scientific information you should know about cholesterol, and contains a cholesterol-lowering program that you can tailor to meet your particular needs. For your convenience, the program is summarized in Appendix B at the back of this book.

We welcome any comments or suggestions you might have for future editions of this book. Please direct your comments to us in care of:

The AMA's Campaign Against Cholesterol
3575 Cahuenga Boulevard West
Los Angeles, CA 90068

We wish you success in your effort to control cholesterol through healthful eating, and we extend our best wishes to you for good health.

Arthur Ulene, MD

INTRODUCTION

EATING FOR A HEALTHY HEART

If you are one of those people who associates a cholesterol-lowering dietary program with deprivation and dullness, get ready for a pleasant surprise. You are about to discover how easy and delicious heart-healthy cooking can be. If you'd like a hint of what to expect, glance at the pictures in this book. That's just a sample of the foods you will be able to eat every day by applying the principles set forth here.

The recipes in this book have been designed to help you achieve the following goals:

1. Reduce the amount of fat you eat—especially saturated fat;
2. Decrease the amount of cholesterol you consume;
3. Increase your intake of soluble fiber.

Research shows that most people who achieve these goals will experience significant drops in their blood cholesterol levels. In the pages that follow, you'll learn why that happens. Many of the recipes in this book will help you achieve all three goals at once; others concentrate more on one factor than another. We hope you'll try every recipe at least once, to experience the full range of foods and flavors that can be yours to enjoy in a cholesterol-lowering program.

Even more important than the recipes in this book are the principles behind them. In the pages that follow, you will learn some basic concepts and techniques that you can apply to all of your cooking. You can use them to modify your favorite old recipes or to create brand new ones. As you put these principles to work on a regular basis, you will see why we are able to say that you can lower your cholesterol level without any great sacrifice.

We'll begin by reviewing the scientific reasons behind the cooking goals we have chosen.

1

Reducing Saturated Fats

Fats are an important element in a well-balanced diet. They perform many essential functions: They are a source of energy, they act as building blocks for vital substances made by the body, and they aid in transporting compounds such as fat-soluble vitamins throughout the body. Fats also add taste to food, but excessive fat intake—especially of *saturated* fats—can make your cholesterol level rise. For that reason, the recipes included here are aimed specifically at reducing the amount of dietary fats you consume.

There are three types of fats—saturated, polyunsaturated, and monounsaturated—based on the characteristics of their chemical structure. When cholesterol levels are high, it is usually saturated fats that are the primary culprits. Saturated fats can cause your blood cholesterol level to rise even more than dietary cholesterol itself.

Saturated fats are found primarily in animal products, including fatty meats (beef, veal, lamb, pork, etc.) and many dairy products (whole milk, cream, ice cream, cheese). Although most vegetable products contain only a little saturated fat, tropical oils (coconut, palm, palm kernel) and vegetable shortening are high in these fats. Once saturated fats are consumed, the liver uses them to manufacture cholesterol in the body. If excess cholesterol builds up in the bloodstream, it can lead to the buildup of plaques in your coronary arteries, which can choke off the flow of blood to the heart and increase your risk of a heart attack.

Not surprisingly, then, you need to keep your intake of saturated fats low. To do so, you won't have to give up all of your favorite foods, though you may have to eat them less often and in smaller quantities. We'll show you how to accomplish that without feeling deprived.

The National Cholesterol Education Program (NCEP) recommends that less than 10 percent of your daily calories come from saturated fat; that compares with 15 to 20 percent presently in the average American diet. Later in the book, we'll show you how to use the "SF system" to translate the NCEP recommendation into a program that is personalized to meet your particular needs, based on your sex, ideal weight, and activity level.

Increasing Soluble Fiber

There are two general types of plant fiber: soluble and insoluble (insoluble fiber doesn't dissolve in water). It is the soluble form of fiber that is effective for lowering blood cholesterol levels if consumed in sufficient quantities. It does this by preventing the body's absorption of substances that could be used by the liver to manufacture cholesterol.

There are other benefits from eating a high-fiber diet that occur primarily because of the insoluble fiber present. These include preventing constipation, controlling weight (high-fiber foods tend to be low in calories), and, perhaps, decreasing the risk of colon cancer.

Beans (such as kidney and pinto beans and black-eyed peas) and oat bran are particularly good sources of soluble fiber, but they are not the only foods with cholesterol-lowering properties. Whole-grain breads, cereals, and pasta are rich in soluble fiber, too. The entire spectrum of fruits and vegetables contains some soluble fiber, and some are especially high in it, such as corn, Brussels sprouts, cabbage, prunes, figs, raisins, and apples. The pulp in orange, grapefruit, and other juices is rich in fiber, too. Consequently, foods such as these have been incorporated into many of the recipes in this book.

As good as this may sound, however, you can actually get too much of a good thing. In excess, fiber can cause side effects that include increased gassiness, stomach cramps, and diarrhea. The amount of fiber you should consume varies according to your sex, ideal weight, and activity level, with a recommended upper limit of 18 grams of fiber per day (see Appendix B for guidelines).

Reducing Dietary Cholesterol

Although saturated fat exerts the greatest influence upon high blood cholesterol levels, you can't ignore the cholesterol in the foods you eat. Cholesterol is present in animal tissues (meat, poultry, fish) as well as animal products such as cheese, milk, butter, and eggs. There is no cholesterol in plant foods, including vegetables, fruits, nuts, and cereals. (Some of these foods, however, may contain saturated fat.)

Eggs are probably the best-known contributor of cholesterol to your diet, but that doesn't mean that you have to give up eggs entirely, because all of the cholesterol is in the yolk. Egg whites are an excellent source of protein, and you can use them in many recipes without the yolks and still retain an "eggy" flavor. We'll show you exactly how to do that.

Cholesterol is present in large amounts in organ meats such as liver, kidneys, brains, hearts, and sweetbreads. Some fish and fish products— sardines, anchovies, and caviar—are high in cholesterol as well. You'll need to eat all of these items sparingly, but you can still get enough of them to appreciate their very unique flavors without jeopardizing your cholesterol-lowering goals.

Generally, cholesterol and saturated fat tend to go hand in hand—foods that are low in saturated fat also tend to be low in cholesterol, and foods that are high in one are likely to be high in the other. So as you reduce your consumption of foods high in saturated fat, you'll also cut back on your intake of dietary cholesterol. However, there are some exceptions to this general rule, and it's important to be aware of them so they don't spoil the effect of the other cholesterol-reducing efforts you are making. For example, while shrimp is low in saturated fat, it contains large amounts of dietary cholesterol. Eggs fall into the same category: low in saturated fat, high in cholesterol.

Making the Most of These Recipes

The recipes in this book have been carefully developed to provide ingredients that will help you lower your blood cholesterol level. These ingredients come from a wide variety of food groups, which helps you maintain a balanced diet, and they can be found in most supermarkets. In spite of their healthy nature, you will find them just as easy to prepare as the higher-fat, higher-cholesterol recipes that you may have relied on for years.

To help you use these recipes and adapt other recipes from other sources, we will next present information in the following areas:

1. How to substitute more healthful ingredients in place of those high in saturated fat and cholesterol;
2. How to extend your dishes with low-fat, low-cholesterol foods, and enhance them with flavorings and seasonings that won't raise your blood cholesterol level;
3. How to alter your cooking techniques to produce healthier dishes.

Once you become familiar with these techniques, you can apply them to any other cookbook you may have on your kitchen shelf. You don't need to throw out those old recipes; you just need to adapt them using the techniques you'll read about now.

As for the recipes in this book, we recommend that you use them in conjunction with the program outlined in the American Medical Association's companion volume, *Count Out Cholesterol*. That means utilizing the "SF system," which is a simple approach for keeping track of the saturated fat (SF1) and soluble fiber (SF2) in your diet. This system can help you determine whether you are meeting your own particular dietary requirements for maintaining a low blood cholesterol level. You won't need computers or complex reference books to do this, but rather just the occasional use of special charts that you will find in Appendix B.

The recipes in this book have been designed with the *Count Out Cholesterol* program in mind. At the end of each recipe, you'll find the "SF1," cholesterol, and "SF2" values for that particular dish. These numbers should be used in determining whether you're reaching your own cumulative SF1 and SF2 goals each day. In Appendix B of this book, you'll find an introduction to the SF system, with enough information to help you get started on it now. If you would like more background on cholesterol itself and how it contributes to heart disease, Appendix A can provide you with that information.

It's time, then, to move ahead with the program. There are more than 250 heart-healthy dishes in this book—all of them appetizing and attractive, all designed to help you lower your cholesterol level. Try them, and you will see how easy and enjoyable taking care of yourself can be.

Best wishes for good health and good eating.

I

ADAPTING RECIPES TO LOWER YOUR CHOLESTEROL

Ingredient Substitutions

As we emphasized in the Introduction, you don't have to give up good eating to adhere to a cholesterol-lowering diet. The recipes in this book are as delicious as any you'll find, and they're easy to prepare.

What's more, you don't have to throw out your old recipes. Even a recipe high in saturated fat and cholesterol can be transformed into one that is perfectly acceptable for someone on a cholesterol-lowering program. With some low-fat, low-cholesterol substitutions, you can continue to use your favorite cookbooks, making them "heart-healthy."

It's a relatively effortless process. Some of the alterations are obvious, such as substituting skim milk for whole milk, roast chicken for roast beef, egg whites or egg substitutes for whole eggs. Others may not be quite as evident, but they are just as easy to make. And with these changes, you can in most cases retain the flavor of the original dish. Now let's get down to specifics.

Meats

You don't need to eliminate red meat from your diet to keep your blood cholesterol level low. When a recipe calls for meat, however, you should choose one of the leanest cuts. For beef, that may mean substituting sirloin, round, chuck, or loin. The best pork choices are tenderloin, leg (fresh), and shoulder (arm or picnic). When buying lamb, you should choose cuts of leg, arm, or loin. All trimmed cuts of veal are acceptable, except for those that are commercially ground.

''Select'' grades of meat are lower in fat than ''choice'' or ''prime'' selections, and they are tasty and rich in protein and iron. They should be your first choices.

Poultry

Ounce for ounce, chicken and turkey contain less saturated fat than beef, lamb, and pork. For instance, skinless, light chicken (broiler or fryer) contains one-half the saturated fat of an equal portion of top round beef. (Keep in mind that dark poultry meat has more fat than light.) So you should use poultry as a substitute for meat whenever you can.

Ground or shredded turkey and chicken can be utilized in a number of imaginative ways. For instance, you can use them (instead of ground beef) to make meatballs, meatloaf, chili, tacos, spaghetti sauce, or any of your other favorite ground-beef recipes. However, keep in mind that unless you have the turkey ground to order, it probably won't be as low in fat as you might think. Manufacturers of commercially ground turkey are allowed to grind some of the turkey skin in with the ground turkey, which increases the fat content by as much as 15 percent.

Seafood

Most fish have less saturated fat and cholesterol than red meat and poultry. Those particularly low in saturated fat include halibut, cod, sea bass, rockfish, snapper, haddock, and perch. Even those fish that are higher in saturated fat, such as swordfish, tuna, salmon, and mackerel, are good choices for a cholesterol-lowering diet. These fish are rich in a particular kind of oil called omega-3 fatty acids. Research suggests that these fatty acids have an effect that lowers LDL cholesterol and triglyceride levels in the blood. (If you use any of these fish in their canned forms, make sure to choose the water-packed variety.)

Sedentary shellfish (clams, scallops, mussels) are quite low in saturated fat and moderately low in cholesterol. Shrimp is high in cholesterol, although it has low amounts of saturated fat.

Cheese

As a rule, cheese must be selected carefully and eaten sparingly. Most cheeses have high amounts of fat, making up 65 to 75 percent or more of their calories. Even cheese that's labeled ''low-fat'' or ''part-skim'' might surprise you. For instance, there's almost 3 grams of saturated fat in an ounce of part-skim mozzarella; that's more than twice as much saturated fat as in a 3-1/2-ounce portion of light-meat, skinless chicken.

When you're making substitutions in recipes that call for some of the harder, higher-fat cheeses, use those with a strong flavor that will allow you to cut down on the amount you use. Also, if you grate cheese, you will probably use less of it.

Parmesan, Cheddar, and Sapsago cheeses can be grated and sprinkled on main dishes and casseroles, allowing you to add taste without contributing too much fat. Feta cheese is another good choice, sprinkled in a salad or on top of a casserole. Other acceptable, lower-fat substitutions are part-skim mozzarella and Romano; they'll work just as well in your recipes as their higher-fat counterparts. But as a rule, hard cheeses have to be eaten in limited amounts, even the part-skim varieties.

Check the labels of any cheese you're considering using, and keep this guideline in mind: Any cheese with more than 2 grams of total fat per ounce must be eaten sparingly.

Other Dairy Products

Milk is an excellent source of protein, vitamins, minerals, and, in many cases, cholesterol-raising saturated fat! In the refrigerator section of the supermarket, you can choose from whole milk (3.3 percent fat by weight), low-fat (2 percent or 1 percent), or nonfat or skim (nearly free of fat). But calculations by *weight* can be deceiving. The differences may not seem like much—until you look at grams of fat and calories. Each cup of whole milk contains just over 8 grams of fat. That adds up to 74 calories per cup, which means that 49 percent of the calories in whole milk come from fat. In spite of its name, low-fat milk still contains almost 5 grams of fat, so 35 percent of its calories come from fat. By contrast, nonfat or skim milk contains less than one-half gram of fat per cup. Clearly, nonfat milk is your best option for recipes.

Incidentally, evaporated skim milk works surprisingly well when recipes call for half-and-half or heavy cream. It has the same rich, creamy texture, with only a trace of fat. You can even whip it, but make sure that the milk, as well as the bowl and the beaters, are well chilled before you begin.

Other substitutions in this category are just as easy to make. For instance, rather than using sour cream, try low-fat or nonfat yogurt instead, or a combination of cottage cheese and buttermilk (see Sour Cream Substitute, page 45). While a single tablespoon of sour cream has about 1.5 grams of saturated fat, an entire cup of plain nonfat yogurt has only 0.3 grams of saturated fat. Yogurt works well as a topping for chili or baked potato, or in place of mayonnaise in a salad dressing. It also makes a flavorful base for a dip. Or it can be used in place of sour cream in soups and sauces, although if overheated, it tends to separate. To keep that from happening, add the yogurt at the end of the cooking time and warm gently. Or before heating it, mix one tablespoon of cornstarch into a cup of yogurt.

Eggs

Because of their high cholesterol content, eggs need to be limited in your cooking. But remember that only the yolk is brimming with cholesterol; the egg whites are cholesterol-free, and also contain very little fat.

When recipes call for a whole egg, substitute two egg whites instead. You'll be surprised at how well this adaptation works, particularly in baking. Try it when preparing muffins or breads. You can even scramble egg whites or use them in a flavorful omelet, topped with herbs and spices, or some green pepper, garlic, or onion.

There's still another alternative—egg substitutes. They're widely available in supermarket frozen food sections and can be used when preparing omelets, pancakes, waffles, and French toast.

Oils

What should you do when a recipe calls for browning or sautéing in animal fat, vegetable shortening, butter, or margarine? Substitute a vegetable oil that is lower in saturated fat. These include polyunsaturated oils such as corn oil, safflower oil, and sunflower oil; and mono-unsaturated oils like canola oil and olive oil. *Avoid* palm, palm kernel, and coconut oils; although these oils are commonly used in commercially prepared cakes, cookies, and cereals, they are very high in saturated fats. The following chart shows the amount of fats in common vegetable oils and shortening.

When you are baking, substitutions become a little trickier, but they are still possible. For instance, in a recipe that calls for melted margarine or butter, or vegetable shortening, use a polyunsaturated cooking oil, but cut down the amount. If the recipe recommends *un*melted butter or solid vegetable shortening, your best choice is probably a polyunsaturated margarine.

Be creative with substitutions. For instance, in dessert recipes, for each square (1 ounce) of chocolate, substitute 1 tablespoon of polyunsaturated oil and 3 tablespoons of cocoa. When preparing French fries, use a polyunsaturated oil rather than animal fat, and bake them in the oven instead of deep-frying them so that they absorb less oil.

HEALTHIER COOKING WITH OILS

Here is a breakdown of the amount of saturated and unsaturated fats in cooking oils and shortening. Each figure represents the percentage of total fat in the product. Whenever possible, substitute an oil rich in polyunsaturated or monounsaturated fats for one with high levels of saturated fat.

	Poly-unsaturated	Mono-unsaturated	Saturated
Safflower oil	75%	12%	9%
Sunflower oil	66%	20%	10%
Corn oil	59%	24%	13%
Soybean oil	58%	23%	14%
Cottonseed oil	52%	18%	26%
Canola oil (rapeseed oil)	33%	55%	7%
Olive oil	8%	74%	13%
Peanut oil	32%	46%	17%
Vegetable shortening	14%	51%	31%
Palm oil	9%	37%	49%
Coconut oil	2%	6%	86%
Palm kernel oil	2%	11%	81%

Source: National Heart, Lung, and Blood Institute

One reminder: Even when the oil is polyunsaturated, don't overdo it. Although you're better off with polyunsaturated instead of saturated fats, you need to watch all types of fat in your diet if you want to control your cholesterol level and your caloric intake. Examine every recipe carefully, and see if you can reduce the amount of oil. Try cutting a tablespoon at a time, or eliminate it completely.

Using Extenders and Enhancers

Some people are reluctant to start a cholesterol-lowering program because they believe (incorrectly) that some of their favorite foods and dishes will be forbidden or severely restricted. In this section, you'll see how the use of food extenders and enhancers can solve that problem. Food extenders are low-fat, low-cholesterol ingredients that you can mix into your favorite dishes to dilute or stretch a main ingredient that is high in fat and cholesterol. That means you can still enjoy the main ingredient while consuming less fat and cholesterol in each portion. Food enhancers are ingredients that add flavor to your dishes, so you can cut back on the amount of fat in the dishes you prepare without feeling cheated on taste (fat is an important contributor of flavor to food).

Extenders

You don't have to look far to find good extenders for your favorite dishes: Grains and products made from grains, vegetables, fruits, beans, and lentils all make great choices, and they have been used successfully this way for centuries. In addition to cutting the amount of fat and cholesterol in each portion you serve, these ingredients will usually also increase the amount of soluble fiber and decrease the cost.

All of these foods can be used with meats to reduce the amount of fat and cholesterol per serving without giving up the basic identity of the dish. Mixing grains such as rice or barley, or vegetables such as potatoes, carrots, and tomatoes into a meat recipe maintains the robust nature of the dish while diluting the cholesterol-raising potential of the meat. Using beans to replace a portion of the meat in a chili recipe significantly dilutes the amount of fat and cholesterol in each serving, while enhancing the overall nutritional value of the dish.

Meat recipes are not the only ones that can be extended this way. For example, you can reduce the cholesterol-raising effect of a "creamy" soup by using cooked, puréed vegetables instead of cream. And the addition of beans and lentils to a meat-based soup or stew will make you forget that the amount of meat in the recipe has been decreased. Again, there's a cholesterol-lowering bonus because of the soluble fiber you're adding at the same time.

You should experiment with other extenders as you prepare the recipes in this book and begin to modify recipes in the other cookbooks you own. The possibilities are as endless as your imagination and creativity.

Enhancers

Because fat is such an important contributor to the flavor of foods, you may need to compensate for the fat you are removing from your dishes by adding other sources of flavor to your recipes. A good place to start is with fresh dried herbs and spices. Experiment with a wide variety of them, to see which appeal most to your taste buds. Dill and parsley add a flavoring that most people enjoy; these herbs can be used on everything from fish to poultry to vegetables. Small amounts of garlic, ginger, onions, and shallots can make foods much more interesting; for instance, just a teaspoon of chopped, fresh herbs is enough to liven up several servings of vegetables.

Here are some other options: Add a little red or green sweet pepper to give some "bite" to your recipes. If you want something stronger, try hot peppers, mustard, salsa, or hot sauce. A wine vinegar, or a mellow vinegar like balsamic, is another popular choice. Spicy marinade is one way to add pungency to chicken once its skin has been removed. And to garnish salads or rice dishes, try bean sprouts, or sprouts from wheat seeds or alfalfa seeds.

If you use dressing to flavor your salad, cut down on blue cheese, Roquefort, and any others made with cheese or sour cream. You can make a good dressing alternative with safflower, sunflower, or corn oil, and a little lemon and vinegar. To keep your total fat intake at a reasonable level, limit your consumption of salad dressing to about 1 to 2 tablespoons per serving.

Butter and sour cream may be what you have always enjoyed with baked potatoes, but on a low-fat, low-cholesterol diet, you need to find other taste enhancers. Earlier, we mentioned nonfat yogurt as a substitute for sour cream. To give the yogurt extra taste, try adding some fresh dill, parsley, scallions, green pepper, or chives. Instead of yogurt, some people find that a few tablespoons of stewed tomatoes give potatoes a unique flavor. Or try a combination of dried herbs and a small amount of lemon juice. Speaking of lemon juice, you should always keep fresh lemons in your refrigerator. A little squeeze can add flavor to all kinds of foods. Soy sauce, broths, and bouillons are good seasonings, too, but since they are high in sodium, avoid them if you're on a low-sodium diet.

Incidentally, most people find that the taste of *fresh* flavor enhancers is worth the extra effort that they may require. For instance, using a peppermill for freshly ground black pepper may take a little additional time, but people who do so say that it's worth it. Other types of fresh spices—from garlic to ginger root—can be purchased in many grocery stores, and they'll stay fresh for weeks. You might even consider growing spices and herbs in your garden, or in indoor window pots.

One final suggestion: You can give added flavor to foods by cooking them in wine. For instance, instead of using oil to sauté mushrooms, onions, and other vegetables, try a small amount of wine. All the alcohol evaporates, and only the flavor remains.

Cooking Techniques for Lowering Your Cholesterol

Even if you're very conscientious about using only low-fat, low-cholesterol recipes, you can quickly undermine them in the kitchen because the cooking method you choose will affect the fat content of what you ultimately serve.

Cooking Meats, Poultry, and Fish

As much as possible, you should use methods that allow the fat to drip off during cooking, such as broiling, baking, roasting, and braising. Since fat is lost continuously during cooking, you'll be better off with medium or well-done meat rather than rare.

Avoid frying whenever possible, since it increases a food's fat content significantly. When you fry meat, for instance, it absorbs some of the oil that you've used to coat the pan. At the same time, the fat within the meat can't drain away during cooking.

Let's look at the recommended cooking options a little more closely.

Broiling. Many foods that you might have pan-fried in the past can be broiled. Try broiling meatballs, for example; the advantage here is that the fat will drip into the pan below, so you're not frying the meatballs in their own fat. You also can broil potato slices to create low-fat French fries, or eggplant slices to create eggplant Parmigiana.

Roasting. Meats should be roasted in a preheated oven at about 350°F—a temperature low enough to encourage the fat to drip off. (At higher temperatures, the meat will be seared, keeping the fat in.) To keep the meat moist during cooking—particularly lean meat—baste it with a fat-free liquid (e.g., fruit juice marinade, soy sauce).

Baking. This approach is similar to roasting, but you use a covered container in the oven and may have to add some cooking liquid. It is a particularly good cooking method for less fatty cuts of meat.

Poaching. This is one of the better ways to cook fish, and you don't need a special fish poacher to use this technique; a regular skillet will do just fine. Just add enough liquid (broth, wine, water seasoned with lemon or dill) to cover the fish itself. Cook until the fish is fork-tender.

Steaming. Fish can be steamed in a steamer basket placed in a pan large enough to accommodate it. Put some water—seasoned with herbs, wine, or other flavorings—into the pan, and then insert the steamer with the fish in it. On average, cook the fish about 1 minute for each ounce that it weighs.

Sautéing. When a recipe recommends sautéing, you'll usually cut the food into small pieces and cook it uncovered over high heat. Instead of using fat or oil, try liquids such as wine, flavored vinegars, unsweetened fruit juice, or chicken (or vegetable) broths that have been defatted. Or use a vegetable-oil cooking spray to coat the pan (these sprays now come with flavors such as olive oil and butter).

Cooking Vegetables, Legumes, and Lentils

Since all vegetables are naturally free of cholesterol and most contain very little, if any, saturated fat, your goal is to keep them that way. To do that requires little more than avoiding the temptation to cook them in oils or cover them with sauces that contain saturated fat and cholesterol. You should also choose cooking techniques that preserve as much of the natural nutrition of these foods as possible.

Steaming. Although boiling is a popular way to cook vegetables, many vitamins and minerals are lost in the process. This loss of nutrients is much less likely to occur with steaming. You should put vegetables in a steamer basket once the water (about 1 inch deep) is boiling; after the vegetables are in place, reduce the heat so that the water is simmering. Make sure the water does not touch the food during cooking, and place a lid on the pot. When the vegetables start to become tender—but still retain some crispness—they are ready. That usually takes about 5 minutes for most vegetables cut in serving sizes.

Stir-frying. When stir-fried, vegetables are cooked in very intense heat, but retain their color, texture, and nutrients. There's another advantage as well: You need only a little bit of unsaturated oil to stir-fry (or use small amounts of broth, wine, or lemon juice instead). Pour the oil around the edges of the wok (or heavy skillet), and once the oil is hot, place the food (sliced, diced, or minced) into it. Stir the food constantly, making sure it is slightly coated to seal in the juices. You may need to add some liquid before cooking is complete.

Microwaving. Like steaming, microwave cooking keeps vitamin loss to a minimum. Follow the instructions that come with your oven for specific cooking times.

Cooking Oils

All vegetable oils are not the same. As we pointed out earlier, the saturated and unsaturated fat content of different oils can vary considerably, and so, too, their effect upon your blood cholesterol level. Rely primarily on those oils high in polyunsaturated or monounsaturated fats, and low in saturated fats. That means concentrating on safflower, corn, soybean, cottonseed, sunflower, and canola (rapeseed) oils. Stay away from coconut, palm, and palm kernel oils as much as possible.

Rather than pouring the oil into your pan, apply it with a brush to keep from using too much. All you need is a thin coat of oil, just enough to keep the food from sticking.

You can cut the amount of fat and calories even further with the use of no stick vegetable-oil cooking spray or no stick cookware.

Other Ways to Limit Fat

Here are some other suggestions for low-fat, low-cholesterol cooking:

- Before cooking meat, trim away all its visible fat. (Keep in mind that you can't cut out the fat *within* the meat, so you should buy the leanest cuts possible.)
- With poultry, remove not only all visible fat, but also the skin; by doing so, you'll reduce the saturated fat by about half, or even more. If you believe that the skin is one of the best parts of the chicken, try the following: Dip the skinless chicken parts in skim milk, and then in crushed oat bran cereal; then bake it and enjoy the tasty result.
- Soups, stews, and sauces should be refrigerated before using so the fat in them can rise to the top and congeal; you can then easily skim off the fat before reheating. For each tablespoon of fat you skim off the surface, you remove 120 fat calories.

Adapting Your Recipes to Lower the Amounts of Saturated Fats and Cholesterol

Almost any recipe can be altered to decrease the amount of fat and cholesterol in it. In fact, it is a smart idea to start cooking with half of the amount of fat called for in a recipe. Add more fat only if you need it. In most cases, the chemistry of the recipe will not be altered by this change.

Substituting "better fats" such as polyunsaturated fat (see page 11) also will not significantly change the chemistry of most recipes. The following pages list some specific alterations you can make. Try your favorite recipe with these nutritious changes; in most cases, you'll not only have a reduction of calories, you'll be consuming better fats (from a cholesterol-lowering point of view).

Recipes with Butter, Lard, or Bacon Fat

If your recipe calls for a flavorful fat such as bacon fat, use one-quarter of that amount. Complete the recipe by using one-quarter vegetable oil such as safflower or canola oil. For the remaining half, use either water, vinegar, or cooking stock. Following are recipes for a regular Wilted

Lettuce Salad and a low-fat, low-cholesterol version. Note that in the second version, the amount of bacon is also reduced. The result? A light, delicious salad with flavor, not fat.

<table>
<tr><td>

WILTED LETTUCE SALAD

Serves 8

8 slices raw bacon, cut into
   1/2-inch pieces
1/2 cup sliced green onion
2 tablespoons white wine vinegar

2 teaspoons sugar
freshly ground pepper
8 cups torn leaf lettuce

Fry bacon until crisp. Drain, reserving 3 tablespoons bacon fat. Combine fat with onion, vinegar, sugar, and pepper. Heat to boiling. Pour over lettuce with crumbled bacon. Serve immediately.

</td><td>

LOW-CHOLESTEROL WILTED LETTUCE SALAD

Serves 8

2 slices raw bacon, cut into
   1/2-inch pieces
1/2 cup sliced green onion
3 tablespoons white wine vinegar
1 tablespoon safflower oil
2 teaspoons sugar
freshly ground pepper
8 cups torn leaf lettuce

Fry bacon until crisp. Drain thoroughly. Combine onion with vinegar and oil. Add sugar and pepper. Heat to boiling. Pour over lettuce with crumbled bacon. Serve immediately.

</td></tr>
</table>

Each serving:

 3

 10 mg

 less than 1

    Calories 87

Each serving

 less than 1

 1 mg

 less than 1

    Calories 32

Throughout the book we use the following symbols at the end of each recipe. For an explanation of the SF system, see p. 231.

 = Saturated Fat   = Cholesterol   = Soluble Fiber

To sauté, replace butter with a vegetable oil such as safflower or canola oil. Start with half of the amount in the recipe and use the additional only if you seem to need it. Following are recipes for Chicken with Grapes and a Low-Fat Chicken with Grapes.

CHICKEN WITH GRAPES

Serves 4

2 large, boneless chicken breasts
salt and pepper
1/2 cup butter
4 cups chicken stock
1/3 cup flour
1 cup dry vermouth
dash cayenne pepper
1 cup green seedless grapes

Remove skin from chicken. Cut chicken into 4 pieces. Season chicken with salt and pepper. Melt butter in a heavy skillet. Sauté chicken over moderate heat until golden brown. Add 1 cup chicken stock. Simmer for 15 minutes. Make a white sauce by whisking together the flour, the vermouth, and the remaining stock. Add to cooked chicken and whisk until smooth. Cook until thick and smooth. Sprinkle with cayenne pepper. Place chicken on platter. Add grapes and cover with sauce.

Each serving:

 10

 101 mg

less than 1

Calories 333

LOW-FAT CHICKEN WITH GRAPES

Serves 4

2 large, boneless chicken breasts
salt and pepper
1/4 cup safflower oil
4 cups chicken stock
1/3 cup flower
1 cup dry vermouth
dash cayenne pepper
1 cup green seedless grapes

Remove skin from chicken. Cut chicken into 4 pieces. Season chicken with salt and pepper. Heat oil to medium in a heavy skillet. Sear chicken quickly on both sides. Add 1 cup chicken stock. Simmer for 15 minutes. Make a white sauce by whisking together the flour, the vermouth, and the remaining stock. Add to cooked chicken and whisk until smooth. Cook until thick and smooth. Sprinkle with cayenne pepper. Place chicken on platter. Add grapes and cover with sauce.

Each serving:

 3

 58 mg

less than 1

Calories 280

You may want to try to sauté with no stick cooking spray. This works well when you want simply to sear the meat. After the initial browning, add stock and cook as directed. Following are the recipes for Chicken with Grapes and No-Added-Fat Chicken with Grapes.

CHICKEN WITH GRAPES

Serves 4

2 large, boneless chicken breasts
salt and pepper
1/2 cup butter
4 cups chicken stock
1/3 cup flour
1 cup dry vermouth
dash cayenne pepper
1 cup green seedless grapes

Remove skin from chicken. Cut chicken into 4 pieces. Season chicken with salt and pepper. Melt butter in a heavy skillet. Sauté chicken over moderate heat until golden brown. Add 1 cup chicken stock. Simmer for 15 minutes. Make a white sauce by whisking together the flour, the vermouth, and the remaining stock. Add to cooked chicken and whisk until smooth. Cook until thick and smooth. Sprinkle with cayenne pepper. Place chicken on platter. Add grapes and cover with sauce.

Each serving:

 10

101 mg

less than 1

Calories 333

NO-ADDED-FAT CHICKEN WITH GRAPES

Serves 4

2 large, boneless chicken breasts
salt and pepper
no stick cooking spray
4 cups chicken stock
1/3 cup flower
1 cup dry vermouth
dash cayenne pepper
1 cup green seedless grapes

Remove skin from chicken. Cut chicken into 4 pieces. Season chicken with salt and pepper. Spray a heavy skillet with no stick cooking spray. Heat to medium. Sear chicken quickly on both sides. Add 1 cup chicken stock. Simmer for 15 minutes. Make a white sauce by whisking together the flour, the vermouth, and the remaining stock. Add to cooked chicken and whisk until smooth. Cook until thick and smooth. Sprinkle with cayenne pepper. Place chicken on platter. Add grapes and cover with sauce.

Each serving:

2

58 mg

less than 1

Calories 200

In unthickened sauces, poach the vegetables rather than sauté them. If you use plenty of flavorful liquid (such as stock or wine), you can further concentrate its taste by reducing the sauce. Here is a recipe for Port Wine Sauce and a recipe for Low-Fat Port Wine Sauce.

PORT WINE SAUCE

Serves 4

1/4 cup butter
1/4 cup minced onion
1 cup sliced mushrooms
2 cups port wine
1 cup ham, cut into 1/2-inch
    chunks
2 tablespoons fresh basil,
    chopped

In a medium saucepan, heat butter. Add onion and mushrooms and sauté until browned and soft. Add port wine and simmer until reduced in half. Add ham, continuing to simmer until ham is heated through. Sprinkle with basil. Serve immediately.

Each serving:

 8

52 mg

0

Calories 162

LOW-FAT PORT WINE SAUCE

Serves 4

no stick cooking spray
1/4 cup minced onion
1 cup sliced mushrooms
2 cups port wine
4 ounces 95% fat-free ham,
    cut into slivers
2 tablespoons fresh basil,
    chopped

Coat a medium saucepan with no stick cooking spray. Heat to medium and sauté onion and mushrooms until brown. Add port wine and simmer until reduced in half. Add ham, continuing to simmer until ham is heated through. Sprinkle with basil. Serve immediately.

Each serving:

 less than 1

8 mg

 0

Calories 39

In a sauce such as the Port Wine Sauce, the vegetables could be poached, or gently simmered, in the liquid. When you want a thicker sauce, poach vegetables in the flavorful liquid, then purée in a blender or food processor.

If the sauce is to be thickened with flour, try reducing the amount of fat in the recipe. Here is a White Sauce and a Reduced-Fat White Sauce. Note that in the Reduced-Fat White Sauce, the milk is whisked with the flour, then both are whisked into the hot margarine. This will ensure a smooth sauce.

WHITE SAUCE

Serves 4

2 tablespoons butter

2 tablespoons flour
1 cup whole milk

Melt butter over low heat. Blend in flour and allow to cook in butter for 2 to 3 minutes. Remove from heat. Slowly stir in milk and heat the sauce, blending until thick and smooth. Serve immediately.

Each serving:

SFI 5

CH 24 mg

SF2 0

Calories 102

REDUCED-FAT WHITE SAUCE

Serves 4

1 tablespoon soft corn oil
    margarine
2 tablespoons flour
1 cup skim milk

Melt margarine over low heat. Whisk flour with milk. Whisk into margarine and heat, whisking to keep sauce thick and smooth. Continue to cook and whisk for 5 minutes in order to cook the flour. Serve immediately.

Each serving:

SFI less than 1

CH 1 mg

SF2 0

Calories 61

In butter and egg sauces, such as Hollandaise Sauce, you may reduce the fat by using a blender. Following is a recipe for Hollandaise Sauce and a recipe for Reduced-Fat Blender Hollandaise. Both are delicious, yet the blender sauce has far less saturated fat.

HOLLANDAISE SAUCE

Serves 4

3 egg yolks
1 tablespoon water
1 tablespoon lemon juice
1/4 teaspoon salt
white pepper
7/8 cup butter, melted

Beat egg yolks until thick. Add the water, lemon juice, salt, and pepper. Beat well. Place sauce in the top of a double boiler over hot water. Add 1 tablespoon butter and whisk until sauce starts to thicken. Slowly pour in remaining butter, whisking until sauce is thick and smooth.

Each serving:

 25

 307 mg

 0

    Calories 383

REDUCED-FAT BLENDER HOLLANDAISE

Serves 4

3 egg whites
1 tablespoon lemon juice
1/4 teaspoon salt
cayenne pepper
1/2 teaspoon prepared mustard
1/2 cup soft corn oil margarine, melted

In a blender cup, place egg whites, lemon juice, salt, cayenne pepper, and mustard. Blend on high speed. Slowly add melted margarine. The sauce will be thin but flavorful. For a thicker sauce, place the mixture in the top of a double boiler over hot water. Watch carefully and whisk until sauce thickens.

Each serving:

 4

 0 mg

 0

    Calories 215

Instead of deep-frying foods, try baking them. Meat has a lot of fat within the grain of the meat, and this natural fat will bake out, causing the coating to crisp and brown. Following is a recipe for Veal Scallopine and a version for Turkey Scallopine. The veal is a traditional recipe using a large amount of fat. The Turkey Scallopine uses a light breading for flavor and almost no fat. The breading also adds significant amounts of soluble fiber to your diet. For best results, use an oat bran that is coarsely milled.

VEAL SCALLOPINE

Serves 4

1-1/2 pounds veal scallops
1/2 cup flour
2 tablespoons butter

3 tablespoons olive oil
2 cups beef stock
6 slices lemon, sliced thin
2 tablespoons lemon juice
1 cup dry white wine
2 cups mushrooms, sliced thin
salt to taste
freshly ground pepper

Dip veal scallops into flour. Coat well. Sauté in 2 tablespoons butter mixed with olive oil until golden. Remove veal. Add stock and scrape bits from bottom of pan. Return meat and cover with lemon slices. Cover and simmer for 10 minutes or until meat is tender. To serve, arrange meat and lemon on a platter, and hold in a warm oven. Reheat stock in veal pan. Add lemon juice, wine, and mushrooms. Reduce by half. Salt and pepper and pour over veal.

Each serving:

 11

 161 mg

 0

Calories 513

TURKEY SCALLOPINE

Serves 4

1-1/2 pounds turkey tenderloins
no stick cooking spray
2 egg whites blended with
   2 tablespoons water
1/2 cup oat bran
6 lemon slices, sliced thin
2 cups chicken stock
2 tablespoons lemon juice
1 tablespoon safflower oil
2 cups mushrooms, sliced thin
3 tablespoons minced shallots
1 cup dry white wine
salt to taste
freshly ground pepper

Cut turkey into very thin slices. Preheat oven to 400°F. Spray a jellyroll pan with no stick cooking spray. Dip turkey slices into egg white, then oat bran to coat well. Place on prepared pan and bake for 10 minutes. Cover with lemon and bake 10 minutes longer. Meanwhile, heat chicken stock with lemon juice. Sauté mushrooms and shallots in the oil. Add to chicken stock along with the wine. Reduce by half. Salt and pepper to taste. Arrange turkey scallops on a platter and top with sauce.

Each serving:

 2

 99 mg

 1

Calories 320

We recommend baking Spring Rolls and other foods that are normally deep-fried. Following are two recipes for Spring Rolls. In the first, the Spring Roll is deep-fat fried. Deep-frying will add between 1 and 2 teaspoons fat to each egg roll and will give the egg roll more volume. A baked Spring Roll will stay smaller and more compact, with a crispy outer crust and a hot interior.

FRIED SPRING ROLL

Makes 8 rolls

8 ounces shredded raw chicken
2 tablespoons soy sauce
1 egg white
1 tablespoon cornstarch
1 tablespoon olive oil
2 cups finely chopped vegetables
    (include garlic, scallions,
    mushrooms, bean sprouts,
    pea pods, celery, bok choy)
8 egg roll wraps
vegetable oil for deep-fat frying

Combine chicken with soy sauce, egg white, and cornstarch. Heat the olive oil in a medium-sized saucepan. Quickly sauté chicken mixture. Add vegetables. Cook until vegetables are very tender and mixture is soft. Roll 1/8 of the mixture into each egg roll. In a wok or other heavy pan, heat the vegetable oil. Fry egg rolls until well browned, turning often, about 5 minutes.

Each roll:

SF1 2

CH 15 mg

SF2 less than 1

Calories 155

BAKED SPRING ROLL

Makes 8 rolls

8 ounces shredded raw chicken
2 tablespoons soy sauce
1 egg white
1 tablespoon cornstarch
1 tablespoon olive oil
2 cups finely chopped vegetables
    (include garlic, scallions,
    mushrooms, bean sprouts,
    pea pods, celery, bok choy)
8 egg roll wraps
no stick cooking spray

Combine chicken with soy sauce, egg white, and cornstarch. Heat the olive oil in a medium-sized saucepan. Quickly sauté chicken mixture. Add vegetables. Cook until vegetables are very tender and mixture is soft. Roll 1/8 of the mixture into each egg roll. Preheat oven to 375°F. Spray a baking sheet with no stick cooking spray. Place egg rolls in pan and bake for 15 minutes, until brown.

Each roll:

SF1 less than 1

CH 15 mg

SF2 less than 1

Calories 86

Instead of making French fries, bake sliced potatoes at 450°F for 20 minutes. Potatoes will be browned and delicious. Battered vegetables such as onion rings may also be baked at 400 to 450°F instead of fried.

If you are preparing pastry or pie crust and the recipe calls for butter, lard, or hardened vegetable shortening, substitute soft corn oil margarine. Here are two recipes for a Pie Crust that demonstrate how simple it is to cut the amount of saturated fat you use in baking.

9-INCH PIE CRUST

Serves 6

1-1/4 cups flour
1/2 teaspoon salt
1/3 cup lard
3 tablespoons ice water

Mix flour with salt. With a pastry blender or with 2 knives, cut the lard into the flour. Sprinkle with ice water. Toss with a fork until well blended. Allow to rest for 5 minutes. On a well-floured board, roll out pie crust to fit a 9-inch pie pan. Heat oven to 425°F. Bake for 10 to 12 minutes.

Each serving:

 5

 11 mg

 0

Calories 200

LOWER-FAT 9-INCH PIE CRUST

Serves 6

1-1/4 cups flour
1/2 teaspoon salt
1/3 cup soft corn oil margarine*
3 tablespoons ice water

Mix flour with salt. With a pastry blender or with 2 knives, cut the margarine into the flour. Sprinkle with water. Toss with a fork until well blended. Allow to rest for 5 minutes. On a well-floured board, roll out pie crust to fit a 9-inch pie pan. Heat oven to 425°F. Bake for 10 to 12 minutes.

Each serving:

 2

 0 mg

 0

Calories 187

*If you use "light" corn oil margarine, you'll require less water, as "light" margarine contains more water.

Recipes with Eggs

In almost any recipe calling for eggs, you can use egg whites instead of whole eggs. This will significantly reduce the cholesterol and fat content of the recipes. Egg whites are not only a good source of low-fat protein, they also add moistness and elasticity to foods. We do not recommend using whole eggs except where necessary.

If you are making scrambled eggs or omelets, one idea is to use only half the number of egg yolks as eggs. Here is a recipe for a French Omelet and a recipe for a Lower-Fat French Omelet.

FRENCH OMELET

Serves 2

4 eggs

2 tablespoons water
1/8 teaspoon pepper
2 tablespoons butter

In a small bowl, combine eggs, water, and pepper. Beat with a whisk until mixed well. Melt butter in a large skillet over medium heat. When a drop of water sizzles in the pan, pour in the egg mixture. Cook, lifting edges, so uncooked portion goes under eggs. Fold omelet, and serve immediately.

Each serving:

 11

 579 mg

(SF2) 0

Calories 258

LOWER-FAT FRENCH OMELET

Serves 2

2 whole eggs
4 egg whites
2 tablespoons water
1/8 teaspoon pepper
no stick cooking spray

In a small bowl, combine eggs, egg whites, water, and pepper. Beat with a whisk until mixed well. Coat a large skillet well with no stick cooking spray. Heat to medium. When a drop of water sizzles in the pan, pour in the egg mixture. Cook, lifting edges, so uncooked portion goes under eggs. Fold omelet, and serve immediately.

Each serving:

(SFI) 2

(CH) 274 mg

(SF2) 0

Calories 111

If the recipe calls for hard-boiled eggs, hard-boil the eggs and use only the egg white. This works well in potato and other salads, in egg salad, even in stuffed eggs. Here is a recipe for regular Stuffed Eggs along with a recipe for our Low-Fat Stuffed Eggs.

STUFFED EGGS

Makes 12 stuffed eggs

6 eggs, hard-boiled
1 teaspoon prepared mustard
1/4 cup mayonnaise
paprika

Cut eggs in half lengthwise. Remove egg yolks and crush with mustard and mayonnaise. Refill the egg whites with egg yolk mixture. Sprinkle with paprika.

Each egg half:

SFI 1

CH 139 mg

SF2 0

Calories 73

LOW-FAT STUFFED EGGS

Makes 12 stuffed eggs

6 eggs, hard-boiled
fillings such as: tuna salad made
    with Light Salad Dressing
    (page 101), Famous Vegetable
    Salad (page 126), Lobster Salad
    (page 118), Hot 'n' Spicy Clam
    Dip (page 45)

Cut eggs in half lengthwise. Discard egg yolks. Refill the egg whites with low-fat fillings.

Each egg half:

SFI 0

CH less than 1 mg

SF2 0

Calories 30

Egg whites can even replace egg yolks in recipes where the eggs are separated, such as when the egg yolk is to be used for the custard and the egg white for the meringue. Note that in our Praline Soufflé (page 218), egg whites have been used to create both the custard and the meringue.

Recipes with Dairy Products (Other Than Butter and Eggs)

Cheese is extremely high in saturated fat—ounce for ounce, considerably higher than most cuts of red meat. Therefore, in recipes that call for cheese, divide the amount of cheese called for in half, or use reduced-fat varieties. Use sharp cheeses such as Provolone and extra sharp Cheddar. You may dilute these cheeses with low-fat yogurt. For example, a great cheese topping (ideal for pizza or hot open-faced sandwiches) can be made by combining 1 cup low-fat yogurt with 1/2 cup grated extra sharp Cheddar, Provolone, or Parmesan cheese.

Hard cheeses such as Romano and Parmesan, though full of flavor, are very hard to grate. Food processors and hand graters do not do a good job grating these cheeses. Yet, even half an ounce of finely grated Parmesan, extra sharp Cheddar, or Romano cheese will perk up the flavor of vegetables and vegetable casseroles. We have found the best way to grate these cheeses is with a battery-operated grater. These graters, costing less than $25, are available at specialty and gourmet shops.

In dips, use Sour Cream Substitute to replace sour cream and cream cheese. Following is the recipe for this substitute:

SOUR CREAM SUBSTITUTE

Makes 16 1-ounce servings.

1-1/2 cups 1% (or 1/2%) low-fat cottage cheese
1/2 cup low-fat buttermilk
1 tablespoon freshly squeezed lemon juice with pulp

Place all ingredients in a blender cup. Blend on low speed to combine ingredients, about 30 seconds. Blend on high speed an additional 1 minute to make sauce smooth and thick. Sour Cream Substitute can be kept in the refrigerator for 1 week.

Each serving:

 less than 1   **1 mg**   **0**   **Calories 19**

Here is a recipe for Spinach Dip and a recipe for Low-Fat Spinach Dip, utilizing the Sour Cream Substitute.

SPINACH DIP

Serves 8

1 pound fresh spinach, cleaned
1 cup sour cream
1/2 cup mayonnaise

1/2 cup sliced water chestnuts
2 tablespoons minced onion
1 clove garlic, minced
1 teaspoon dill seed
2 tablespoons chopped pimiento
salt to taste
1 round loaf (1 pound) rye bread

Cook and drain spinach, pressing out all water. Blend with sour cream, mayonnaise, water chestnuts, onion, garlic, dill, and pimiento. Salt to taste. Hollow out bread, reserving interior chunks for dipping. When ready to serve, place bread round on a large platter, scoop dip inside hollow, and place bread chunks around edges.

Each serving:

 5

 21 mg

 less than 1

Calories 317

LOW-FAT SPINACH DIP

Serves 8

1 pound fresh spinach, cleaned
1 cup Sour Cream Substitute
1/2 cup reduced-cholesterol mayonnaise
1/2 cup sliced water chestnuts
2 tablespoons minced onion
1 clove garlic, minced
1 teaspoon dill seed
2 tablespoons chopped pimiento
salt to taste
1 round loaf (1 pound) rye bread

Cook and drain spinach, pressing out all water. Blend with Sour Cream Substitute, mayonnaise, water chestnuts, onion, garlic, dill, and pimiento. Salt to taste. Hollow out bread, reserving interior chunks for dipping. When ready to serve, place bread round on a large platter, scoop dip inside hollow, and place bread chunks around edges.

Each serving:

 less than 1

 6 mg

less than 1

Calories 216

When cooking a recipe with sour cream, try Sour Cream Substitute. It will add the flavor of sour cream with the nutrition of low-fat milk to your recipe. If Sour Cream Substitute tends to lump in the sauce, simply whisk to smooth. Here's a recipe for Quick and Easy Beef Stroganoff and a recipe for Reduced-Fat Beef Stroganoff.

QUICK AND EASY BEEF STROGANOFF

Serves 4

no stick cooking spray
1 pound round steak
1 medium onion, chopped
2 cups beef stock (homemade
   or prepared)
2 tablespoons all-purpose flour
1 cup dry red wine
1 cup sliced fresh mushrooms
1 cup sour cream

Spray a large skillet with no stick cooking spray. Brown meat and onion. Add the beef stock, reduce heat, cover, and simmer for 1-1/2 hours or until meat is tender. Dissolve the flour in 1/3 cup of the wine, stirring until smooth, then whisk into the meat juices until thickened. Add the mushrooms, simmer 5 minutes, then add the remaining wine and sour cream and simmer an additional 5 minutes.

Each serving:

 10

 123 mg

 0

    Calories 383

REDUCED-FAT BEEF STROGANOFF

Serves 4

no stick cooking spray
1 pound round steak
1 medium onion, chopped
2 cups beef stock (homemade
   or prepared)
2 tablespoons all-purpose flour
1 cup dry red wine
1 cup sliced fresh mushrooms
1 cup Sour Cream Substitute

Spray a large skillet with no stick cooking spray. Brown meat and onions. Add the beef stock, reduce heat, cover, and simmer for 1-1/2 hours or until meat is tender. Dissolve the flour in 1/3 cup of the wine, stirring until smooth, then whisk into the meat juices until thickened. Add the mushrooms, simmer 5 minutes, then add the remaining wine and the Sour Cream Substitute and simmer an additional 5 minutes.

Each serving:

 3

 100 mg

 0

    Calories 297

In cream sauces and cream soups, use evaporated skim milk to replace cream. Here are recipes for Cream of Carrot Soup and our Reduced-Fat Carrot Soup.

CREAM OF CARROT SOUP

Serves 4

6 medium carrots, shredded
1 small onion, chopped
1 bay leaf
2 tablespoons butter
3 cups chicken stock
2 teaspoons sugar
freshly ground pepper
1 cup heavy cream
1 tablespoon lemon zest
1 tablespoon chopped parsley

Combine carrots, onion, bay leaf, and butter in a heavy pan with a lid. Cook over low heat until carrots are tender, about 8 minutes. Remove bay leaf. Add chicken stock. Blend in a blender until smooth. Add sugar, pepper, and cream and heat until hot. Divide among 4 bowls and garnish with lemon zest and parsley.

Each serving:

 18

 100 mg

2

Calories 346

REDUCED-FAT CARROT SOUP

Serves 4

6 medium carrots, shredded
1 small onion, chopped
1 bay leaf

3 cups chicken stock
2 teaspoons sugar
freshly ground pepper
1 cup evaporated skim milk
1 tablespoon lemon zest
1 tablespoon chopped parsley

Combine carrots, onion, bay leaf, and stock in a heavy stock pot with a lid. Heat to a simmer. Cook for 15 minutes. Cool slightly. Remove bay leaf. Blend in a blender until smooth. Add sugar, pepper, and evaporated milk and heat until hot. Divide among 4 bowls and garnish with lemon zest and parsley.

Each serving:

 less than 1

CH 3 mg

2

Calories 182

Recipes with Meat

Meat makes a delicious flavoring for foods. It also adds vitamins, minerals, and essential protein. However, we don't need nearly as much meat as most of us eat. Meat should be thought of as a flavoring instead of a staple. In most recipes, the amount of meat can be cut in half with vegetables or carbohydrates increased likewise.

When a recipe calls for bacon, either eliminate it entirely or decrease it considerably. If the recipe calls for 1 pound of bacon, use no more than 1/4 pound. When you cook the bacon, make sure you either microwave it until very crisp or fry it until very crisp. Drain it to make sure all external fat has been removed. In a bacon, lettuce, and tomato sandwich, for example, use just 1 slice of bacon. Crumble the bacon on top of the tomato to make it stretch.

When a recipe calls for ground meat, substitute ground turkey. Or blend ground turkey with ground beef, ground pork, or ground veal. Four ounces of ground turkey has 1.8 grams of saturated fat compared to 8 grams in 4 ounces of ground beef and 12 grams in ground pork.

Hints for Reducing Saturated Fat in Your Diet

- Eliminate butter on bread or rolls, if possible. A good substitute is "light" margarine used sparingly.
- Ask to have toast served "dry." Use jelly or jam to replace butter.
- On French toast and pancakes, eliminate butter. Use Fruit Sauce (page 68) for a nutritious alternative to pancake syrup.
- When a rich milk is required, use low-fat buttermilk. Make sure the buttermilk you purchase says "low-fat."
- Try to add low-fat dairy products such as part-skim mozzarella cheese, ricotta cheese, low-fat yogurt, low-fat cottage cheese, and other reduced-fat cheeses. Use high-fat cheeses sparingly.
- Use Sour Cream Substitute (page 45) instead of sour cream.
- In most recipes, egg whites can be used for whole eggs (1 egg = 2 egg whites).
- When you have salad, go easy on the salad dressing. Ask to have salad dressing served "on the side." Better still, ask for a squeeze of lemon or lemon wedges for a salad dressing.

- When you make salad dressing, cut the oil called for by half.
- For desserts, use fruit, fruit purée, or fruit flambés. Ice milk or nonfat yogurt is a good alternative to ice cream.
- Eat low-fat snacks such as raisins and prunes, fresh fruit, cut up raw vegetables, Salsa with Chips (page 35), and dips made with Sour Cream Substitute (page 45).
- Chill soups and soup stocks. When cold, the fat on top of the soup will congeal and can be easily removed.
- Refer to the saturated fat chart (Appendix B) in this book and use it as a guide to menu planning. For example, you'll note that the leanest meat is roast turkey breast. If you roast your own turkey breast, you'll consume far less saturated fat than if you purchase turkey breast from the deli. You'll also save money. So keep your own home-roasted turkey on hand for sandwiches—turkey reubens, turkey clubs, and hot turkey sandwiches.

2

APPETIZERS & GRAZING TREATS

Throughout the book we use the following symbols at the end of each recipe. For an explanation of the SF system, see p. 231.

 = Saturated Fat   = Cholesterol   = Soluble Fiber

HUMMUS

This Middle Eastern dip is quick and easy to make. Serve it with pieces of pita bread, with vegetable crudité, or as a spread on crackers. The secret to a great tasting hummus: richly toasted sesame seeds.

Makes 2 cups, 8 servings

1/2 cup sesame seeds
1 can (19 ounces) garbanzo beans with liquid
1 clove garlic, sliced into 3 pieces
1 freshly squeezed lemon (3 tablespoons lemon juice)
1 teaspoon salt
1 small onion, chopped
sesame seeds for garnish
chopped green onions for garnish

In a small skillet, toast sesame seeds over high heat. Stir and shake pan as it heats to toast the seeds evenly.

Place sesame seeds in a blender cup. Add remaining ingredients, cover, and blend on low for 30 seconds. Uncover and stir. Blend on high for 1 minute or until all ingredients are blended into a smooth spread. Garnish with sesame seeds and chopped green onions.

Each serving:

 less than 1   **0 mg**   1   **Calories 104**

ROASTED CECI BEANS

Keep these crunchy treats around and you'll find yourself nibbling on healthy snacks. They are also great on salads and in sandwiches. This is a fun and easy snack because there are so many ways to flavor it—with cajun seasonings, herb-garlic, Italian seasonings, and so on.

Serves 6

no stick cooking spray
1 can (19 ounces) garbanzo or ceci beans
seasoned salt or salt-free seasoning

Preheat oven to 350°F. Spray a jellyroll pan with no stick cooking spray.

Drain the beans. Spread them over the pan and sprinkle with the salt or seasoning. Bake for 45 minutes to 1 hour, stirring occasionally so that beans are evenly cooked. The beans should be browned and crunchy.

Store beans in an airtight container.

Each serving:

 0   **0 mg**   1   **Calories 65**

SALSA WITH CHIPS

Homemade salsa is very nutritious. In fact, it has lots of vitamin A, vitamin C, dietary fiber, and soluble fiber. If you toast your own chips, you'll have an appetizer that is nutritious and tasty. For additional Mexican flavor, sprinkle corn tortillas with a little cumin before baking.

Serves 10

10 corn tortillas
3 large tomatoes, very ripe
1/2 cup fresh cilantro, washed
1 teaspoon salt
1 small onion, coarsely chopped (optional)
2 tablespoons canned or fresh jalapeño peppers, chopped
1 clove garlic, minced (optional)

Salsa with Chips (*continued*)

Preheat the oven to 400°F. Cut each tortilla into 8 pieces. Place on an ungreased cookie sheet. Bake for 15 minutes or until the chips are browned and crisp. Cool. Stored in airtight plastic bags, these chips will stay fresh for up to 1 week.

Meanwhile, cut each tomato into 8 wedges. Place the tomatoes in a blender or food processor along with the cilantro, salt, and onion. Pulse several times to make chunky salsa. Stir in jalapeños and garlic.* Serve immediately or store in refrigerator until serving. Salsa will keep for up to 1 week refrigerated. Stir thoroughly before serving.

Each serving:

 1   0 mg   1   **Calories 75**

*For a smooth salsa, continue to blend for 1 minute.

SMOKED FISH SALAD
Edward Giobbi

Any combination of smoked fish will work in this recipe—eel, white-fish, etc.

>   *Makes 4 generous servings.*
>
>   1 smoked trout
>   1/2 pound smoked sturgeon
>   2 medium potatoes, boiled, cooled, peeled, and sliced
>   Juice of 1 lemon
>   1/2 tablespoon good mustard
>   1 teaspoon small capers
>   1 tablespoon extra virgin olive oil
>
>   2-1/2 teaspoons safflower oil
>   1/2 cup thinly sliced whole scallions
>   2 tablespoons finely chopped Italian parsley or fresh coriander
>   Freshly ground black pepper to taste

Skin trout by cutting through it on the back with a sharp knife and then pulling off skin. Remove flesh from bones, cut in pieces, and place in a bowl. Cut sturgeon in pieces 1/4 inch thick and about 1 inch long and discard any bones. Combine with the trout and potatoes. Put lemon juice, mustard, capers, and oils in a small bowl and whip until well blended. Mix the dressing, scallions, parsley or coriander, and black pepper carefully with the fish and serve at room temperature.

Each serving:

 2   26 mg   1   **Calories 261**

BAYOU SHRIMP

Here's an appetizer that you can prepare up to 2 days in advance. It is filling and nutritious.

Serves 6

1/3 cup tarragon vinegar
1 tablespoon catsup
2 tablespoons freshly grated horseradish
   (or prepared horseradish sauce)
1 teaspoon prepared mustard
2 teaspoons cajun seasoning
1/4 cup sliced green onions or scallions with tender green tops
2 large tomatoes, chopped
1-1/4 cups chopped celery
1 pound medium-sized cooked, cleaned shrimp
6 cups shredded salad greens (iceberg lettuce, romaine lettuce, radicchio, and Bibb lettuce)

In a medium-sized bowl, combine and whisk the vinegar, catsup, horseradish, mustard, cajun seasoning, and onions. Add tomatoes, celery, and shrimp and stir to coat. Marinate in refrigerator for 4 to 5 hours.

To serve, arrange 1 cup lettuce on each of 6 salad plates. Arrange the shrimps and sauce over the lettuce.

Each serving:

 less than 1   **148 mg**   **less than 1**   **Cal. 97**

SHRIMP AND PEPPER SALAD
Edward Giobbi

It is important to use a very thin pasta so as not to overwhelm this dish—let the pasta serve more as a bridge between the roasted peppers and the shrimp.

Makes 4 servings.

1/2 pound shrimp, with shells on
2 large sweet red peppers, about 1 pound*
1/4 pound capellini (break pasta in half)
1 tablespoon coarsely chopped fresh mint
1 teaspoon finely chopped garlic
1 tablespoon finely chopped fresh ginger
4 tablespoons thinly sliced whole scallions
Juice of 1/2 lemon
2 tablespoons extra virgin olive oil
1 teaspoon safflower oil

*Green peppers may be used, but red are better.

Shrimp and Pepper Salad (*continued*)

Steam the whole shrimp for about 2 minutes; do not overcook—they will be cooked when they turn pink. Let cool, then remove and discard shells and heads.

In the meantime, roast peppers over a gas flame, turning, until blackened all over. When cool, remove charred skin and seeds and slice the peppers. Add peppers to shrimp.

Cook pasta in rapidly boiling water (it will cook in several minutes). Drain.

Add pasta to shrimp and peppers, along with the rest of the ingredients, and gently mix. Serve at room temperature. Do not refrigerate.

Each serving:

 1   83 mg   less than 1   Cal. 212

CARIBBEAN MEAT PÂTÉ

Meat pâté is a traditional food of the West Indians living in the American Virgin Islands. For this version, we have reduced the fat and cholesterol, increased the fiber, yet maintained great flavor. This recipe takes a little time, but it is well worth the effort.

Makes 10, 2-pâté servings

Dough

1-1/2 to 2 cups all-purpose flour
1 cup yellow cornmeal
2 tablespoons sugar
1 teaspoon salt
1 egg
2 egg whites, beaten
5 tablespoons skim milk

Filling

2 tablespoons vegetable oil
1 large onion, finely chopped
1 cup chopped celery
2 cloves garlic, minced
1 jalapeño pepper, seeded and minced (optional)
1 pound ground chicken or turkey
3 tablespoons chili powder
1 cup grated potato
1 cup chicken stock (or water)
salt to taste
vegetable oil for frying

Appetizers and Grazing Dishes (Clockwise, starting at upper left):

Mahogany Chicken Wings (Page 47)
Stuffed Mushrooms, Greek Style (Page 49) with
Smoked Fish Salad (Page 36) in the center
Baked Oysters (Page 40)

To make the dough, combine 1-1/2 cups flour with the cornmeal, sugar, and salt in a medium-sized bowl. Whip egg and egg whites lightly with milk. With a pastry blender, cut the egg mixture into the flour mixture. Add a little extra flour, if necessary, to make an elastic dough. Form dough into 20 balls.

Next, make the filling: Heat 2 tablespoons vegetable oil in a large pan. Add the onion, celery, garlic, jalapeño pepper, ground chicken or turkey, and chili powder. Sauté until the meat is well browned. Add the potato and the stock, cover, and cook an additional 10 minutes. Drain meat and cool for 10 minutes. Salt to taste.

Heat the vegetable oil in a deep-fat fryer or in a heavy saucepan until it is 375°F (at this temperature, a bread cube will brown in about 5 minutes).

Next, on a floured board, roll a dough ball (with a rolling pin) as thin as possible, about 5 inches in diameter. Fill with 2 to 3 tablespoons of the hot meat mixture. Fold the dough over in half to make a half moon and crimp edges of the pâté by pressing with the tines of a fork. Repeat with the other dough balls and the remaining meat filling.

To Fry

Place a few of the pâté in a deep-fat frying basket. Lower into the fat and fry for 3 to 4 minutes until pâté is golden brown. Meat pâté may be served immediately or refrigerated and reheated by placing in a 350°F oven for 10 minutes. Cooked or uncooked pâté may be frozen for up to 1 month.

Each serving (deep-fried):

 2   57 mg   1   **Calories 301**

To Bake

Preheat oven to 375° F. Place meat pâté on a large cookie sheet that has been sprayed with no stick cooking spray. Bake for 25 minutes or until pâté are browned.

Each serving (baked):

 less than 1   39 mg   1   **Calories 228**

BAKED OYSTERS

During oyster season, you may be tempted to buy freshly shucked oysters. Here's a recipe for them that is easy and delicious. It is also very nutritious. If you can't buy fresh oysters with the shell, use oysters in liquor and bake them on small, ovenproof plates or shells and pour a little oyster liquor around each.

Serves 6

24 fresh oysters, shucked (or 1 pint select oysters)
rock salt (optional)
2 tablespoons extra virgin olive oil
1 tablespoon minced onion
2 tablespoons unbleached white flour
1 cup chicken broth
1/3 cup dry white wine
1/2 cup fresh mushrooms, minced
1/2 cup cooked shrimp, chopped
1 egg white
1 tablespoon evaporated skim milk
1/4 cup wheat germ
1/4 cup freshly grated Parmesan cheese
salt to taste
freshly ground pepper
parsley sprigs for garnish

Preheat the oven to 350°F. Remove half of the oyster shells and discard. Place oysters with their half shell on a large jellyroll pan or two (a bed of rock salt will hold shells in place). Bake the oysters in their own juices for 8 minutes. (If you are using oysters in liquor, divide the pint of oysters between 6 ovenproof plates or shells. Pour a little oyster liquor around each.)

Heat oil in a medium-sized saucepan. Sauté onion until translucent. Sprinkle flour over this mixture. Gradually whisk in the chicken broth and wine, and whisk until smooth. Stir in mushrooms and shrimp. Whisk mixture over low heat until smooth and blended, about 4 minutes. Remove from heat. Beat egg white with milk and slowly add to hot chicken sauce, whisking constantly. Blend until smooth and thick.

Remove oysters from oven and cover each with 1 heaping tablespoon of the hot sauce. Sprinkle with wheat germ and Parmesan cheese. Bake for an additional 10 minutes until topping is golden brown.

Each serving:

 2   41 mg   less than 1   Cal. 181

TASTY CHEESE BISCUITS

You'll love the flavor of these crackers. They are so easy to make, and they keep well. Use these tasty biscuits with appetizer dips, as rolls for small turkeyburgers, with soup or salad, or sliced in half and filled with Famous Vegetable Salad (page 126), or with Hot Crabbies (page 44).

Makes 40 biscuits

1 package (1/4 ounce) active dry yeast
1 cup very warm water (115°F)
1 cup oat bran (for best results, use an oat bran
   that is coarsely milled)
1-1/2 to 2 cups all-purpose white flour
1/4 cup freshly grated Parmesan cheese
1 teaspoon salt
1/4 cup vegetable oil
no stick cooking spray

In a medium-sized bowl, dissolve the yeast in the warm water.

Mix the oat bran and the flour with the Parmesan cheese, salt, and the oil until well blended. Add the yeast mixture and knead lightly until dough sticks together.

Spray another medium-sized bowl with no stick cooking spray. Place the mixture in a warm bowl, cover, and allow the dough to rise in a warm, draft-free place for 30 minutes. After the biscuit dough has risen, knead it for 2 to 3 minutes, incorporating additional flour until dough is easy to handle.

Spray 2 large cookie sheets with no stick cooking spray. Between 2 layers of plastic wrap, roll out the dough to 1/8-inch thickness. Cut into 1-1/2-inch rounds (or into other shapes you desire). Place the shapes on the cookie sheet 2 inches apart. Cover and allow to rise in a warm, draft-free place for 15 minutes.

Preheat oven to 400°F. Bake the biscuits for 8 to 10 minutes until well browned on tops and bottoms.

Each biscuit:

 less than 1   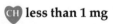 **less than 1 mg**   **less than 1**   **Cal. 39**

TURKEY MEATBALLS, MEXICAN STYLE

Ground turkey is lean, low in cholesterol, and very tasty. In this appetizer recipe, we've teamed ground turkey with Mexican spices and salsa for a wonderfully nutritious treat.

Turkey Meatballs, Mexican Style (*continued*)
Makes 24 meatballs

> no stick cooking spray
> 1 pound ground turkey
> 2 egg whites
> 1/4 cup chopped cilantro (available in most supermarket
>   produce departments, or use parsley)
> 1 medium-sized onion, chopped
> 2 cloves garlic, minced
> 2 fresh or canned medium or hot jalapeño peppers, minced
> 1 teaspoon salt
> 1/2 teaspoon ground cumin

> *The Salsa*

> 2 large tomatoes, very ripe
> 1 can (4 ounces) diced green chilis, undrained
> 1/3 cup chopped cilantro
> 1 teaspoon salt

Preheat oven to 325°F. Spray a 9×9-inch baking pan with no stick cooking spray.

Combine the ground turkey with the egg whites, cilantro, onion, garlic, 2 jalapeño peppers, salt, and cumin. Mix until the mixture holds together well. Wet your hands and form the meat into 24 1-inch balls. Place them in the prepared pan and bake for 10 minutes.

Meanwhile, to make the salsa, use a blender cup or food processor and blend the tomatoes, canned chilis, cilantro, and salt until very smooth.

Pour the salsa over the hot meatballs, stir, and bake for 5 more minutes. Serve immediately.

Each meatball:

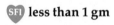 less than 1 gm   11 mg   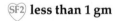 less than 1 gm   **Cal. 31**

ARTICHOKE NIBBLES

Artichoke hearts are delicious, but they are often served in sauces that are high in fat and cholesterol. For this recipe, we've combined low-fat water-packed artichoke hearts with delicious seasonings. If you are an artichoke lover, this is a recipe you must try.

> *Serves 8*

> no stick cooking spray
> 1/4 cup mayonnaise-type Light Salad Dressing (page 101,
>   or use prepared)

1 teaspoon Dijon mustard
1 tablespoon prepared horseradish
1/4 cup low-fat yogurt
2 cans (14 ounces each) water-packed artichoke hearts
1/2 cup freshly grated Parmesan cheese
1/2 cup fresh bread crumbs
salt to taste
freshly ground pepper

Preheat oven to 350°F. Prepare a 9-inch glass pie pan or decorative quiche dish by spraying it with no stick cooking spray.

Blend together the salad dressing, mustard, horseradish, and the yogurt. Drain and rinse the artichoke hearts. Pat dry between paper towels. Cut the artichoke hearts into small, bite-sized pieces.

Mix the artichoke heart pieces with the sauce. Toss the Parmesan cheese with the bread crumbs. Salt and pepper to taste. Sprinkle half of the crumbs in the prepared dish. Top with the artichoke mixture. Sprinkle with remaining bread crumb mixture.

Bake until crusty and browned, about 30 minutes. Allow to cool for 5 to 10 minutes, then cut into 8 wedges and serve on colorful plates. Or, allow to cool completely, cut it into squares, and serve cold.

Each serving:

 less than 1 gm 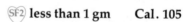 **10 mg** **less than 1 gm** **Cal. 105**

CHILI CON QUESO WITH CHORIZO

Chorizo sausages are delicious but very high in fat and cholesterol. In this recipe, we've teamed small amounts of chorizos with chili hot beans. Beans are an excellent addition as they not only reduce the overall fat and cholesterol and add significantly to the fiber, but also add to the rich Tex-Mex flavor.

Serves 16

4 ounces chorizo sausage (available at many supermarket
   meat counters, or use hot Italian sausage)
1 small onion, chopped
2 tablespoons chopped green pepper
1 can (22 ounces) chili hot beans
1/4 cup shredded Monterey Jack cheese
salt to taste
freshly ground pepper
chopped green onion for garnish
chopped tomato for garnish
corn chips, nachos, or toasted tortillas

Chili con Queso with Chorizo (*continued*)

Preheat oven to 350°F.

Remove the casing from the sausage. Crumble the meat into a medium-sized skillet and sauté over medium heat until the meat is well cooked. Drain the fat from the skillet and rinse the sausage. Return the meat to the skillet with the onion and green pepper. Add the beans, heat, and simmer until beans are hot and vegetables are tender, about 10 minutes. Fold cheese into sausage mixture and stir until cheese melts. Salt and pepper to taste.

Pour into a serving dish, garnish with chopped onion and tomato, and serve hot with corn chips, nachos, or warmed tortillas.

Each serving:

 2   7 mg   2   **Calories 177**

HOT CRABBIES

This mixture will keep for up to a week, and it makes a great spur-of-the-moment snack. We serve Hot Crabbies on toasted English muffin halves, but it is also great on Tasty Cheese Biscuits (page 41) and on wheat crackers.

Serves 6

no stick cooking spray
3 tablespoons all-purpose flour
1 cup skim milk
7 to 8 ounces fresh, frozen, or canned crabmeat, drained
1 tablespoon minced pimiento
1 tablespoon chopped green onion or scallions
2 tablespoons green pepper, chopped into 1/4-inch pieces
1/2 teaspoon Dijon mustard
1/4 cup freshly grated Parmesan cheese
salt to taste
freshly grated pepper
6 toasted whole wheat English muffin halves
paprika for garnish
mint or parsley sprigs

Preheat oven to 350°F. Spray a cookie sheet with no stick cooking spray.

Whisk the flour into the milk in a 2-quart saucepan. Heat, whisking constantly, until smooth and thick. Remove from heat and add the drained crabmeat to the sauce along with the pimiento, green onion, green pepper, mustard, and cheese. Blend well. Salt and pepper to taste.

Place the toasted English muffin halves on the prepared sheet and divide crabmeat filling among them. Bake for 10 minutes. Garnish with the paprika and parsley or mint sprigs.

Each serving:

 1   42 mg   **less than 1**   **Cal. 164**

SOUR CREAM SUBSTITUTE

This is a good recipe to make and have on hand. It can be used in all recipes calling for cold sour cream. Note: When you heat the Sour Cream Substitute, be sure to stir it well.

Makes 4 1/2-cup servings

1-1/2 cups 1% low-fat cottage cheese
1/2 cup low-fat buttermilk
2 tablespoons freshly squeezed lemon (1/2 lemon)

Place ingredients in blender cup. Blend until smooth.
    This mixture will keep, refrigerated, for up to 2 weeks. Stir before using.

Each serving:

 less than 1   **5 mg**   **0**   **Calories 76**

HOT 'n' SPICY CLAM DIP

Using our Sour Cream Substitute (above) in this recipe gives you less fat and fewer calories. It also increases the amount of calcium in this dip. And with all the delicious seasonings, you'll never miss the fat.

Serves 16

1 cup Sour Cream Substitute (above)
2 tablespoons chopped pimiento
2 tablespoons chopped green pepper
1 tablespoon minced onion
1 clove garlic, minced
1 tablespoon prepared horseradish
1 teaspoon Worcestershire sauce
2 tablespoons skim milk
1 can (6-1/2 to 8 ounces) minced clams
salt to taste
freshly ground pepper
parsley sprigs
crackers, Tasty Cheese Biscuits (page 41), or vegetable crudité

Hot 'n' Spicy Clam Dip (*continued*)

In a 2-cup bowl, mix the Sour Cream Substitute with the pimiento, green pepper, onion, garlic, horseradish, Worcestershire, and the milk.

Drain and rinse the clams. Fold into the Sour Cream Substitute mixture. Refrigerate for at least 1 hour. Salt and pepper to taste. Garnish with parsley sprigs and serve cold with crackers, Tasty Cheese Biscuits, or vegetable crudité. Or serve warm. To warm, heat the oven to 350°F. Spray a 1-quart baking dish with no stick cooking spray. Bake for 10 to 15 minutes, just until dip is hot.

Each serving:

 1   17 mg   less than 1   Cal. 149

IDAHOS WITH HERBS

Hot potatoes make a wonderful appetizer. These are spicy as well as tasty.

Serves 6

2 large Idaho potatoes
no stick cooking spray
1/4 cup low-fat yogurt
1 egg white, beaten
1/4 cup freshly grated Parmesan cheese
1/2 cup finely crushed saltines
1/4 cup finely chopped fresh basil (or 2 tablespoons dry basil)
2 tablespoons finely chopped fresh tarragon
    (or 1 teaspoon dry tarragon)
1/2 teaspoon paprika
1 tablespoon freshly grated Parmesan cheese for garnish
chopped parsley for garnish
salt to taste
freshly ground pepper

Scrub the potatoes with a vegetable brush to remove any surface dirt or blemishes. Slice into 1/2-inch slices, wash, and pat dry.

Preheat oven to 350°F. Spray a large cookie sheet with no stick cooking spray.

Blend the yogurt with the egg white in a medium-sized bowl. Add the potatoes and coat them well with the yogurt mixture.

In a paper or plastic bag, mix the Parmesan cheese with the saltines, basil, tarragon, and paprika. Shake to ensure proper blending of ingredients.

Drop the potatoes into the bag in batches and shake to coat evenly.

Place the potato slices in a single layer on the prepared sheet. Bake for 35 minutes until the potatoes are golden and tender.

Remove to a serving tray and sprinkle with the grated Parmesan cheese and chopped parsley. Salt and pepper to taste.

Each serving:

 1   7 mg   (SF2) 2   **Calories 160**

MAHOGANY WINGS

If you have a taste for chicken wings, try these. They are hot, spicy, and delicious. To reduce the fat and cholesterol even further, use lean chicken breast strips in place of the wings.

> *Serves 6 (3 wing pieces)*
>
> 2 pounds chicken wings (or 1 pound boneless, skinless chicken
>   breast cut into 1 × 1/2-inch strips)
> 2 tablespoons teriyaki sauce
> 1/2 cup plum sauce (available in oriental food departments and
>   in some supermarkets, or use plum preserves)
> 2 tablespoons brown sugar
> 1 tablespoon Worcestershire sauce
> 1 clove garlic, minced
> 1 slice ginger root, minced (or 1/2 teaspoon ground ginger)
> 1 tablespoon arrowroot
> 2 tablespoons water
> no stick cooking spray

Cut off wing tips and discard. Separate the wings at the joints. Cut off any visible fat. Wash and pat dry. Or simply use the chicken strips.

In a medium-sized saucepan, combine the teriyaki sauce, plum sauce, sugar, Worcestershire sauce, garlic, ginger, arrowroot, and water. Heat, whisking the sauce, until smooth and thick and the sugar and arrowroot are dissolved. Put chicken wings (or strips) in the hot marinade, cover, and refrigerate for 4 hours or overnight.

Preheat oven to 400°F. Spray a large baking pan with no stick cooking spray. Drain marinade from chicken wings. Bake wings for 15 minutes until they are tender and crispy. (Or, bake chicken strips for 10 minutes.) Serve hot.

Each serving (3 wings):

(SFI) 8   (CH) 129 mg   (SF2) 0   **Calories 485**

For chicken strips, each serving:

(SFI) 1   (CH) 51 mg   (SF2) 0   **Calories 165**

MEXICAN PIZZA

One way to reduce fat and cholesterol is to use high-fiber beans in recipes. We've done just that in this recipe.

Serves 16

no stick cooking spray
2 jalapeño peppers, seeded and chopped
   (or use canned jalapeños)
2 medium-sized, ripe tomatoes, quartered
1/4 cup fresh cilantro (available in produce department
   of most supermarkets)
1/2 teaspoon salt
4 Corn Tortillas (page 92)
2 cups mashed chili hot beans (or Mexican kidney beans)
2 tablespoons chopped green onion, or scallions
1 cup shredded Monterey Jack cheese
cilantro sprigs for garnish
chopped jalapeño peppers as accompaniment

Preheat oven to 400°F. Spray a large cookie sheet with no stick cooking spray.
   Put the jalapeños, tomatoes, cilantro, and salt in a blender or food processor. Pulse salsa several times until it is chunky.
   Place the tortillas on a baking sheet. Top each tortilla with 1/4 of salsa, mashed beans, green onions, and cheese. Bake for 15 minutes. The cheese will be melted and lightly browned and the crust will be crisp. Cut each pizza into 4 wedges and serve with cilantro sprigs for garnish and chopped jalapeño peppers as an accompaniment.

Each serving:

 less than 1   **0 mg**   **1**   **Calories 104**

SPINACH BACON DIP

In this recipe, we've used just a taste of bacon. Cook or microwave the bacon as crisp as possible to remove as much of the fat as you can.

Serves 8

1 package (10 ounces) frozen chopped spinach,
   cooked and drained
1 cup Sour Cream Substitute (page 45)
1/2 cup minced fresh parsley
4 green onions, chopped with tops

    1 can (4 ounces) water chestnuts, chopped
    1/2 cup Light Salad Dressing (page 101 or prepared)
    2 tablespoons freshly squeezed lemon juice (1 small lemon)
    1 teaspoon fresh dill (or 1 teaspoon dried dill)
    1 slice bacon, fried crisp, drained, and crumbled
    salt to taste
    freshly ground pepper
    thin slices red radish for garnish
    Tasty Cheese Biscuits (page 41), whole-grain crackers, or
        vegetable crudité

Make sure all water is squeezed from the spinach and blend the spinach with the Sour Cream Substitute, parsley, onion, water chestnuts, Light Salad Dressing, lemon, and dill. Fold in crumbled bacon. Salt and pepper to taste. Refrigerate for at least 1 hour before serving.

Serve dip in a small bowl garnished with sliced radishes. Serve with Tasty Cheese Biscuits, whole-grain crackers, or vegetable crudité.

Each serving:

 less than 1   **2 mg**   **less than 1**   **Calories 57**

STUFFED MUSHROOMS, GREEK STYLE

These stuffed mushrooms are excellent! They are easy to make, delicious to eat, and an excellent source of vitamins and calcium.

Makes 8 3-mushroom servings

    no stick cooking spray
    1 package (10 ounces) frozen chopped spinach,
        cooked and drained
    24 large mushrooms
    1/2 cup chopped green onions, or scallions,
        including tender tops
    2 cloves garlic, minced
    1/2 cup 1% low-fat cottage cheese
    1/4 cup freshly grated Parmesan cheese
    1/4 cup feta cheese
    1/2 cup chopped fresh mint (or 2 tablespoons dried mint)
    salt to taste
    freshly ground pepper
    mint leaves for garnish

Preheat oven to 375°F. Spray a baking pan with no stick cooking spray. Make sure all water is squeezed from the spinach.

Stuffed Mushrooms, Greek Style *(continued)*

Clean and stem the mushrooms. Chop the mushroom stems. Spray a 1-quart saucepan with no stick cooking spray. Place mushroom stems, green onions, and garlic in the saucepan and cook until tender, about 5 minutes.

To make the filling, blend the spinach with the cooked vegetables, cottage cheese, Parmesan cheese, feta cheese, and mint. Salt and pepper the filling to taste. Fill mushroom caps with spinach mixture, mounding high in center. Bake in the oven for 15 minutes. Garnish with mint leaves and serve immediately.

Each serving:

 2   9 mg   less than 1   **Cal. 63**

STUFFED MUSHROOMS WITH RAISINS AND SHERRY
Edward Giobbi

Serves 2

4 to 6 large mushrooms
1 tablespoon olive oil
1 tablespoon safflower oil
2 tablespoons finely chopped onion
1 tablespoon finely chopped Italian parsley
3 tablespoons bread crumbs
1 tablespoon yellow raisins
salt and freshly ground pepper to taste
dry sherry

Preheat oven to 450°F.

Separate stems from mushroom caps and chop stems. Heat the oils in a small skillet, then add the onion and chopped mushroom stems. Sauté over moderate heat until onion begins to brown. Turn off heat. Mix in the parsley, bread crumbs, raisins, salt, and pepper. Stuff mushroom caps with this mixture. Arrange the mushrooms in a shallow baking dish and bake them in the oven for about 15 minutes. Sprinkle with dry sherry. Cook another 5 minutes. Serve hot.

Each serving:

 2   0 mg   1   **Calories 188**

3

SOUPS

VEGETABLE STOCK

Vegetable stock can be used for any vegetable-based soup, such as Old-Fashioned Split Pea Soup (page 64), Cauliflower Cheese Soup (page 59), Broccoli Soup (page 58), or Cabbage Soup (page 63). It also makes a very nice vegetable bouillon. You'll need to plan about 3 hours for this stock to develop a fine flavor. This stock and the chicken and meat stocks that follow should be made in large quantity and then refrigerated (up to 1 week) or frozen (up to 3 months) in small containers. If you freeze the stock in ice cube trays, you'll have a source of low-fat, low-salt flavoring for vegetables and other dishes.

Makes 3 quarts (12 servings)

1 tablespoon olive oil
3 cups chopped onion
2 cloves garlic, minced
2 cups carrot chunks
2 cups celery tops with leaves
2 cups fresh or frozen corn
2 cups mushrooms, sliced in half
2 cups chunked zucchini or yellow squash
3 bay leaves
3 quarts water
salt to taste
freshly ground pepper

In a large soup kettle, heat the olive oil. Sauté the onion and the garlic until they are translucent. Add the remaining vegetables and the bay

51

Vegetable Stock (*continued*)

leaves. Cover with 3 quarts water. Bring to a boil, lower heat, cover, then simmer for 3 hours, adding more water as necessary. Strain stock through a sieve that has been lined with a piece of cheesecloth. Salt and pepper the stock to taste.

Each serving:

 less than 1   **0 mg**   **0**   **Calories 25**

MEAT STOCK

We associate beef stock with high-fat, high-cholesterol stock. If you simply refrigerate the stock and then defat it, you'll have a wonderful, low-fat flavor base for meat soups as well as sauces. Use meat stock as a base for Hoppin' John (page 60) or Hearty Beef Stew with Barley (page 58). Meat stock is a hearty flavored stock that may be used in rich vegetable soups, in stews, and as a base for sauces such as spaghetti sauce.

Makes 12 cups

3 pounds beef bones (beef shanks, neck bones, roast bones, etc.)
2 pounds pork neck bones
1 large onion, chopped
1 cup chopped celery
1 chopped carrot
3 bay leaves
12 cups water
salt to taste
freshly ground pepper

Preheat the oven to 250°F. Place the beef bones in the stock pot and roast for about 4 hours.

Add the onion, celery, carrot, and the bay leaves to the beef bones and cover with 12 cups water. Heat to boiling, reduce heat, cover, then simmer for 3 hours, adding more water as necessary. Strain the stock through a sieve that has been lined with cheesecloth. Salt and pepper the stock to taste. Refrigerate the stock until the fat congeals. Before using, defat the stock by removing the congealed fat from the top and edges of the stock container.*

Each cup:

 less than 1   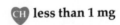 **less than 1 mg**   **0**   **Calories 23**

*Another way to skim fat is to add 6 cups of ice cubes to the hot soup stock. Fat will congeal on the ice cubes and may be removed with the ice cubes. This is a faster method to remove fat, but it will water stock down considerably.

CHICKEN STOCK

Chicken stock is the classic stock for hot and cold soups. It is the base of all chicken and turkey soups and may also be used in place of fish stock, vegetable stock, and beef stock. This version is low in fat and salted to taste. Use chicken stock for Black Bean Stew (page 61) and for Chilled Vichyssoise (page 63). It is also delicious with cooked noodles or rice.

Makes 12 cups

5 pounds chicken backs and necks
1 large onion, chopped
2 cloves garlic, sliced
1 cup roughly chopped celery with leaves
2 large carrots, chopped
1 cup mushrooms, sliced in half
3 bay leaves
12 cups water
salt to taste
freshly ground pepper

Rinse the chicken well. Place the chicken in a large stock pot and cover with water. Bring the water to a boil. Discard this first water, which will have an off-flavor residue from the chicken.

Cover the chicken parts with 12 cups more water. Add the onion, garlic, celery, carrots, mushrooms, and bay leaves. Bring this to a boil, reduce heat, cover, then simmer for 3 hours, adding more water as necessary. Strain the chicken stock through a sieve that has been lined with cheesecloth. Discard the bones, bay leaf, and vegetables. Salt and pepper stock to taste. Refrigerate the chicken stock overnight. Before using, defat the stock by removing the congealed fat from the top and edges of the stock container.*

Each cup:

 less than 1   **0 mg**   **0**   **Calories 25**

*Another way to skim fat is to add 6 cups of ice cubes to the hot soup stock. Fat will congeal on the ice cubes and may be removed with the ice cubes. This is a faster method to remove fat, but it will water down the stock considerably.

VEGETABLE CHOWDER

Vegetable chowder is slightly different from the other stocks in that the vegetables are not strained, which results in a thick, chowder-type soup. Vegetable chowder makes a wonderful eating chowder. If it is puréed in the blender, it is also a delicious base for hearty bean and pasta soups

Vegetable Chowder (*continued*)

such as Hearty Golden Lentil Soup with Potatoes (page 55) and Cabbage Soup (page 63).

Makes 12 cups

1 tablespoon olive oil
3 large onions, chopped
3 cloves garlic, minced
1 cup fresh or frozen corn
1 cup sliced carrots
1 cup fresh or frozen green beans
1 cup sliced zucchini
1 cup chopped tomato
1 cup sliced fresh mushrooms
salt to taste
freshly ground pepper

Heat the olive oil in a large stock pot. Add the onion and garlic and cook until well browned. Add the remaining vegetables and 12 cups of water. Heat to boiling, reduce heat, cover, then simmer for 3 hours, adding more water as necessary. Salt and pepper the stock to taste. Cool stock.

Serve as is or purée in 3 or 4 batches in a blender or food processor.

Each cup:

 less than 1   0 mg   1   **Calories 46**

GREEN VEGETABLE SOUP
Edward Giobbi

Serves 6

1/2 cup chopped green cabbage
1 medium onion, chopped
1/2 cup chopped celery
1/2 cup chopped broccoli
1/2 cup green beans, cut into 1-inch pieces
1/2 cup diced zucchini
2 tablespoons chopped Italian parsley
2 tablespoons chopped fresh basil
4 cups water
1 medium potato, diced
2 tablespoons olive oil
1 tablespoon safflower oil
salt and freshly ground black pepper to taste

1/2 cup ditalini pasta or other small-cut pasta
2 tablespoons Pesto (page 195)

Put all ingredients except the pasta and pesto in a pot and bring to a boil. Cover and boil gently about 1 hour. Add pesto and turn off the heat.

Bring a large pot of water to a boil, add the pasta, and cook until *al dente*—do not overcook. Drain and rinse in cold water. Add to the minestrone. Serve at room temperature with garlic bread.

Each serving:

 1   0 mg   1   **Calories 156**

HEARTY GOLDEN LENTIL SOUP WITH POTATOES

This soup is easy to prepare, and it's packed with flavor and good nutrition.

Serves 12

12 ounces golden lentils, picked over and cleaned
8 cups beef stock (fresh or prepared)
1 can (16 ounces) tomatoes, chopped with liquid
2 tablespoons chopped parsley
1 large onion, diced
1 bay leaf
2 cloves garlic, crushed
2 medium carrots, sliced thin
4 medium red potatoes, cubed with skins on
salt to taste
freshly ground pepper
chopped tomato for garnish
parsley sprigs for garnish

In a large soup pot, combine the lentils with the beef stock, tomatoes, parsley, onion, bay leaf, and garlic. Bring to a boil, reduce heat, cover, and simmer for 1 hour until lentils are tender. Add the carrots and potatoes and water as necessary to maintain level of liquid. Cook for an additional 30 minutes, stirring occasionally until potatoes are tender. Salt and pepper the soup to taste. Remove bay leaf before serving. Top each bowl of soup with chopped tomato and a large sprig of parsley.

Each serving:

 less than 1   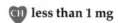 less than 1 mg   2   **Calories 203**

LENTIL SOUP ABRUZZI STYLE
Edward Giobbi

Serves 6 to 8

2 cups dried lentils, washed and drained
5 cups water
1 bay leaf
1 teaspoon thyme
1 teaspoon basil
1 teaspoon marjoram
1 finely chopped onion
salt and freshly ground pepper to taste
12 roasted chestnuts
3 tablespoons olive oil
1 tablespoon safflower oil
1 tablespoon tomato paste, diluted in 1 cup warm water
4 tablespoons chopped Italian parsley
8 slices toasted bread

Put the lentils, water, bay leaf, thyme, basil, marjoram, onion, salt, and pepper in a pot, cover and boil gently about 1 hour, or until lentils are tender.

In the meantime, score chestnuts on concave side with a sharp knife and roast them in a preheated 450°F oven about 12 minutes. Let them cool just till you can handle them, then peel off and discard skins. Chop the nuts and set aside. Heat oils in a small skillet, add chestnuts, simmer for a minute or so, add diluted tomato paste, parsley, salt, and pepper. Cover and simmer several minutes. Add this mixture to the lentils. Cover and simmer 10 minutes.

Place a piece of toasted bread in each soup plate and pour the lentil soup over the bread.

Each serving (for 8 servings):

 1   0 mg   3   **Calories 392**

BEAN SOUP FRANKOWITCH
Edward Giobbi

Serves 6

2 cups dried white beans, preferably cannellini or Great
    Northern, or 2 cans Progresso cannellini beans
5 cups cold water
3 cloves garlic
2 bay leaves

1 tablespoon crushed rosemary
salt and freshly ground pepper to taste

The Flavored Oil

2 tablespoons olive oil
1 tablespoon safflower oil
2 cloves garlic, minced
hot pepper flakes to taste (optional)

8 to 10 slices French or Italian bread

Put the dried beans in a bowl, cover with water, and soak overnight. Drain. Place beans in a soup pot, preferably terracotta, add the water, garlic, bay leaves, rosemary, salt, and pepper. Bring to a boil, then cover and boil gently about 2-1/2 hours, or until beans are tender. Stir occasionally.

Remove half the beans with a slotted spoon. Set aside and keep warm. Place remaining beans with their broth in a food processor or blender and purée.

To make the flavored oil, heat the oils, garlic, and pepper flakes in the soup pot. As garlic begins to take on color, add the reserved whole beans and bean purée. Mix well and remove from heat, keeping the pot covered.

Toast slices of French or Italian bread. After bread is toasted, sprinkle with olive oil, then rub garlic on each slice. Place toasted bread on the bottom of the soup plates and pour the hot bean soup on top.

To serve the toasted bread as an appetizer or side dish, place 1 piece of toast on a flat dish and pour over just enough of the bean mixture to cover bread.

Each serving:

 2   **0 mg**   **4**   **Calories 471**

PASTA AND CORN SOUP
Edward Giobbi

Serves 4

1 tablespoon margarine or butter
1 tablespoon safflower oil
1 small onion, minced
2 cups corn kernels, preferably fresh, although frozen will do
4 cups water
3/4 cup small pasta, such as small elbows, tubettini, etc.
salt and freshly ground black pepper to taste
2 tablespoons minced Italian parsley

Pasta and Corn Soup (*continued*)

Heat the margarine or butter and oil in a small pot, then add the onion. Sauté until onion wilts, then add corn and water. Boil gently 15 minutes. Add pasta and salt and pepper to taste. Boil gently until pasta is *al dente*. Add parsley and serve.

Each serving:

 2   **10 mg**   **3**   **Calories 209**

HEARTY BEEF STEW WITH BARLEY

This stew is a meal in a bowl with lean chunks of beef, vegetables, and tender barley. Serve this very hearty dish to your hungry friends with Minted Citrus Salad (page 102) or a tossed vegetable salad. It's delicious.

Serves 6

no stick cooking spray
2 pounds beef stew meat, trimmed of all fat
4 cups beef stock (homemade or prepared)
1 cup pearl onions (fresh or canned)
1 teaspoon dry basil leaves
1/4 cup fresh parsley, chopped
1 cup uncooked barley
1-1/2 cups sliced carrots
salt to taste
freshly ground pepper

Spray a dutch oven or heavy cooking pot with no stick cooking spray. Heat to hot, then add the beef and brown on all sides. Remove beef to paper towels and pat off excess fat. Rinse dutch oven.

Return the browned beef to the pot and add the beef stock, onions, basil, parsley, barley, and carrots. Bring to a boil, cover, and reduce the heat to simmer stew. Simmer for 1 hour. Salt and pepper to taste. Ladle into wide bowls and serve immediately.

Each serving:

 4   **76 mg**   **1**   **Calories 301**

BROCCOLI SOUP WITH PASTA

Here's a favorite soup. In this version, we've added whole-grain pasta and beans to make a complete protein. This is a very colorful soup, with a lot of flavor.

Serves 10

1 cup 13 (or 15) bean mix
1 bunch broccoli
2 tablespoons olive oil
1 medium-sized onion, chopped
3 cloves garlic, minced
2 quarts chicken stock (homemade or prepared)
1 cup whole-grain pasta elbows,
    cooked according to package directions
salt to taste
freshly ground pepper

In a medium-sized bowl, soak the beans overnight. Drain.

Wash the broccoli and cut into small florets. Peel the stems and cut into slices. In a soup pot, heat the olive oil. Add the broccoli stems, onion, and garlic and cook until the vegetables are soft. Add the chicken stock and drained beans. Heat to boiling, reduce heat, cover, then simmer for 45 minutes to cook beans. Add water to maintain level as necessary. Add broccoli florets and cooked pasta and simmer for 10 minutes or until broccoli is just cooked. Salt and pepper to taste. Ladle into soup bowls and serve immediately.

Each serving:

 less than 1   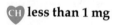 **less than 1 mg**   **3**   **Calories 178**

CAULIFLOWER CHEESE SOUP

For this soup, use a very sharp Cheddar cheese.

Serves 10

1 quart chicken stock (homemade or prepared)
1 medium onion, chopped
2 carrots, sliced into 2-inch lengths
1 head cauliflower, trimmed and cut into florets
3 tablespoons whole wheat flour
2 cups skim milk
1/2 cup shredded extra sharp Cheddar cheese
salt to taste
freshly ground pepper
chopped parsley for garnish
ground nutmeg for garnish (fresh, if possible)

In a large soup pot, bring the chicken stock with the onion, carrots, and cauliflower to a boil, then reduce heat, cover, and simmer. Allow the soup to simmer for 20 minutes until vegetables are tender. Cool slightly.

Cauliflower Cheese Soup (*continued*)

Purée the stock and vegetables until smooth in a food processor or blender. Do this in 2 or 3 batches.

Return the purée to the soup pot. In a small bowl, whisk the flour with the milk. Slowly add the mixture to the cooled cauliflower purée. Return to the heat, and heat to a boil, whisking the soup until it is thick. Add cheese and stir to melt. Salt and pepper to taste. Serve soup in deep bowls. Garnish with chopped parsley and a sprinkle of nutmeg.

Each serving:

 1   7 mg   1   **Calories 80**

HOPPIN' JOHN

The traditional New Year's Day soup of the southwest, Hoppin' John combines high-soluble fiber black-eyed peas with vegetables and spices. For this recipe, the usual fatty ham bone has been replaced with lean cubes of reduced-fat ham. We recommend that you serve this with a cool, tossed green salad and plenty of French bread.

Serves 8

4 cups chicken stock (homemade or prepared)
1 package (10 ounces) frozen black-eyed peas,
    thawed and drained
1 large onion, chopped
1/4 teaspoon black pepper
1/4 teaspoon cayenne pepper
1 clove garlic, minced
1 bay leaf
8 ounces fat-free ham, cubed
salt to taste
freshly ground pepper
4 cups cooked brown rice

In a medium-sized saucepan, heat 1 cup chicken stock to boiling, then add the peas, bring to a boil again, and cook for 10 minutes. Now add the remainder of the stock, along with the onion, black pepper, cayenne pepper, garlic, and bay leaf. Bring to a boil, cover, and simmer for 20 minutes or until peas are tender. Remove the bay leaf, add the cubed ham, and season to taste with salt and pepper. Serve in wide bowls over cooked brown rice.

Each serving:

 less than 1   9 mg   1   **Calories 229**

BLACK BEAN STEW

This is a hearty stew that has almost no fat. Tomatoes and pumpkin give it a rich flavor. It is very high in fiber, low in fat, and excellent when served with just a dollop of yogurt and a slice of lime.

Serves 10

6 oz | 1 package (12 ounces) black beans, washed and picked over
no stick cooking spray
3/4 | 1-1/2 cups chopped green onion or scallions, including tender tops
1 1/2 | 3 cloves garlic, minced
13 oz | 1 can (26 ounces) tomatoes
1/2 | 1 cup fresh or canned unseasoned pumpkin purée
3/4 | 1-1/2 cups beef stock (fresh or prepared)
1/2 | 1 tablespoon cumin
3/4 | 1-1/2 tablespoons balsamic (or red wine) vinegar
6 | 8 ounces fat-free ham, cut into small squares
freshly ground black pepper
1/2 | 1 cup dry sherry
salt to taste
1/2 | 1 cup low-fat yogurt
sliced green onion for garnish
5 | 10 lime slices

Place the beans in a large saucepan and cover with boiling water to a level of 3 inches above the beans. Simmer until the beans are tender, about 3 hours. Drain.

Spray the large saucepan thoroughly with no stick cooking spray. Sauté the onion and garlic until just soft. Add the tomatoes, pumpkin purée, beef stock, cumin, vinegar, and black beans. Simmer for 25 minutes. Add the ham, black pepper, and sherry and heat thoroughly. Salt to taste. Serve in large bowls with a dollop of low-fat yogurt, a sprinkle of green onions, and a slice of lime.

Each serving:

 less than 1   **7 mg**   **1**   **Calories 175**

HAM AND BEAN SOUP

This soup will be ready in 45 minutes. It is tasty and best when served with a good corn bread, such as the Old-Fashioned Corn Bread (page 93). So easy to make, this soup is also an excellent source of soluble fiber.

Ham and Bean Soup (*continued*)

> *Serves 4*
>
> 1 can (14 ounces) pinto beans with liquid
> 3 cups chicken stock (homemade or prepared)
> 1 grated carrot
> 1 finely chopped onion
> 2 cloves garlic, minced
> 1 cup celery, chopped with tops
> 1/2 cup fat-free ham
> salt to taste
> freshly ground pepper

Put beans with their liquid in a medium-sized saucepan. Add chicken stock, carrot, onion, garlic, and celery. Heat to boiling, reduce heat, cover, and allow to cook for 30 minutes until vegetables are tender. Add ham and heat for 5 minutes. Salt and pepper to taste. Serve immediately.

Each serving:

 less than 1   **6 mg**   **3**   **Calories 230**

CHICK PEA SOUP
Edward Giobbi

> *Serves 3 to 4*
>
> 20-ounce can chick peas (ceci beans), drained
> 1-1/2 cups water
> 1 teaspoon minced garlic
> 1 teaspoon crushed rosemary
> salt and freshly ground black pepper to taste
> 1/2 cup small pasta, such as tubettini, elbows, etc.
> 1 teaspoon safflower oil
> 1 tablespoon excellent olive oil
> 1 tablespoon finely chopped Italian parsley for garnish

Put all ingredients except pasta, oils, and parsley in a soup pot. Simmer about 20 minutes. Add pasta and cook until it is almost *al dente.* Add safflower oil. When pasta is *al dente,* stir in olive oil.

Garnish each bowl of soup with parsley.

Each serving (for 4 servings):

 1   **0 mg**   **5**   **Calories 226**

CABBAGE SOUP

This soup will become a favorite. The cabbage blends well with the flavors of the other vegetables.

Serves 8

8 cups vegetable or chicken stock (homemade or prepared)
1 medium onion, chopped
2 medium-sized all-purpose potatoes, cubed, with skins on
3 ribs celery, sliced
1 large tomato, chopped
1/4 teaspoon celery seed
1 small head of cabbage, shredded
1/4 cup chopped parsley
1/2 teaspoon paprika
1/4 teaspoon pepper
salt to taste
freshly ground pepper
1/4 cup freshly grated Parmesan cheese

In a large soup pot, heat the stock with the onion, potatoes, celery, tomato, celery seed, cabbage, parsley, paprika, and pepper. When the soup boils, reduce heat, cover, and simmer for 30 minutes until vegetables are tender. Add water, if necessary. Salt and pepper to taste. Top each serving with Parmesan cheese.

Each serving:

 less than 1   **less than 1 mg**   SF2 **1**   **Calories 115**

CHILLED VICHYSSOISE

Make this early on a hot day for a quick and easy lunch or dinner.

Serves 8

3 cups chicken or vegetable stock (homemade or prepared)
1/2 leek bulb, sliced
3 celery ribs with tops, sliced
2 large red potatoes, cubed with skins on
1 cup skim milk
1/4 teaspoon white pepper
1/4 teaspoon hot sauce
salt to taste
freshly ground pepper
chopped parsley

Chilled Vichyssoise (*continued*)

In a large soup pot, bring the stock with the leek, celery, and potatoes to a boil, then reduce heat, cover, and simmer for 30 minutes. The potatoes should be very tender. Add the milk, pepper, and hot sauce. Salt to taste.*
Chill for at least 4 hours before serving. To serve, place the soup in chilled bowls and top with freshly ground pepper and chopped parsley.

Each serving:

 less than 1   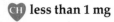 **less than 1 mg**   **1**   **Calories 88**

*For smooth vichyssoise, purée in blender or food processor in 2 or 3 batches.

OLD-FASHIONED SPLIT PEA SOUP

This smooth soup has old-fashioned flavor, yet it takes less than 2 hours to make from start to finish. It's loaded with soluble fiber and flavor.

> *Serves 8*
>
> 12 ounces split green peas
> 1 quart water
> 1 medium onion, chopped
> 2 carrots, cut into 2-inch pieces
> 2 ribs celery, cut into 2-inch pieces
> 2 parsley sprigs
> 1 clove garlic
> 1/2 teaspoon sugar
> 1/8 teaspoon thyme leaves
> 4 cups chicken stock (homemade or prepared)
> 1 cup fat-free ham, slivered into 1/4 × 1-inch pieces
> salt to taste
> freshly ground pepper

Put the peas and water in a large soup pot, bring to a boil, reduce heat, cover, and simmer for 45 minutes. Watch the peas carefully so that they do not boil over. Add the onion, carrots, celery, parsley, garlic, sugar, thyme, and chicken stock. Cover and simmer for 1 hour. Cool slightly.

Purée the soup in 3 or 4 batches in a food processor or blender. Return the pea purée to the soup pot, heat, and garnish with slivered ham. Salt and pepper the soup to taste.

Each serving:

 less than 1   **6 mg**   **2**   **Calories 176**

CHICK PEA AND CANNELLINI SOUP
Edward Giobbi

Serves 8

2 cups dried chick peas (ceci beans)*
2 cups cannellini beans (white beans)*
1 teaspoon bicarbonate of soda
6 cups water
2 cloves garlic, finely minced
1/2 cup finely chopped carrots
1 cup finely chopped celery
1 cup chopped tomatoes, fresh if possible (drain if canned)
1-1/2-ounce package dried boletus mushrooms
2 cups chopped Swiss chard
1 bay leaf
salt and freshly ground black pepper to taste
3 tablespoons olive oil
1 teaspoon safflower oil
8 slices toasted Italian or French bread
finely chopped Italian parsley for garnish

Soak the dried beans in separate bowls for 24 hours in cold water, adding 1 teaspoon bicarbonate of soda to the chick peas. Drain, wash, cover the chick peas with water, and cook, covered, 4 hours.

Drain the cannellini beans. Cover with cold water and boil slowly until cooked, about 2 hours.

Put the 6 cups water in a soup pot and add the garlic, carrots, celery, tomatoes, mushrooms, Swiss chard, bay leaf, salt, and pepper. Cover and boil gently 1 hour. Add the drained, cooked chick peas, cover and boil 30 minutes. Drain the cannellini beans, add them to the soup, and cook 20 minutes. Add the two oils, cover, and boil gently 20 more minutes.

Place toast on bottom of each soup plate. Ladle soup over toast. Garnish with the Italian parsley.

Each serving:

 1   0 mg   5   **Calories 303**

*Or you may use a 20-ounce can each of ceci beans and cannellini beans, adding beans when indicated in recipe.

CHILLED BEET SOUP WITH YOGURT
Good Housekeeping

Most people think you need a beet base for this first-course soup. Not so! Our trick? We peeled the beets after cooking, adding to the soup's richness and color.

Serves 6

1-1/4 pounds medium-sized beets
2 tablespoons sugar
2 tablespoons lemon juice
1 teaspoon salt
1 teaspoon grated lemon peel
1/8 teaspoon pepper
5 cups water
1 8-ounce container low-fat plain yogurt
lemon slices for garnish

With a soft brush and running cold water, scrub the beets well. In a 4-quart saucepan over high heat, bring the beets, sugar, lemon juice, salt, lemon peel, pepper, and water to boil. Reduce the heat to low; cover and simmer for 1 hour, or until the beets are tender.

With slotted spoon, remove the beets; set the broth aside. Run the beets under cold water for easy handling; peel, then shred. Return the shredded beets to the broth in saucepan. Refrigerate until chilled. To serve, pour into a tureen; add the yogurt and lemon.

Each serving:

 less than 1   **2 mg**   **1**   **Calories 70**

4

BREAKFASTS,
BRUNCHES,
& BREAKFAST
BEVERAGES

Throughout the book we use the following symbols at the end of each recipe. For an explanation of the SF system, see p. 231.

 = Saturated Fat = Cholesterol = Soluble Fiber

OAT BRAN PANCAKES

Here's a basic recipe you'll use again and again. Note the variations at the end of the recipe.

Makes 24 3-inch pancakes

no stick cooking spray
1-1/2 cups low-fat buttermilk
1-1/2 teaspoons baking powder
3/4 teaspoon salt
1 tablespoon granulated sugar
3 tablespoons vegetable oil
4 large egg whites, whipped until soft peaks form
3-1/2 cups oat bran (for best results, use coarsely milled oat bran)
1 cup (or more) water*

*Because different brands of oat bran are milled with differing amounts of oat flour in them, you may need up to 2 cups more water as the pancake batter rests.

Oat Bran Pancakes (*continued*)

Spray the griddle or a large skillet with no stick cooking spray. Preheat the griddle until medium hot.

Mix the buttermilk with the baking powder. Allow the mixture to cure for 5 minutes until it is bubbly. Add the salt, sugar, and vegetable oil. Fold the whipped eggs into the mixture. Gently fold the oat bran into this mixture. Blend in 1 cup water.

Pour 1/3 cup batter for each pancake onto the hot grill. Cook the pancakes until they are puffed and bubbles form on top side. Turn and cook until both sides are browned. Repeat to make 24 3-inch pancakes. If the pancake batter becomes too thick, you may need to add 1 or more cups water to make a batter of pouring consistency.

Serve the pancakes hot with heated maple syrup or with Fruit Sauce (below).

Pancakes may be frozen for up to 2 months. You can reheat the frozen pancakes in the microwave (30 seconds on high) or in the toaster.

Each pancake:

 less than 1   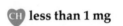 **less than 1 mg**   **1**   **Calories 99**

Variations

- Fold in 1 cup of fresh or frozen blueberries or strawberries with the oat bran.
- Pour the oat bran pancake batter around grilled apple slices.
- Add 1 cup mashed bananas at the time you add the oil to the pancake batter.
- Use low-fat yogurt or skim milk in place of buttermilk.

FRUIT SAUCE FOR PANCAKES OR WAFFLES

Here's a healthy alternative to heavy and artificially flavored maple syrups. Keep a supply in the freezer and reheat it whenever you serve pancakes or waffles.

Makes 8 3/4-cup servings

2 cups fresh or frozen strawberries, thawed
1 cup sliced kiwi fruit, peeled
2 ripened bananas
1 cup fresh or frozen blueberries, thawed
1/2 cup pure maple syrup
1 cup water
1/3 cup oat bran (for best results, use an oat bran that is coarsely milled)

Place all ingredients in a blender or food processor. Whirl until the ingredients are smoothly blended. Heat, if desired,* and serve over hot pancakes or waffles.

Each serving:

SFI less than 1   CH 0 mg   SF2 1   **Calories 127**

*To preserve vitamin C, serve fruit sauce cold.

OAT BRAN APPLE WAFFLES

Oat bran is the perfect flour for waffles as its firm, tasty texture is enhanced by the waffle iron's deep grooves. These waffles are best when made in a Belgian waffle iron maker, although they will work with any waffle iron. Make all the waffles, then wrap and freeze what you don't eat.

See the directions (*) for making the waffle batter the "night before."

Makes 12 Belgian waffles

1 package (1/4 ounce) active dry yeast
1/2 cup very warm water (115°F)
no stick cooking spray
3-1/2 cups oat bran (for best results, use an oat bran that is
    coarsely milled)
1 teaspoon baking powder*
1/3 cup light brown sugar, packed
3/4 teaspoon salt
1 cup apple juice, room temperature
4 large egg whites
2 tablespoons vegetable oil
2 cups water*

Blend the yeast with very warm water. Allow mixture to cure for 5 minutes until the yeast is bubbly.

Spray the grids of a waffle iron with no stick cooking spray. Preheat the waffle maker for 10 minutes.

Mix the oat bran with the baking powder, brown sugar, and salt. Then mix the apple juice with the egg whites and oil. Combine the yeast with the apple juice mixture and gently fold the oat bran into this mixture. Allow to rise in a warm place for 15 minutes.

Just before baking the waffles, add 2 cups water to the batter and stir well. Place 1/2 cup of the waffle batter into each side of the Belgian waffle maker. Spread the mixture with a spatula so that it covers the waffle

*To make the waffle batter in advance, blend all ingredients except baking powder and 1 cup water. Make the batter as directed. Store in refrigerator. Then, 1 hour before serving, blend baking powder with warm water and stir into the waffle mix.

Oat Bran Apple Waffles (*continued*)

grid. Close lid of waffle maker and allow it to bake until no more steam arises. This will take 5 to 8 minutes. When you open the waffle maker, the waffles should release easily. Serve the waffles hot with maple syrup, Fruit Sauce (page 68), or creamed chicken. Or serve the waffles cold with fruit, ice milk, or cottage cheese.

Belgian waffles can be frozen for up to 3 months or refrigerated for 3 weeks. To reheat, microwave each waffle 30 seconds (high) or place each waffle in a 350°F oven for 5 to 7 minutes.

Each waffle:

 1   0 mg   3   **Calories 204**

GINGERBREAD PANCAKES

Here's a hearty, spicy pancake that is sure to please. It is low in fat and calories and high in fiber. It's best served with plain or vanilla yogurt.

> *Makes 12 4-inch pancakes*
>
> 1-1/2 cups oat bran (for best results, use an oat bran that is
>   coarsely milled)
> 1 teaspoon baking powder
> 1/4 teaspoon baking soda
> 1/4 teaspoon salt
> 1/2 teaspoon ground ginger
> 1 teaspoon ground cinnamon
> 2 large egg whites
> 1-1/4 cups skim milk
> 1/4 cup molasses
> 3 tablespoons vegetable oil
> no stick cooking spray

Mix the oat bran with the baking powder, baking soda, salt, ground ginger, and cinnamon. Beat the egg whites with the milk, molasses, and oil. Blend the wet ingredients with the dry ingredients until just moistened.

Spray a griddle or a large skillet with no stick cooking spray. Heat until medium hot. Pour 1/3 cup batter onto the hot grill. Cook the pancakes until they are puffed and bubbles form on top side, about 2 minutes. Turn and cook until both sides are browned. Serve at once.

Pancakes may be frozen for up to 2 months. You can reheat the frozen pancakes in the microwave (30 seconds on high) or in the toaster.

Each pancake:

 less than 1   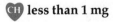 less than 1 mg   1   **Calories 90**

Breakfasts and Brunches (Clockwise, starting at upper left):

Sunshine French Toast (Page 79)
Italian-style Frittata (Page 78)
Oat Bran Apple Waffles (Page 69)

Oat Bran Hot Cereal

Of course, the easiest way to incorporate oat bran into your diet is to serve it as a hot cereal. Here are some variations of oat bran cereals.

MAPLE RAISIN OAT BRAN HOT CEREAL

This hot cereal will appeal to your taste buds. It has an interesting texture and a mellow flavor.

> *Serves 1*
>
> 2/3 cup water
> 1/3 cup oat bran
> pinch salt (optional)
> 2 teaspoons pure maple syrup
> 1/4 cup raisins

In a small saucepan, mix the water with the oat bran and salt. Heat to boiling. Add the maple syrup and the raisins. Cover and simmer for 2 minutes. Serve immediately. You may serve this with skim milk or low-fat flavored yogurt.

Each serving:

 less than 1   0 mg   3   Calories 256

CRANBERRY CEREAL

You'll enjoy the fresh flavor of this cereal. When fresh cranberries are in season, freeze a few packages so you can make this cereal all year long.

> *Serves 2*
>
> 1/2 cup fresh or frozen cranberries
> 1-1/2 cups water
> 1/4 cup sugar
> 2/3 cup oat bran

Put the cranberries and the water in a medium-sized saucepan. Heat to boiling, cover, and simmer for 10 minutes until the cranberries are softened. Add the sugar and the oat bran and simmer for 2 minutes longer. Serve immediately with skim milk.

Each serving:

 less than 1   0 mg   SF2 2   Calories 221

MIXED OAT CEREAL WITH FRUIT

Add the firm texture of oatmeal to oat bran hot cereal, and you'll have a wonderful blend of textures. This is particularly good with bananas and brown sugar.

Serves 2

1-1/2 cups water
1/8 teaspoon salt (optional)
1/3 cup quick-cooking oatmeal
1/3 cup oat bran
1/4 cup firmly packed brown sugar
cinnamon
2 medium-sized bananas, sliced

In a medium-sized saucepan, heat the water with salt, oatmeal, and the oat bran. When the water boils, add the brown sugar, cover, and simmer the cereal for 2 minutes. Ladle the cereal into 2 shallow bowls, sprinkle with cinnamon, top with sliced banana, and serve with skim milk.

Each serving:

 less than 1   **0 mg**   **2**   **Calories 286**

HOT CHOCOLATE CEREAL

Here's a wonderful variation for breakfast. Use carob powder in place of chocolate, if desired.

Serves 1

1 cup water
2 teaspoons unsweetened cocoa (or carob powder)
1 tablespoon honey
1/3 cup oat bran

In a small saucepan, mix the water with the cocoa and honey. Heat to boiling. Add the oat bran, cover, and simmer for 2 minutes. Serve immediately with skim milk.

Each serving:

 less than 1   **1 mg**   **2**   **Calories 187**

BROCCOLI CRABMEAT QUICHE

This quiche is reduced in fat and calories, yet it has great flavor and nutrition.

Serves 8

Oat Bran Pastry

3/4 cup oat bran hot cereal (for best results, use a coarsely milled oat bran)
3/4 cup all-purpose flour
1/4 teaspoon salt
1 teaspoon baking powder
1/4 cup vegetable oil
1 to 2 tablespoons ice water
no stick cooking spray

Broccoli-Crabmeat Filling

1 bunch broccoli, separated into florets and peeled and sliced stems
1/4 cup chopped green onions
6 ounces fresh, frozen, or canned crabmeat, drained
1/4 teaspoon white pepper
1/4 cup chopped fresh parsley
1 cup shredded Provolone cheese
8 large egg whites
1-1/3 cups low-fat buttermilk
1/2 teaspoon salt
1 teaspoon Dijon mustard
1/4 teaspoon paprika
salt to taste
freshly ground pepper

To make the pastry: In a mixing bowl, combine the oat bran with the flour, salt, and baking powder. Using a pastry blender, cut in the oil until the mixture has a coarse texture. Sprinkle 1 tablespoon ice water over the pastry and blend until the mixture holds together well. Add more water, if necessary. Turn pastry onto a well-floured surface and allow to rest for 5 minutes. Spray a 10-inch quiche dish or a 10-inch pie pan with no stick cooking spray. Roll pastry to an 11-inch round and place it in the pan. Flute edges.

For the quiche: Preheat oven to 450°F. Steam the broccoli until it is bright green in color and still crunchy. Drain. Mix broccoli with green onions, crabmeat, white pepper, and parsley. Distribute evenly over the oat bran pastry. Sprinkle cheese over the crabmeat mixture. Whip eggs

Broccoli Crabmeat Quiche (*continued*)

with buttermilk, salt, mustard, and paprika. Pour over quiche. Bake for 10 minutes. Then reduce heat to 350°F and continue baking for 20 minutes longer. Let stand for 5 minutes before cutting. Salt and pepper to taste.

Each serving:

 4   35 mg   1   **Calories 231**

BUCKWHEAT AND OAT BRAN BLINI

This treat—a Russian delicacy—is like a heavyweight crêpe. Made with nutritious oat bran and the traditional buckwheat, it is very low in calories yet high in fiber. Try a topping of low-fat vanilla yogurt, cottage cheese, or fruit.

Makes 12 blini

1 package (1/4 ounce) active dry yeast
1-1/2 cups very warm water
1 cup plain low-fat yogurt, room temperature
1 teaspoon granulated sugar
1/2 teaspoon salt
1 tablespoon peanut oil
1/2 cup oat bran (for best results, use a coarsely milled oat bran)
1/2 cup buckwheat
2 large egg whites
no stick cooking spray

Sprinkle the yeast over 1/2 cup warm water. Stir and allow the mixture to cure for 5 minutes until the yeast is bubbly. Blend the yogurt with the sugar, salt, and oil. Stir the yeast mixture into this mixture. Add the oat bran and buckwheat and beat by hand or with an electric mixer until the batter is smooth.

Cover the bowl and allow to stand in a warm, draft-free place for 20 minutes. Meanwhile, whip the egg whites until soft peaks form. Fold the final cup of warm water into the batter, then fold the egg whites into it as well. Let the batter stand for another 10 minutes.*

Preheat the oven to 250°F. Spray a blini pan or a 6-inch crêpe pan with no stick cooking spray. Heat the pan over a medium-hot burner (if you

*To prepare this breakfast treat the night before, make the blini recipe excluding the final cup of warm water and the egg whites. Cover and refrigerate. In the morning, remove and add warm water. Whip eggs until soft peaks form, fold them into the batter, and continue as above.

are using an electric pan, heat to 375°F). Place a scant 1/4 cup batter in the pan and bake until the top is firm and bubbly. Turn the blini and cook until crisp and golden brown, about 5 minutes. Keep the blini warm in the oven until ready to serve. Repeat to make 12 blini.

Top with low-fat cottage cheese, flavored yogurt, or fresh fruit. You may store the blini, covered, in the refrigerator for up to 3 weeks. You may wrap and freeze the blini for up to 3 months. To reheat, microwave each blini for 20 seconds (high) or heat in a 350°F oven for 5 minutes.

Each blini:

 1   1 mg   less than 1   Cal. 109

OAT BRAN CRÊPES WITH FILLINGS

Here's a basic recipe for oat bran crêpes. You can fill them with just about anything. The following two recipes give you just a couple of examples of crêpe fillings. Make plenty of crêpes; then you can freeze or refrigerate them and have a delicious breakfast treat whenever you want. You can fill these same crêpes with fruit and yogurt for a great dessert!

Makes 12 crêpes

1 cup oat bran (for best results, select a coarsely milled oat bran)
3/4 cup water
2/3 cup skim milk
6 large egg whites
1 tablespoon vegetable oil
1/4 teaspoon salt
no stick cooking spray

Place all the ingredients in a medium-sized bowl and mix thoroughly by hand or with an electric mixer. Refrigerate for 1 hour or overnight.

Spray a 5- or 6-inch crêpe pan with no stick cooking spray. Heat the pan over a medium-hot burner (if you are using an electric crêpe pan, heat it to 375°F). Pour 2 to 3 tablespoons of the crêpe batter into the pan, tilting and swirling the hot pan as you add the batter. Use just enough batter to cover the bottom of the pan with a thick layer.

When the surface of the crêpe is dry and the underside is brown, turn the crêpe. Allow the other side to brown. This whole process will take about 5 minutes. Remove the crêpe and start to form a stack. Repeat with the remaining batter. As you stack the crêpes, cover with plastic wrap.

Fill crêpes and roll, or fill and fold edges in to form a square.

Each crêpe:

 less than 1   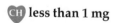 less than 1 mg   1   Calories 99

ASPARAGUS AND MUSHROOM CRÊPES

What could be more delightful than fresh vegetables, light cheeses, and a tasty sauce napped with wine? This recipe is a breakfast or brunch winner. It is high in calcium, fiber, and flavor.

Makes 6 crêpes

2 tablespoons extra virgin olive oil
2 cups fresh asparagus, cleaned and cut
    into 1/2-inch diagonal pieces (or you may use 2
    10-ounce packages of frozen asparagus spears)
1 cup sliced fresh mushrooms
1/2 teaspoon lemon juice
1 teaspoon fresh tarragon, chopped,
    or 1/4 teaspoon dried tarragon
1/4 teaspoon white pepper
1/4 cup grated Swiss cheese
4 green onions, sliced into 1/2-inch slices
no stick cooking spray
6 Oat Bran Crêpes (page 75)
3 tablespoons all-purpose flour
1 teaspoon Dijon mustard
1/8 teaspoon cayenne pepper
1-1/2 cups plain low-fat yogurt
1/4 cup dry white wine
1/4 cup grated Parmesan cheese
freshly ground pepper
chopped chives for garnish
paprika for garnish
salt to taste

Place the olive oil in a large, heavy pan over medium-high heat. Add the asparagus and mushrooms and sauté vegetables lightly for 5 minutes. Mix in the lemon juice, tarragon, and pepper. Blend in the Swiss cheese and green onion and remove from the heat.

Preheat oven to 350°F. Spray a 9×9-inch baking dish with no stick cooking spray. Place 1/4 cup asparagus mixture down the center of each crêpe, fold, and lay side by side, seam side down in the baking dish.

Mix the flour with the Dijon mustard, cayenne pepper, yogurt, white wine, and Parmesan cheese. Spoon this mixture on top of the crêpes. Cover and bake for 30 minutes or until the sauce is lightly browned. Garnish with chopped chives, paprika, and freshly ground black pepper. Serve immediately. Salt to taste.

Each crêpe:

 5   16 mg   3   **Calories 320**

MEXI CHICKEN CRÊPES

Here's south-of-the-border taste rolled in a crêpe. This easy-to-make recipe is very low in calories and has a wonderful flavor. It's even better reheated the second day!

Makes 6 crêpes

3 large, ripe tomatoes
1 teaspoon salt
1 tablespoon green chilis or jalapeño peppers
1/2 cup fresh cilantro
no stick cooking spray
6 Oat Bran Crêpes (page 75)
1-1/2 cups cooked chicken, cut into bite-sized pieces
1/4 cup shredded Monterey Jack cheese
1/2 cup Sour Cream Substitute (page 45)
3 green onions, chopped
sprigs of cilantro for garnish
salt to taste
freshly ground pepper

Chop the tomatoes into quarters. Place the chopped tomatoes with the salt, chilis or jalapeños, and the cilantro in a blender cup. Pulse several times with an on–off motion until the mixture (salsa) is chunky.

Spray a 9×9-inch baking dish with no stick cooking spray. Spread half of the salsa mixture in the bottom of the baking dish.

Preheat the oven to 375°F. Place 1/4 cup of the chicken in the middle of each crêpe and roll. Place the seam side down in the baking dish atop the salsa. Spoon remaining salsa over crêpes. Sprinkle with cheese. Cover and bake for 25 minutes. The filling will be hot and the cheese will be melted.

Spoon the Sour Cream Substitute down the centers of the crêpes. Sprinkle with the green onions. Garnish with sprigs of cilantro. Serve immediately. Salt and pepper to taste.

Each crêpe:

 2   49 mg   2   **Calories 227**

ITALIAN-STYLE FRITTATA

Prepare all the ingredients for this frittata in advance. Just before serving, quickly sauté veggies, add eggs, cook, and finish with cheese.

Serves 6

no stick cooking spray
1 cup chopped zucchini, with peel
1/3 cup green pepper, seeded and chopped into 1/4-inch chunks
1/3 cup coarsely chopped onion
1 large tomato, chopped into 1/2-inch pieces
1/2 teaspoon dried oregano
1 tablespoon fresh basil, chopped (or 1 teaspoon dried basil)
1/4 teaspoon black pepper
1/2 cup whole wheat elbow macaroni, cooked
12 egg whites, beaten until just blended
1/4 cup freshly shredded Romano cheese

Spray a large skillet with no stick cooking spray. Heat to hot. Reduce heat, cover, and cook the zucchini, pepper, and onion until tender, about 8 minutes, stirring occasionally. Add chopped tomato. Stir in the oregano, basil, pepper, and macaroni.

Preheat the broiler. Pour the eggs over the zucchini-tomato mixture and cook over low heat until the egg bottom is set, about 5 minutes. Place the frittata under the broiler about 4 inches from the source of heat. Broil for 2 minutes. Sprinkle with the cheese and broil until cheese melts.

Cut into wedges and serve hot.

Each serving:

 less than 1   **10 mg**   **1**   **Calories 106**

OLD-FASHIONED GRANOLA

Over the years, this recipe for granola has been an absolute favorite; it is rich with dietary fiber and so delicious that you'll want to make extra to give to your friends!

Makes 24 1/3-cup servings

2 cups oat bran (for best results,
    use an oat bran that is coarsely milled)
2 cups rolled oats
1/2 cup sliced almonds
1/2 cup sunflower seeds
1/2 cup sesame seeds

1/2 cup shredded coconut
1/4 cup nonfat dry milk
2 tablespoons dark brown sugar, packed
1/2 teaspoon cinnamon
1/4 cup peanut oil
1/2 cup maple syrup*
1/2 teaspoon salt
1/2 cup seedless raisins

Preheat oven to 300°F.

In a large bowl, combine oat bran, rolled oats, almonds, sunflower seeds, sesame seeds, coconut, dry milk, brown sugar, and cinnamon. In a small bowl, mix the peanut oil, maple syrup, and salt. Pour maple syrup mixture over dry ingredients and mix thoroughly.

Spread the granola in a rimmed, ungreased 10 × 15-inch jellyroll pan and bake for 45 minutes, stirring every 10 minutes. It is important to stir the granola every 10 minutes to blend the flavors and toast the granola evenly. Stir in raisins and bake an extra 10 minutes. Remove from oven and cool. Store in an airtight container for up to 3 months. Serve granola with low-fat milk.

Each serving:

 2   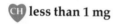 **less than 1 mg**   **1**   **Calories 138**

*You may substitute honey or brown sugar for maple syrup.

SUNSHINE-STYLE FRENCH TOAST

Start your day with this tasty, natural orange French toast.

Serves 4

1/2 cup skim milk
6 egg whites
2 tablespoons sugar
1/2 cup orange juice, with pulp
1 teaspoon grated orange peel
8 1/2-inch thick slices day-old French bread,
   or Honey Wheat Bread (page 95)
no stick cooking spray
1/4 cup powdered sugar

In a medium-sized mixing bowl, beat the milk, egg whites, sugar, orange juice, and orange peel until the mixture is thick, blended, and smooth. Pour the mixture into a shallow bowl.

Sunshine-style French Toast (*continued*)

Dip the bread slices into the egg mixture and allow to rest on a large jellyroll pan. Make sure to use all of the egg mixture on the 8 bread slices.

Spray a large griddle or a large skillet with no stick cooking spray. Heat to medium hot (about 325°F). Without crowding, brown the toast slices on both sides. Allow at least 5 minutes per slice to ensure cooking throughout. Dust with the powdered sugar. Serve with hot maple syrup or Fruit Sauce (page 68).

Each serving:

 less than 1   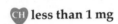 less than 1 mg   1   **Calories 263**

Breakfast Beverages

At our house, we love to have breakfast in a glass. Try our ideas here, then experiment on your own. For your beverages, you'll need a cup of milk or orange or other fruit juice, then select any fruit or fruit combination that you like. For special fizz, add seltzer after blending the fruit mixture.

APPLE BERRY FIZZ

Here's a winning combination. It is a complete breakfast in a glass, rich with dietary fiber. And it's filling!

Serves 1

1 cup canned apple juice
1/2 cup strawberries or raspberries, fresh or frozen
1/2 cup ice cubes (if using frozen berries,
   use water instead of ice cubes)
1/2 cup seltzer

Place the apple juice, berries, and ice cubes or water into a blender cup. Blend until smooth, about 30 seconds. Pour into a 16-ounce glass, stir in seltzer, and serve immediately.

Each serving:

 less than 1   0 mg   1   **Calories 138**

STRAWBERRY SMOOTHIE

Here's another breakfast in a glass—a family favorite. It is rich in fiber and vitamins and moderate in calories.

Serves 2

> 1/2 cup orange juice, fresh or frozen
> 1 very ripe banana
> 1 cup fresh strawberries, washed and capped
>   (or whole frozen strawberries without sugar)
> 1/3 cup oat bran (use a coarsely milled oat bran)
> 1/2 cup skim milk
> 1 cup ice cubes (if using frozen strawberries,
>   use water instead of ice cubes)

Place the orange juice, banana, strawberries, oat bran, milk, and ice cubes in a blender cup. Blend until smooth, about 30 seconds. Pour into 2 12-ounce glasses. Serve immediately.

Each serving:

 less than 1   **1 mg**   **2**   **Calories 179**

FROZEN PINEAPPLE REFRESHER

This is a refreshing way to start any day; it's low in calories and high in fiber.

Serves 2

> 1 cup fresh pineapple pieces (or canned or frozen)
> 1/2 cup orange juice
> 1 banana
> 1 cup ice cubes
> 1 cup seltzer

Place pineapple, orange juice, banana, and ice cubes in a blender cup. Blend until smooth, about 30 seconds. Pour into 2 16-ounce glasses. Stir in seltzer.

Each serving:

 less than 1   **0 mg**   **1**   **Calories 119**

5

MUFFINS, BREADS, & CRACKERS

HIGH-FIBER BREAD

This flavorful bread is low in saturated fat, high in fiber, and very tasty. Follow the instructions for any easy-to-make, satisfying bread.

Makes 16 slices

1 package (1/4 ounce) active dry yeast
1/4 cup very warm water (115°F)
2/3 cup lukewarm water
1/2 cup oat bran (for best results,
   select a coarsely milled oat bran)
1/4 cup granulated sugar
1/2 teaspoon salt
1 tablespoon margarine, melted
1 cup whole wheat flour
1 cup all-purpose white flour
1/2 cup bread flour
2 egg whites
no stick cooking spray
1 tablespoon oat bran to sprinkle

Soften the yeast in the very warm water. In a medium-sized mixing bowl or in the bowl of an electric mixer or food processor, combine lukewarm water with the oat bran, sugar, salt, and margarine. Let this mixture stand for 5 minutes in order to soften the oat bran.

Mix the whole wheat flour with the white flour and bread flour. Knead 1 cup of the flour mixture into the oat bran mixture. This can be done by hand or with dough hooks fitted to the mixer or food processor. Add 1 egg white, the softened yeast, and the remaining flour and knead until dough is smooth and satiny (about 10 minutes by hand or 5 minutes by mixer).

Spray a medium-sized mixing bowl with no stick cooking spray. Put the bread dough in the bowl in a very warm, draft-free place, cover with a wet towel, and allow to rise for 1-1/2 to 2 hours. The dough should be very warm and light.

Spray a cookie sheet with no stick cooking spray. Knead the dough down and roll it with a rolling pin into a 6 × 12-inch rectangle. Next, roll the dough lengthwise, turn it seam down, and place it on the cookie sheet, tucking the ends under. Cover with a wet towel and allow the dough to rise in a very warm, draft-free place for 1/2 hour.

Preheat the oven to 350°F. Brush the remaining egg white over the surface of the bread. Sprinkle with the oat bran. Bake the bread for 30 to 35 minutes or until it is golden brown. Cool on a baking rack. Slice when cool.

Each slice:

 less than 1   **0 mg**   **.5**   **Cal. 96**

Variation

To make garlic toast, first slice the bread. Then spread the slices with a very thin layer of light margarine. Sprinkle with freshly minced garlic and chopped parsley. Broil until browned.

RASPBERRY BANANA MUFFINS

Here's a rich, crumbly muffin—almost a meal in itself. It is rich in carbo-hydrates, fiber, and calcium, and you'll love the raspberry flavor.

Makes 12 muffins

no stick cooking spray
1 cup low-fat buttermilk
1 teaspoon baking powder
1 teaspoon salt
2 tablespoons vegetable oil
1/2 cup dark brown sugar, firmly packed
1 very ripe banana, mashed
1 pint fresh raspberries (or 10 ounces
    frozen raspberries, thawed)
4 large egg whites, whipped until soft peaks form
3-1/2 cups oat bran (for best results,
    use a coarsely milled oat bran)

Raspberry Banana Muffins (*continued*)

Preheat oven to 400°F. Spray 12 muffin tins with no stick cooking spray.

Combine the buttermilk with the baking powder. Allow this mixture to cure for 5 minutes. Mix in the salt, vegetable oil, brown sugar, banana, and raspberries. Stir until the mixture is well blended. Fold the egg whites into the raspberry mixture. Gently fold in the oat bran. Mix until oat bran is just blended with the other ingredients.

Divide this mixture among the 12 muffin tins. Bake at 400°F for 20 minutes until the muffins are lightly browned and firm to the touch. Allow the muffins to cool for 5 minutes before removing from the muffin tins. Muffins may be stored in the refrigerator for up to 3 weeks or in the freezer for 3 months. To reheat, microwave each muffin (high) for 30 seconds or heat the muffins in a 350°F oven for 10 minutes.

Each muffin:

 1   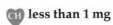 less than 1 mg   3   **Calories 231**

APPLESAUCE MUFFINS

These muffins have a high concentration of oat bran. Just 2 of them will give you 6 grams of soluble fiber, the daily recommendation to reduce blood cholesterol. They are easy to prepare and have great flavor. Serve these muffins hot for best flavor.

Makes 12 muffins

no stick cooking spray
1/2 cup low-fat buttermilk
1-1/2 teaspoons baking powder
1 cup unsweetened applesauce
1/3 cup brown sugar, packed
2 teaspoons cinnamon
2 tablespoons vegetable oil
1 teaspoon salt   *½ cup raisins*
4 large egg whites
1/2 cup apple juice
1 large apple, seeded and chopped into 1/2-inch chunks
3-1/2 cups oat bran (for best results,
    use a coarsely milled oat bran)

Preheat the oven to 400°F. Spray 12 muffin tins with no stick cooking spray. Mix the buttermilk with the baking powder. Allow this mixture to cure for 5 minutes or until it is bubbly.

In a large mixing bowl, combine the applesauce, brown sugar, cinnamon, oil, salt, egg whites, apple juice, and chopped apple. Mix thoroughly. Fold in the buttermilk mixture.

Pour in the oat bran a little at a time. Stir until the oat bran is just blended into the liquid. Divide among 12 muffin tins. Bake at 400°F for 20 minutes until the muffins are lightly browned and firm to touch. Allow the muffins to cool for 5 minutes before removing from the muffin tins. Muffins may be stored in the refrigerator for up to 3 weeks or in the freezer for 3 months. To reheat, microwave each muffin (high) for 30 seconds or heat in a 350°F oven for 10 minutes.

Each muffin:

 1   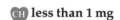 less than 1 mg   3   **Calories 205**

PEANUT BUTTER AND JELLY MUFFINS

Here's a delicious breakfast muffin that's designed for the child in us all. It is high in protein and dietary fiber, low in fat, and an excellent food for snacking.

Makes 16 muffins

no stick cooking spray
1/2 cup low-fat yogurt
1/4 cup honey or brown sugar
1/4 cup strawberry jelly
1/2 cup peanut butter, creamy or chunky
1/2 teaspoon salt
2 large egg whites
2 tablespoons vegetable oil
1 cup water
3-1/2 cups oat bran (for best results,
    use a coarsely milled oat bran)
2 teaspoons baking powder
1/2 teaspoon baking soda
4 teaspoons strawberry jelly

Preheat oven to 400°F. Spray 16 muffin tins with no stick cooking spray.

Combine the yogurt with the honey, jelly, peanut butter, salt, egg whites, oil, and water. Mix well.

Mix the oat bran with the baking powder and baking soda. Blend the wet ingredients with the dry ingredients. Make sure all oat bran is incorporated into this mixture.

Divide the mixture among the 16 muffin tins. Make an indentation in the top of each muffin and spoon in 1/4 teaspoon strawberry jelly into

Peanut Butter and Jelly Muffins (*continued*)

this indentation. Bake at 400°F for 20 minutes until the muffins are lightly browned and firm to touch. Allow the muffins to cool for 5 minutes before removing from the muffin tins. Muffins may be stored in the refrigerator for up to 3 weeks or in the freezer for 3 months. To reheat, microwave each muffin (high) for 30 seconds or heat in a 350°F oven for 10 minutes.

Each muffin:

 2    **less than 1 mg**   2   **Calories 201**

CARROT GINGER MUFFINS

This flavorful muffin will remind you of a moist carrot cake. For sensational flavor, use freshly grated ginger root. Also, serve these muffins hot.

Makes 16 muffins

no stick cooking spray
1 cup low-fat buttermilk
1 teaspoon baking powder
1/4 cup corn syrup
1/2 cup brown sugar, firmly packed
1/4 cup walnuts
1/2 cup raisins
3 cups finely grated carrots
1 tablespoon freshly grated ginger
   (or 1 teaspoon dry ginger spice)
4 large egg whites
2 tablespoons vegetable oil
1 cup water
3-1/2 cups oat bran (for best results,
   use a coarsely milled oat bran)

Preheat the oven to 400°F. Spray 16 muffin tins with no stick cooking spray.

Combine the baking powder with the buttermilk. Then add the corn syrup, brown sugar, walnuts, raisins, carrots, ginger, egg whites, oil, and water. Stir this mixture well.

Gently fold in the oat bran, a little at a time. Mix until it is all just moistened.

Divide among the 16 muffin tins. Bake at 400°F for 25 minutes until the muffins are lightly browned and firm to touch. Allow the muffins to

Breads, Muffins and Quick Breads, and Sandwiches (Clockwise, starting at
  upper left):

Oat Bran Raisin Bagel (Page 99)
Reuben Rolls (Page 122)
Ham and Broccoli Fiesta (Page 121)

cool for 5 minutes before removing from the muffin tins. Muffins may be stored in the refrigerator for up to 3 weeks or in the freezer for 3 months. To reheat, microwave each muffin (high) for 30 seconds or heat in a 350°F oven for 10 minutes.

Each muffin:

 1   less than 1 mg $(SF2)$ 2   **Calories 209**

CINNAMON OAT BRAN MUFFINS

Here's a muffin with a firm crumb and lots of flavor. It's easy to make and packed with good nutrients. Serve hot.

Makes 12 muffins

no stick cooking spray
1 cup low-fat buttermilk
1 teaspoon baking powder
1/2 teaspoon salt
1 tablespoon vegetable oil
1-1/2 teaspoons cinnamon
3/4 cup firmly packed brown sugar
1/2 cup water
4 large egg whites, whipped until soft peaks form
3-1/2 cups oat bran (for best results,
    use a coarsely milled oat bran)

Preheat the oven to 400°F. Spray 12 muffin tins with no stick cooking spray.

Mix the buttermilk with the baking powder, salt, oil, cinnamon, brown sugar, and water. Allow this mixture to cure for 3 minutes until the buttermilk becomes bubbly. Fold the egg whites into the buttermilk mixture. Fold the oat bran cereal into the mixture until just blended.

Divide this mixture among the 12 muffin tins. Bake for 20 minutes until the muffins are lightly browned and firm to touch. Allow the muffins to cool for 5 minutes before removing from the muffin tins. Muffins may be stored in the refrigerator for up to 3 weeks or in the freezer for 3 months. To reheat, microwave each muffin (high) for 30 seconds or heat in a 350°F oven for 10 minutes.

Each muffin:

 1   less than 1 mg $(SF2)$ 3   **Calories 220**

QUICK AND EASY BLUEBERRY YOGURT MUFFINS

Go from mixing bowl to serving platter in 25 minutes! These easy-to-make muffins are great in flavor but low in calories.

Makes 16 muffins

no stick cooking spray
2 (8-ounce) cups blueberry flavored yogurt (1.5% milkfat)
2 teaspoons baking powder
3 large egg whites
1/4 cup granulated sugar
2 tablespoons vegetable oil
1/2 cup water
3-1/2 cups oat bran (for best results,
    use a coarsely milled oat bran)
1 cup blueberries, fresh or frozen

Preheat the oven to 400°F. Spray the 16 muffin tins with no stick cooking spray.

In a medium-sized mixing bowl, blend the blueberry yogurt with the baking powder. Allow this mixture to cure for 5 minutes or until it becomes bubbly.

Blend the egg whites, sugar, oil, and water into the yogurt mixture. Fold the oat bran and the blueberries into this mixture until the oat bran is just wet.

Divide into the 16 muffin tins. Bake at 400°F for 20 minutes until the muffins are lightly browned and firm to touch. Remove the muffins from the muffin tins immediately. Muffins may be stored in the refrigerator for up to 3 weeks or in the freezer for 3 months. To reheat, microwave each muffin (high) for 30 seconds or heat in a 350°F oven for 10 minutes.

Each muffin:

 1   2 mg   2   **Calories 155**

OAT BRAN TORTILLAS

Tex-Mex food is always popular. And what better accompaniment to it than oat bran tortillas? These tortillas have authentic size and texture. There's also plenty of soluble fiber in them.

Makes 12 tortillas

1-1/2 cups unbleached white flour
1 cup oat bran (for best results, use a coarsely milled oat bran)
1 teaspoon salt

1 teaspoon baking powder
1 to 1-1/4 cups warm water
no stick cooking spray

In a large mixing bowl, combine the white flour with the oat bran, salt, and baking powder. Stir in the warm water until the mixture is blended and sticks together well.

Form into 12 balls. Place the balls between pieces of waxed paper. With a tortilla press or a rolling pin, roll each tortilla into a round that is about 5 to 6 inches in diameter. Spray a griddle or a large frying pan with no stick cooking spray. Heat. Bake each tortilla for 1-1/2 to 2 minutes per side. Tortilla will be speckled and brown when cooked.

Each tortilla:

 less than 1   **0 mg**   **1**   **Calories 80**

MEXI MUFFINS

Here's authentic south-of-the-border flavor with lots of nutrition. Mexi muffins are hot, spicy, and full of flavor. If you want a milder muffin, cut back on the jalapeños and black pepper. Make sure to serve these muffins hot.

Makes 16 muffins

no stick cooking spray
1/2 cup homemade (or prepared) salsa
3 large egg whites
1 cup low-fat yogurt
1/2 cup shredded Monterey Jack cheese with jalapeño peppers
1/4 cup chopped jalapeño peppers (canned or fresh)
1/2 teaspoon black pepper
1/4 cup chopped fresh cilantro or parsley
1/2 teaspoon cumin
1 cup water
3-1/2 cups oat bran (for best results,
    use a coarsely milled oat bran)
2 teaspoons baking powder
1 teaspoon baking soda

Preheat the oven to 400°F. Spray 16 muffin tins with no stick cooking spray.

Combine the salsa with the egg whites, yogurt, cheese, jalapeño peppers, black pepper, cilantro, cumin, and water. Mix thoroughly.

In a second bowl, mix the oat bran with the baking powder and baking soda. Add wet ingredients to dry ingredients, mixing until oat bran is just blended.

Mexi Muffins (*continued*)

Divide into the 16 muffin tins. Bake at 400°F for 20 minutes until the muffins are lightly browned and firm to touch. Allow muffins to cool for 5 minutes before removing from the muffin tins. The muffins may be stored in the refrigerator for up to 3 weeks or in the freezer for 3 months. To reheat, microwave each muffin (high) for 30 seconds or heat in a 350°F oven for 10 minutes.

Each muffin:

 less than 1   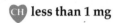 **less than 1 mg**   **2**   **Calories 150**

ZUCCHINI SPICE LOAF

Here's a spicy loaf that will leave your kitchen fragrant and your tummy happy. It's a great snack!

> *Makes 1 loaf, 16 slices*

> no stick cooking spray
> 1 cup oat bran (for best results, select a coarsely milled oat bran)
> 1/2 cup all-purpose flour
> 1 teaspoon ground cinnamon
> 1/2 teaspoon allspice
> 1/2 teaspoon nutmeg
> 1/2 teaspoon baking soda
> 1 teaspoon baking powder
> 1/2 teaspoon salt
> 1 cup dark brown sugar, firmly packed
> 1-1/2 cups finely shredded, unpeeled zucchini
> 2 large egg whites
> 1 cup apple juice
> 1/4 cup vegetable oil
> 1/4 cup chopped walnuts or almonds

Preheat the oven to 325°F. Spray an 8×4×2-inch loaf pan with no stick cooking spray.

In a medium-sized mixing bowl, combine the oat bran with the flour, cinnamon, allspice, nutmeg, baking soda, baking powder, and salt. In a second mixing bowl, combine the sugar with the zucchini, egg whites, apple juice, and oil.

Stir the flour mixture into the zucchini mixture and blend in the chopped nuts.

Pour the batter into the prepared pan. Bake for 60 minutes. When the loaf is done, it will be lightly browned and a wooden pick inserted near the center will come out clean.

Cool the bread for 10 minutes before removing from pan. Allow the bread to cool completely before slicing.

Each slice:

 less than 1   **0 mg**   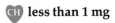 **1**   **Calories 136**

BANANA NUT BREAD

This is a delicious treat. It is rich in dietary fiber and potassium. It also makes excellent toast!

Makes 1 loaf, 12 slices

no stick cooking spray
1-3/4 cups oat bran (for best results,
   select a coarsely milled oat bran)
1 teaspoon baking powder
1 teaspoon baking soda
1/2 teaspoon salt
2/3 cup honey
1/4 cup vegetable oil
4 large egg whites
1/4 cup low-fat yogurt
2 very ripe, mashed bananas
1/4 cup chopped walnuts or pecans
1/2 cup currants

Preheat oven to 375°F. Spray an 8×4×2-inch loaf pan with no stick cooking spray.

Mix the oat bran with the baking powder, baking soda, and salt.

In the bowl of an electric mixer, place the honey and oil. Beat for 1 minute at high speed. Reduce the speed to medium and add egg whites, one at a time, then the yogurt. Add the oat bran mixture and the mashed bananas. Blend in the nuts and the currants.

Pour the batter into the prepared pan. Bake for 45 to 50 minutes or until the top of the bread is lightly browned and a wooden pick inserted near the center comes out clean. Cool in the pan 10 minutes before removal. Allow bread to cool completely before slicing.

Each slice:

 1   **less than 1 mg**   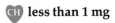 **1**   **Calories 205**

SWEET POTATO BISCUITS

Sweet potatoes are a good source of fiber and vitamin A. In biscuits, they add flavor, texture, and good nutrition. Serve with honey.

Makes 12 biscuits

> 1 cup unbleached white flour
> 1 cup whole wheat flour
> 4 teaspoons baking powder
> 1 teaspoon salt
> 1/4 cup brown sugar, firmly packed
> 1/4 cup vegetable oil
> 1-1/4 cups sweet potatoes, cooked and mashed with skins
>   removed
> 3 tablespoons cold skim milk

Preheat oven to 400°F.

Combine the white flour with the whole wheat flour, baking powder, salt, and brown sugar. Then add the vegetable oil and the sweet potatoes together. With a pastry blender or with two knives, cut the oil and potatoes into the flour mixture. The mixture will be crumbly. Add 3 tablespoons or more of the cold milk and blend to make a soft dough.

Place the dough on a floured cutting board and knead lightly for 2 minutes. Allow the mixture to rest for 5 minutes. Roll the dough to 1/2-inch thickness. Cut with a floured, 3-inch biscuit cutter. Place the biscuits on an ungreased cookie sheet and bake 15 minutes.

Each biscuit:

 less than 1   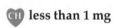 **less than 1 mg**   **less than 1**   **Cal. 145**

CORN TORTILLAS

Some people prefer the flavor of corn tortillas to flour tortillas. These tortillas also make good Taco Chips (page 35).

Makes 12 tortillas

> 1 cup yellow cornmeal
> 1 cup unbleached white flour
> 1 teaspoon baking soda
> 1 teaspoon salt
> 3/4 cup warm water
> no stick cooking spray

In a large mixing bowl, combine the cornmeal with the white flour, baking soda, and salt. Stir in the warm water until mixture is blended and sticks together well.

Form into 12 balls. Place the balls between pieces of waxed paper. With a tortilla press or a rolling pin, roll each tortilla into a round that is about 5 to 6 inches in diameter. Spray a griddle or a large frying pan with no stick cooking spray. Heat. Bake each tortilla for 1-1/2 to 2 minutes per side. Tortilla will be speckled and brown when cooked.

Each tortilla:

 less than 1   **0 mg**   **less than 1**   **Cal. 77**

OLD-FASHIONED CORN BREAD

Bake this in a 9-inch square pan or in a heated iron skillet. One serving suggestion is to serve the corn bread with Ham and Bean Soup (page 61).

Serves 8

1 tablespoon peanut oil
1 cup yellow cornmeal
1 cup all-purpose flour
2 teaspoons baking powder
1/2 teaspoon salt
1 tablespoon honey
2 egg whites, lightly beaten
1 cup low-fat buttermilk
2 tablespoons vegetable oil, preferably safflower or canola

Preheat the oven to 400°F. Pour the peanut oil into a 9-inch square pan or into a 9-inch round or square cast iron skillet. Place the pan or the skillet in a hot oven and allow it to heat.

Meanwhile, mix the cornmeal and flour with the baking powder and salt. Blend the honey, egg whites, buttermilk, and oil. Stir wet ingredients into the dry ingredients just until the mixture is blended. The batter will be thick.

Carefully, pour the cornmeal mixture into the hot pan. Bake for 25 to 35 minutes or until browned. Remove the hot pan from the oven, cut the corn bread into 8 servings, and serve immediately.

Each serving:

 less than 1   **1 mg**   **1**   **Calories 169**

HOT CROSS BUNS

Here's a simple yet foolproof recipe for this traditional Easter treat. Easy as they are, you can make these buns all year.

Makes 16 buns

1-1/2 cups unbleached white flour
1-1/2 cups whole wheat flour
1 package (1/4 ounce) active dry yeast
1/4 cup sugar
3/4 teaspoon salt
1/4 teaspoon nutmeg
1/2 teaspoon cinnamon
1/4 teaspoon ground cloves
1 cup low-fat buttermilk
2 tablespoons light margarine
1 egg, beaten
1/3 cup currants
no stick cooking spray
1 egg white, beaten
1 cup confectioners sugar
2 tablespoons hot milk

In a mixing bowl or a food processor bowl, blend 1-1/4 cups of the unbleached flour, 1-1/4 of the whole wheat flour, the yeast, sugar, salt, nutmeg, cinnamon, and cloves. Heat the buttermilk to almost boiling, add the margarine, and stir until it melts. Pour the buttermilk mixture into the flour mixture and blend with a wooden spoon or with dough hooks in a food processor. Add the eggs and the currants and knead in enough of the remaining flour to make a dough that is smooth and satiny (about 10 minutes by hand or 5 minutes with a food processor).

Spray a medium-sized bowl with no stick cooking spray. Place the dough in the bowl, cover, and let it rise in a warm, draft-free place for 1-1/2 hours.

Spray a 13×9×2-inch baking pan with no stick cooking spray. Place the dough on a cutting board and cut into 16 parts. Form into 16 smooth balls and place in the baking pan. Cover, and allow dough to rise in a warm, draft-free place for 15 minutes. Brush the tops with the egg white.

Preheat oven to 425°F. Bake the Hot Cross Buns for 12 to 15 minutes until they are evenly browned. Cool them in the pan.

To make the icing, blend the confectioners sugar and the hot milk into a smooth paste. Then make a cross with the icing on top of each cooled Hot Cross Bun.

Each bun:

 less than 1   18 mg   less than 1   **Cal. 141**

HONEY WHEAT BREAD

If you like a great bread for toasting, this is the one. You'll make two hearty loaves, and it's great for sandwiches.

Makes 2 loaves, 12 slices each

1 cup very warm water
5 tablespoons honey
5 tablespoons light margarine, melted
2 packages (1/4 ounce each) active dry yeast
3-1/4 cups whole wheat flour
2 cups all-purpose white flour
1-1/4 to 1-1/2 cups bread flour
1/2 teaspoon salt
4 large egg whites
6 tablespoons low-fat milk, scalded*
1/4 cup shelled, finely ground pistachio nuts (optional)
no stick cooking spray

Mix the warm water with the honey, margarine, and yeast. Allow this mixture to stand for 5 minutes until the yeast is bubbly.

In a large mixing bowl or food processor fitted with a dough hook, mix whole wheat flour, white flour, 1 cup bread flour, and salt. Then blend in the egg whites, hot milk, yeast mixture, and the optional pistachio nuts. Beat until the mixture cleans the sides of the mixing bowl. Turn onto a floured board and knead in enough additional flour to make a smooth and elastic bread dough. This will take about 5 minutes.

Spray a large cookie sheet with no stick cooking spray.

Spray a large bowl with no stick cooking spray. Place dough in bowl, cover, put in a warm, draft-free place, and allow to rise for 1 hour. Then form the dough into 2 9×3-inch loaves, place the loaves on the prepared cookie sheet, and allow to rise a second time for 30 minutes.

Preheat oven to 350°F. Bake the bread 25 minutes or until it is golden brown.

Each slice:

 less than 1   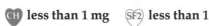 **less than 1 mg**   **less than 1**   **Cal. 154**

---

*To scald milk, heat in a small saucepan or in the microwave oven. Milk is scalded when the small bubbles start to form around the edge of the heating container. Do not boil milk.

APPLE OAT BREAD
Good Housekeeping

This bread makes a delicious high-fiber breakfast, snack, or dessert.

Makes 1 loaf, 12 slices

no stick cooking spray
1-1/2 cups quick-cooking or old-fashioned oats, uncooked
1-1/2 cups all-purpose flour
1-1/2 teaspoons baking soda
1-1/2 teaspoons ground cinnamon
3/4 teaspoon ground allspice
1/2 cup honey
1/2 cup skim milk
1/4 cup vegetable oil
3 egg whites
3 medium-sized unpeeled green cooking apples
    (about 1-1/4 pounds), diced

Preheat the oven to 350°F. Spray an 8-1/2 × 4-1/2-inch loaf pan with no stick cooking spray. In a large bowl, mix the oats, flour, soda, and spices. In a small bowl, beat the honey, milk, oil, and the egg whites until blended; stir into the flour mixture just until flour is moistened (the batter will be lumpy). Fold in the apples.

Spoon batter evenly into the loaf pan. Bake 65 minutes or until a toothpick inserted into the center of the bread comes out clean. Cool the bread in the pan on a wire rack for 10 minutes; remove bread from pan. Cool bread completely on wire rack.

Each slice:

 1   0 mg   1   **Calories 210**

OAT BRAN PITAS

This is a very practical recipe; the pitas can be used as pizza crusts, as sandwiches, or in delicious pita chips. They are so easy to prepare that they are a staple at our house.

Makes 12 pitas

1-1/2 cups oat bran (for best results,
    select a coarsely milled oat bran)
1 package (1/4 ounce) active dry yeast
2 to 2-1/2 cups all-purpose white flour
1-1/4 cups very warm water (115°F)
1/4 cup vegetable oil
1-1/2 teaspoons salt
no stick cooking spray

In a food processor fitted with a steel blade or in a blender, mill the oat bran until fine and flourlike, about 2 minutes. Mix the milled oat bran with the yeast and 1/2 cup of the flour. Combine the warm water, oil, and salt. Pour over the flour-yeast mixture.

Beat the mixture at the low speed of an electric mixer fitted with the dough hooks or in a food processor for 1 minute, scraping sides of bowl. Beat for 3 minutes at medium speed to incorporate as much of the remaining flour as possible.

Turn onto a floured board and knead in enough of the remaining flour to make a smooth, elastic, and satiny dough. This will take 5 to 7 minutes.

Spray a medium-sized bowl with no stick cooking spray. Place the dough in the bowl, cover it, and allow to rise in a warm, draft-free place for 30 minutes. Dough should be very warm and light to touch. Divide into 12 equal portions. Cover, and allow dough to rise a second time in a warm place for 15 minutes.

Preheat the oven to 500°F. To roll the pitas, cut 12 pieces of plastic wrap or waxed paper. Place one side of the paper on the bottom surface of a 6-inch tortilla press or a flat plate. Place pita dough on paper, then fold paper over. Use tortilla press to form a smooth, 1/8-inch thick pita or use a second flat plate to do same. Or you may use a rolling pin to flatten pita dough. Make sure the pitas have no creases or folds.

Place the pitas, 4 at a time, directly on hot oven racks. The pitas should be distributed throughout the oven. Bake for 3 minutes to set the dough. The oven will be extremely hot. Open oven, turn pitas over, and bake for 2 to 3 minutes. The pitas will be browned and should puff up during the baking process.* Allow the oven to reheat for 5 minutes between baking periods.

To serve, open pitas to form pockets. Fill the pocket with meats, sautéed vegetables, or other toppings. If the pocket does not open easily, use a sharp knife to open.

Each pita:

 less than 1   **0 mg**   **1**   **Calories 170**

---

*For pitas to puff up, the dough must be warm, the pitas must be distributed throughout the oven, and the oven must be very, very hot.

SCOTTISH SCONES

Here we've taken the recipe for authentic Scottish scones and adapted it for oat bran. You'll like the flaky pastry, the soft texture, and especially the flavor. Serve with your favorite preserves or marmalade.

Scottish Scones (*continued*)

Makes 12 scones

3 cups oat bran (for best results, use coarsely milled oat bran)
1/2 cup currants
2 tablespoons granulated sugar
3 teaspoons baking powder
1/2 teaspoon salt
1/2 teaspoon baking soda
1/2 cup low-fat yogurt
1/4 cup vegetable oil
2 large egg whites
2 tablespoons low-fat milk for brushing tops of scones
2 tablespoons granulated sugar for sprinkling tops of scones

Preheat the oven to 400°F.

In a food processor fitted with a steel blade or in a blender, mill the oat bran until fine and flourlike, about 2 minutes.

In a large bowl, combine the finely milled oat bran with the currants, sugar, baking powder, salt, baking soda, yogurt, peanut oil, and egg whites. Blend until the mixture holds together well.

Place mixture on a pastry board that has been sprinkled with oat bran. Knead dough lightly, 1/2 to 1 minute. Divide the dough into 12 portions. Smooth each portion into a 2-inch circle then flatten to a 1-inch thickness. Brush the tops with additional milk and sprinkle with sugar.

Place the scones, 2 inches apart, on an ungreased cookie sheet. Bake for 10 to 12 minutes or until the scones are golden brown. Serve hot.

Each serving:

 1   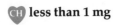 **less than 1 mg**   2   **Calories 161**

BASIC PIZZA DOUGH

Oat bran makes a tasty pizza crust. Top it with Mixed Seafood Topping (page 139), Pizza Primavera Topping (page 175), or your favorite pizza combination.

Makes 1 14-inch pizza crust, 8 slices

1-1/2 cups oat bran (for best results, select a coarsely milled oat bran)
1 package (1/4 ounce) active dry yeast
1 cup very warm water (115°F)
1-1/2 cups all-purpose flour
1/2 teaspoon granulated sugar

1/2 teaspoon salt
2 tablespoons olive oil
no stick cooking spray

In a food processor fitted with a steel blade or in a blender, mill the oat bran until fine and flourlike, about 2 minutes.

Dissolve yeast in warm water. Allow to rest for 5 minutes. Then stir in white flour, sugar, salt, olive oil, and 1 cup oat bran. Knead in remaining oat bran by hand. This will take about 5 minutes; the dough should be smooth and elastic.

Spray a medium-sized bowl with no stick cooking spray. Place pizza dough in bowl, cover, and allow to rise in a warm, draft-free place for 15 minutes. Spray 1 14-inch pizza pan or 2 10-inch pizza pans with no stick cooking spray. Stretch and roll out the pizza dough to fit pan size; flute outer edges of pizza dough to hold fillings.

Each slice:

 less than 1   **0 mg**   **2**   **Calories 173**

OAT BRAN RAISIN BAGELS

Bagels take a little time and skill, but these are so worth the effort. You'll love the soft, moist texture and the crisp outer crust. This recipe is very low in fat.

Makes 12 bagels

no stick cooking spray
1-1/2 cups oat bran (for best results,
    select a coarsely milled oat bran)
1 package (1/4 ounce) active dry yeast
2 to 2-1/2 cups all-purpose flour
1-1/2 cups very warm water (115°F)
3 tablespoons granulated sugar
1/2 teaspoon cinnamon
1 teaspoon salt
1/2 cup seedless raisins
1 gallon water

Spray a large cookie sheet with a thick coating of no stick cooking spray.

In a food processor fitted with a steel blade or in a blender, mill the oat bran until it is fine and flourlike, about 2 minutes. Mix the milled oat bran with the yeast and 1-1/2 cups flour. Combine the warm water, sugar, cinnamon, and salt and pour over the flour mixture.

Oat Bran Raisin Bagels (*continued*)

Beat the mixture with an electric mixer or with a food processor fitted with dough hook for 1/2 minute. Add the remaining flour and the raisins and knead with the mixer or the food processor (or knead by hand) until the dough is smooth and satiny (4 minutes with electric dough hook, 10 minutes by hand).

Cover; allow the dough to rise in a warm, draft-free place for 60 minutes. Divide the dough into 12 portions and shape each portion into a smooth ball. Make a hole in the center of each ball and gently shape it into a 1-inch hole or a 4-inch bagel. Place bagel on the prepared cookie sheet. Cover; allow to rise in a warm, draft-free place for 30 minutes. Preheat the oven to broil.

Broil the bagels for 5 minutes, 5 inches from the source of heat. Turn the bagels one time, but do not allow them to brown.

Reduce the temperature of the oven to 375°F. On top of the stove, heat the gallon of water to boiling. Cook the bagels in boiling water, 4 to 5 at a time, for 7 minutes, turning once. Drain.

Place the hot bagels on a greased baking sheet. Bake in a 375°F oven for 25 to 30 minutes. When baked, bagels will be deep brown with a crisp outer crust.

Freeze any bagels not consumed in 2 days. To reheat, defrost, split, and toast the bagels in an electric toaster.

Each bagel:

 less than 1   0 mg   1   **Calories 159**

6

SALADS

MAYONNAISE-TYPE LIGHT SALAD DRESSING

This nutritious alternative to mayonnaise-type salad dressings will work in almost any mayonnaise-based recipe. Try this recipe by itself, or use it 50/50 with your favorite mayonnaise or high-fat salad dressings.

Makes 1 cup, 4 2-tablespoon servings

1 tablespoon freshly squeezed lemon juice
1/4 teaspoon salt
1 teaspoon sugar
1 egg white
1 cup 1% low-fat cottage cheese
3/4 teaspoon prepared mustard (preferably Dijon)

Place all ingredients in a blender cup. Cover and blend on low until ingredients are mixed. Turn off blender and stir to blend ingredients. Then blend on high until mixture is creamy and thick, about 2 minutes.

This salad dressing will keep, refrigerated, for up to 1 week. Use it to replace mayonnaise-type salad dressings in potato salads, dips, as a spread for sandwiches, and in chicken or tuna salads.

Each serving:

 less than 1   10 mg   0   **Calories 50**

WALDORF SALAD

Traditional Waldorf Salad is laden with heavy salad dressing and walnuts. This version reduces the fat yet still preserves the crisp apple flavor.

101

Waldorf Salad (*continued*)

> *Serves 6*
>
> 1/4 cup no-cholesterol mayonnaise
> 1/4 cup Light Salad Dressing (page 101)
> 1 tablespoon granulated sugar
> 4 large, red or yellow Delicious apples,
>   cored and cubed, about 2 pounds
> 1 teaspoon freshly squeezed lemon juice
> 1 cup chopped celery
> 1/2 cup raisins
> 1/4 cup chopped walnuts
> 6 medium-sized lettuce cups

Combine the mayonnaise, salad dressing, and granulated sugar.

Toss the apples with the lemon juice to prevent from browning. Add the celery, raisins, and walnuts. Fold the dressing over the apple mixture. Chill for at least 1 hour.

Serve on chilled plates on top of lettuce cups.

Each serving:

 1   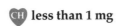 **CH** less than 1 mg   **SF2** 2   **Calories 142**

MINTED CITRUS SALAD

Satisfying and light, this salad combines two excellent sources of vitamin C. Make sure you include the orange pulp for the dressing.

> *Serves 2*
>
> 1/3 cup granulated sugar
> 1/2 cup water
> 3 tablespoons fresh mint sprigs
>   (or 1 tablespoon dry mint leaves)
> juice of 1 orange, including pulp
> 1 grapefruit, peeled and cut into 6 slices
> 2 small oranges, peeled and cut into 4 slices
> mint sprigs for garnish

In a small saucepan, combine sugar and water, stirring to dissolve the sugar. Bring to a boil. Remove from heat and add mint. Allow to cool for 1 hour.

Strain dressing. Then add orange juice.

Meanwhile, arrange grapefruit and orange slices on 2 plates. Top with

3 to 4 tablespoons dressing and garnish with mint. Refrigerate any remaining dressing.

Each serving:

 less than 1   **CH 0 mg**   **SF2 1**   **Calories 175**

BARLEY SALAD VINAIGRETTE

Barley makes an especially pleasing base for a salad. This salad combines barley and other good sources of soluble fiber with a superb vinaigrette dressing.

Serves 6

2 cups Chicken Stock (page 53 or prepared)
12 ounces medium pearl barley
1 cup sliced carrots
2 cups sliced mushrooms
2 garlic cloves, minced
2 tablespoons vegetable oil
1/2 cup freshly squeezed lemon juice (about 2 large lemons)
1 teaspoon Dijon mustard
1/2 teaspoon dried tarragon leaves
1/4 cup sliced green onion
salt to taste
freshly ground pepper
shredded lettuce
sliced radishes

Heat stock in a medium-sized saucepan. When boiling, add barley, reheat to boil, reduce heat, cover, and simmer for 20 to 30 minutes until barley is tender. If barley absorbs chicken stock, add 1/2 cup water. If moisture remains, drain.

Meanwhile, steam carrots for 5 minutes. Add mushrooms and steam an additional 5 minutes.

Combine the garlic with the vegetable oil, lemon juice, mustard, tarragon, and green onion. Mix the cooled barley with the vegetables and vinaigrette. Chill for at least 1 hour. Salt and pepper to taste. Serve on a bed of shredded lettuce. Garnish with radish slices.

Each serving:

SFI less than 1   **CH 0 mg**   **3**   **Calories 261**

CONFETTI SALAD

This salad makes a colorful presentation. Make it in advance; it will keep for up to 4 days.

Serves 6

3 sliced green onions
1 teaspoon marjoram
2 teaspoons granulated sugar
1 tablespoon vegetable oil
1/4 cup red wine vinegar
1 medium zucchini, scrubbed and grated with skin on
1 package (10 ounces) frozen corn, thawed
1 medium-sized red pepper,
   seeded and chopped into 1/2-inch pieces
salt to taste
freshly ground pepper

In a medium-sized bowl, mix the onion, marjoram, granulated sugar, vegetable oil, and vinegar. Add zucchini, corn, and red pepper. Chill for at least 1 hour. Salt and pepper to taste.

Each serving:

 less than 1   0 mg   1   **Calories 74**

VINAIGRETTE SALMON AND BEAN SALAD
Good Housekeeping

A low-fat, high-fiber main dish does not mean long hours of preparation—the chief ingredients here come right off the shelf. Another secret: By using a good-quality wine vinegar, we could make our vinaigrette with only one part oil to one part vinegar.

2 sliced green onions
1 16-ounce can small white beans, drained
1 7-1/2 ounce can red salmon, drained and separated
1 celery stalk, thinly sliced

Vinaigrette Dressing

2 tablespoons wine vinegar
2 tablespoons olive or salad oil
1/4 teaspoon salt
1/4 teaspoon sugar
1/4 teaspoon dry mustard
1/8 teaspoon pepper

lettuce leaves
celery sprig and green onion ''flower'' for garnish

In a medium-sized bowl, lightly toss the green onions, small white beans, salmon, and the celery. In a small bowl, with a fork, mix the wine vinegar, the olive oil or salad oil, salt, sugar, dry mustard, and the pepper. To serve, pour the Vinaigrette Dressing over the salmon mixture; toss lightly. Arrange the lettuce leaves on a platter and spoon the mixture on top. Garnish with the celery and the green onion ''flower.''

Each serving:

 2   **20 mg**   **2**   **Calories 240**

15 BEAN SALAD

This colorful salad is very flavorful. If you don't have packaged 15 bean mix in your market, try blending a few beans of your own. The 15 bean mix includes the following: Great Northern beans, pintos, small reds, large limas, baby limas, black-eyed peas, light red kidneys, garbanzos, Michigan navies, black beans, small pinks, small whites, white kidneys plus lentils, green split peas, and whole green peas.

With so many different beans, this salad has wonderful flavor. However, with so many different sizes of beans, it is important to give the beans an overnight soak and then cook them very carefully to make sure they cook evenly. Our 15 bean mixture (after an overnight presoak) cooked in 45 minutes. The beans should be evenly cooked and tender, not mushy.

Serves 8

12 ounces 15 bean mix
1 medium red onion, thinly sliced
1 red pepper, seeded and chopped into 1/2-inch pieces
2 tablespoons vegetable oil
1/2 cup freshly squeezed lemon juice with pulp
1/2 teaspoon Worcestershire sauce
1/4 cup granulated sugar
1 clove garlic, minced
1/3 cup chopped parsley
salt to taste
freshly ground pepper
lettuce leaves for garnish
lemon slices for garnish

Rinse and sort beans. Place the beans in a medium-sized saucepan and cover with water. Allow to soak overnight.

13 Bean Salad (*continued*)

Drain and rinse beans. Cover with fresh water. Bring to a boil, cover, and simmer for 45 minutes to 1 hour until the beans are just cooked. Make sure beans are covered with 1/2 cup water at all times. Drain and cool. Add the onion and red pepper and toss to mix.

In a small mixing bowl, whisk together the vegetable oil, lemon juice, Worcestershire sauce, sugar, and garlic. Toss with cooled bean mix and chopped parsley. Salt and pepper to taste.

Chill for at least 4 hours, preferably overnight, before serving. To serve, line a large bowl with lettuce leaves. Arrange salad into the bowl. Garnish with thinly sliced lemon.

Each serving:

 less than 1   **0 mg**   **3**   **Calories 304**

PASTA SALAD
Edward Giobbi

An interesting pasta recipe, this dish is made with raw salad greens.

    Serves 4

    about 10 cups loosely packed salad greens*
       (Bibb, red leaf lettuce, escarole hearts, radicchio, etc.)
    1 pound spaghettini
    3 tablespoons olive oil
    1 tablespoon safflower oil
    3 tablespoons good red wine vinegar, or lemon juice
    1 teaspoon dried oregano
    1 teaspoon minced garlic
    salt and freshly ground black pepper to taste

Wash and drain salad greens. Tear large leaves in half.

Boil pasta in a large pot of boiling salted water until *al dente*, then drain. Blend the oils, vinegar, oregano, and garlic together. Put the greens in a bowl and pour half the dressing over them. Add the pasta, the rest of the dressing, salt to taste, and a generous amount of freshly ground pepper.

Each serving:

 1   **0 mg**   **3**   **Calories 565**

*You can use all rucola (arugola) if it is plentiful in your garden.

BLACK-EYED PEAS AND BRUSSELS SPROUT SALAD

Black-eyed peas have more soluble fiber than most other foods and they have a marvelous smooth, mellow taste. This California-style salad teams black-eyed peas with another good source of soluble fiber, Brussels sprouts.

Serves 8

1 cup water
1 package (10 ounces) frozen black-eyed peas
1 large onion, sliced
2 cloves garlic, minced
6 black peppercorns
2 cloves
1 pound fresh Brussels sprouts
1/2 cup sliced radishes
3 ribs celery with tops, sliced
1 bunch green onions, sliced
1/4 cup extra virgin olive oil
1/4 cup wine vinegar
2 tablespoons granulated sugar
salt to taste
8 medium-sized iceberg lettuce cups
freshly ground black pepper

In a medium-sized saucepan, heat the water to boiling, add the peas, bring to a second boil, and cook for 10 minutes. Add onion, garlic, peppercorns, and cloves. Simmer gently until the peas are tender but not mushy, about 15 to 20 more minutes.

Meanwhile, wash and clean Brussels sprouts. Remove outer leaves and make a small X with a knife in the stem end of the Brussels sprout. This will enable sprouts to cook more evenly. Steam Brussels sprouts in a vegetable steamer for 15 minutes, until tender.

When the black-eyed peas are cooked, remove the peppercorns and cloves. Gently combine with the Brussel sprouts, radishes, celery, and green onion.

Make a vinaigrette by combining the olive oil, vinegar, and sugar. Gently toss the black-eyed pea mixture with the vinaigrette. Salt to taste. This salad may be served warm or chilled. To serve, place about 1/2 cup of the mixture into a medium-sized lettuce cup. Top with the freshly ground black pepper.

Each serving:

 1   0 mg   3   **Calories 125**

EASTERN LENTIL SALAD

We like golden lentils, although any lentil will work for this salad. This salad may be prepared up to 24 hours in advance. Garnish just before serving.

Serves 6

12 ounces golden lentils
2 tablespoons vegetable oil
2 tablespoons white wine vinegar
1/4 teaspoon dry mustard
1/2 teaspoon cumin
1 medium onion, finely chopped
1/4 cup fresh parsley, minced
3 tablespoons fresh mint, minced (or 1 tablespoon dry mint)
salt to taste
freshly ground pepper
lettuce leaves for garnish (red leaf if possible)
tomato wedges or cherry tomatoes for garnish

Place lentils in a medium-sized saucepan and cover with water. Bring to a boil, cover, reduce heat, and allow to simmer for 10 to 15 minutes until tender. Watch carefully to be sure that lentils do not become mushy. Drain.

In a small bowl, whisk together the vegetable oil, vinegar, mustard, and cumin. Stir in onion. Toss with lentils while lentils are warm. Chill the lentil salad for at least 1 hour. When ready to serve toss with parsley and mint. Salt and pepper to taste. Place on a plate that has been lined with lettuce leaves. Garnish with tomato wedges or cherry tomatoes that have had small X's cut into their tops.

Each serving:

 less than 1   **0 mg**   **1**   **Calories 97**

SWEET AND SOUR BLACK-EYED PEA SALAD

Frozen black-eyed peas are very useful in these recipes; they are quick to cook and cook very evenly. But please note: Black-eyed peas, which are very high in soluble fiber, will not cook evenly in the microwave!

Serves 4

1 cup water
1 package (10 ounces) frozen black-eyed peas,
    thawed and drained
1 cup chopped celery

1/4 cup chopped onion
1/4 cup sweet pickle relish
1 teaspoon chili powder
1 teaspoon Dijon mustard
salt to taste
freshly ground pepper
shredded lettuce (romaine, if possible) for garnish
1 tablespoon Light Salad Dressing (page 101) for garnish
Roasted Ceci Beans (page 35) for garnish

In a medium-sized saucepan, heat the water to boiling. Place peas in the saucepan, bring to a second boil, lower heat, cover, and cook until the black-eyed peas are very tender, about 30 minutes. Make sure peas have 1/2 cup water covering them at all times. Drain.

Combine the celery, onion, relish, chili powder, and Dijon mustard. Blend with black-eyed peas. Chill at least 1 hour. Salt and pepper to taste.

To serve, place 1/2 cup of the black-eyed pea mixture on a chilled plate topped with some shredded lettuce. Place a small dollop of salad dressing on each serving. Top with crunchy Roasted Ceci Beans.

Each serving:

 less than 1 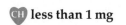 **less than 1 mg**   **6** **Calories 122**

HOT BLACK-EYED PEA SALAD

This recipe contains a touch of bacon for flavor, but it is still very low in saturated fat.

Serves 6

1-1/2 cups water
1 package (10 ounces) frozen black-eyed peas
2 tablespoons extra virgin olive oil
3 tablespoons wine vinegar
2 teaspoons sugar
2 ribs celery with tops, chopped
1 small red pepper, seeded and chopped into 1/4-inch pieces
2 cups shredded romaine lettuce
1 slice bacon, cooked and crumbled
salt to taste
freshly ground pepper

In a small saucepan, bring the water to boil, then add the black-eyed peas. Return to a boil, cover, reduce heat, and simmer peas until tender but not mushy, about 25 to 30 minutes. Make sure peas have water covering them at all times. Drain, reserving 1/2 cup cooking liquid.

Hot Black-Eyed Pea Salad (*continued*)

In a medium-sized saucepan, combine the oil, vinegar, sugar, and cooking liquid from the black-eyed peas. Simmer for 5 minutes.

Remove from heat. Add black-eyed peas, celery, red pepper, crumbled bacon, and romaine lettuce. Salt and pepper to taste and serve immediately.

Each serving:

 less than 1   **1 mg**   **3**   **Calories 76**

RIGATONI WITH BROCCOLI
Edward Giobbi

The component parts of this recipe can be made ahead of time—the pasta in the morning and dressed just with the olive oil, the sauce made, the vegetables prepared. It is best to blanch the broccoli, however, before mixing everything together so it keeps its freshness.

Serves 6

1/2 bunch fresh broccoli, cleaned and cut into bite-sized pieces
6 tablespoons good olive oil
salt and freshly ground black pepper to taste
1 pound rigatoni

The sauce

2 teaspoons coarsely chopped garlic
1/2 cup chopped fresh basil
2 tablespoons chopped Italian parsley
3/4 cup chopped fresh tomatoes
2 tablespoons olive oil
1 tablespoon safflower oil

4 thinly sliced whole scallions
1 7-ounce can Italian-style tunafish
2 tablespoons finely chopped Italian parsley
2 to 3 ripe tomatoes at room temperature,
    cut into bite-sized pieces

Cook the broccoli in boiling salted water about 5 minutes, until broccoli is just done—do not overcook. Drain, place in a large bowl and allow to cool. Add 3 tablespoons of the olive oil and season with salt and pepper.

Cook the pasta in a large pot of boiling salted water. When cooked a little firmer than *al dente,* drain and cool in a wide serving bowl. Season with salt and pepper.

Make the sauce: Blend the garlic, basil, parsley, tomatoes, and oils in the food processor.

When the pasta and broccoli are cool, gently mix together—it is better to do it with your hands. Add the scallions, crushed tunafish and mix with the pasta and broccoli.

Add the sauce and gently mix. Add the chopped parsley and the tomatoes. Check for salt. Do not refrigerate but serve at room temperature.

Each serving:

 3   14 mg   1   **Calories 393**

RICE SALAD
Edward Giobbi

> *Serves 4-6*

> 2 cups green beans, cut in half
> 1 cup fresh peas
> 1 cup cooked rice
> 2 cups cubed fresh tomatoes
> 1 cup thinly sliced whole scallions
> 2 tablespoons chopped Italian parsley or fresh basil
> juice of 1 lemon
> 2 tablespoons olive oil
> 1 tablespoon safflower oil
> 7-ounce can Italian-style tunafish

Steam or boil the beans until tender, then let them cool. Cook the peas until tender, then cool. Mix together the rest of the ingredients, breaking up the tunafish. Carefully mix in the beans and peas, using a fork to keep the salad light.

Each serving:

 2.1   18 mg   1   **Calories 251**

Variation

Early in the season use just peas and asparagus, omitting beans, tomatoes, and scallions.

PICKLED BEETS AND ONIONS

This recipe combines two vegetables high in soluble fiber, beets and onions. It is a traditional favorite that may be served hot or cold. For best results, use fresh beets.

Serves 4

1 pound fresh beets with tops and roots
1/2 cup wine vinegar
1/4 cup water
2 teaspoons dry mustard
1/3 cup sugar
1 small onion, sliced
1/4 cup chopped fresh parsley

Heat about 2 quarts water in a medium-sized saucepan to boiling. Trim stems and beet roots to 2 inches. Place in boiling water, cover, reduce heat, and simmer until tender, about 1 hour. Remove from water and cool.

Heat vinegar and water to a boil. Add mustard and sugar.

When beets cool, peel and slice. There will be about 2 cups. Combine the warm beets with the onion. Pour the hot vinegar mixture over the beets and onion. Chill for at least 1 hour or preferably overnight. Sprinkle with parsley. Serve cold or hot.

Each serving:

 less than 1   **0 mg**   **1**   **Calories 120**

POTATO SALAD

Here's a traditional cold potato salad. The dressing is a wonderful combination of low-fat, tasty ingredients.

Serves 6

5 medium-sized, all-purpose potatoes,
    about 2 pounds, well scrubbed
1/4 cup cooking water from potatoes
1/4 cup white wine vinegar
1 small onion, minced
1 teaspoon prepared mustard (preferably Dijon)
1 grated carrot
3 ribs celery, diced
1 tablespoon sweet pickle relish
1/2 cup Light Salad Dressing (page 101)
2 tablespoons dry skim milk

2 tablespoons low-fat buttermilk
salt to taste
freshly ground pepper

Scrub the potatoes. In a 1-gallon stockpot filled with 3 quarts boiling water, cook the potatoes with their skins. Cook until tender, reserving 1/4 cup cooking liquid. Cool until able to handle, then cut into 1-inch cubes.

Blend the water from the potatoes with the vinegar, onion, and mustard. Pour over the cooked potatoes. When this mixture is cooled, add the carrot, celery, and relish. Refrigerate until cold, about 1 hour.

Meanwhile, make a paste of the salad dressing, the dry skim milk, and the buttermilk. Toss with the cooled potatoes. Refrigerate until well chilled. Salt and pepper to taste.

Each serving:

 less than 1 **3 mg** **2** **Calories 229**

HOT POTATO SALAD

This traditional salad is generally made with lots of bacon. We substituted lean ham for bacon to give this salad both good flavor and excellent nutrition. This recipe makes a big batch, but it reheats well and tastes even better the second day.

Serves 12

8 medium-sized, all-purpose potatoes,
    about 2-1/2 pounds, well scrubbed
2 tablespoons vegetable oil
2 tablespoons unbleached white flour
1/2 cup water
1/2 cup red wine vinegar
3/4 teaspoon sugar
1 medium-sized yellow onion, sliced thinly
4 ounces fat-free ham, cubed
1/4 cup chopped parsley
2 tablespoons chopped chives or scallions for garnish
sliced radishes for garnish
salt to taste
freshly ground pepper

Cook the potatoes with their skins in a heavy pot or dutch oven in boiling water until tender but not mealy. Drain potatoes. Cool, then slice into 1/4-inch slices.

In the same pot, heat the vegetable oil. Remove from heat. Mix the

Hot Potato Salad (*continued*)

flour with the water, vinegar, and sugar. Carefully, whisk this mixture into the hot oil, return skillet to heat, and continue to whisk on moderate heat until the mixture is smooth and thick. Add the onion, the potatoes, and the ham and heat through. Sprinkle with chopped parsley and stir to blend all ingredients. Pour into a large serving bowl, garnish with chives or scallions and radishes, and serve immediately. Salt and pepper to taste.

Each serving:

 2   **5 mg**   **1**   **Calories 180**

POTATO AND TUNA SALAD
Edward Giobbi

Serves 3

2 medium potatoes
2 whole scallions, coarsely chopped
7-ounce can Italian-style tunafish
1 teaspoon good imported mustard
3 tablespoons wine vinegar
3 tablespoons extra virgin olive oil
1 teaspoon safflower oil
1-1/2 teaspoons finely chopped Italian parsley
12 dried black olives
salt and freshly ground black pepper to taste

Boil potatoes until tender. Drain and, when cool, peel and slice. Toss with the rest of the ingredients and serve at room temperature. Do not refrigerate.

Each serving:

 5   **36 mg**   **1**   **Calories 432**

Variation

Instead of the black olives, use 2 tablespoons drained capers.

MARINATED VEGETABLE SALAD

The tender vegetables in this salad, steamed and flavored with a wine vinaigrette, make an excellent first serving or side dish.

Serves 8

1 cup water
1 package (10 ounces) frozen black-eyed peas,
    thawed and drained
2 cups cauliflower florets
1 medium zucchini, washed and sliced into 1/8-inch pieces
1 small onion, sliced and separated into rings
1 cup frozen corn, thawed and drained
1 cup sliced carrots
12 cherry tomatoes, halved
1/3 cup vegetable oil
1 cup white wine vinegar
2 tablespoons freshly grated Parmesan cheese
1 teaspoon granulated sugar
2 teaspoons paprika
2 cloves garlic, minced
1 teaspoon celery seed
1 teaspoon Dijon mustard
salt to taste
freshly ground pepper
1 cup frozen green peas, thawed and drained
lettuce cups or leaves

In a 4-quart saucepan, heat the water to boiling. Place black-eyed peas in the saucepan, bring to a second boil, cover, and cook for 20 minutes. Add the cauliflower, zucchini, onion, corn, and carrots; continue cooking until vegetables are just tender crisp, about 10 more minutes. Add more water if necessary. Drain. Cool slightly and toss with cherry tomatoes in a large mixing bowl.

While vegetables are cooling, whisk vegetable oil with vinegar, Parmesan cheese, sugar, paprika, garlic, celery seed, and mustard. Pour over vegetables and toss gently to blend. Salt and pepper to taste.

Marinate for at least 8 hours. When ready to serve, mix in the green peas. Marinated vegetable salad may be served in small bowls or atop lettuce leaves.

Each serving:

 1   **1 mg**   4   **Calories 211**

HOT CABBAGE SLAW

Although this salad can be served hot or chilled, it has a more pronounced flavor when hot. It is also very good in sandwiches.

> *Serves 6*
>
> 1 large head green cabbage, shredded (about 6 cups)
> 1/2 cup wine vinegar
> 1 tablespoon vegetable oil
> 3 teaspoons sugar
> 1 teaspoon dill seed
> 1 small onion, grated
> 1/2 cup finely shredded carrot
> 1/4 cup red pepper, seeded and chopped into 1/4-inch cubes
> 1 cup finely shredded red cabbage
> salt to taste
> freshly ground pepper

Steam the green cabbage until just limp, about 5 minutes.

In a large skillet, heat the vinegar, oil, sugar, dill seed, and onion. Pour hot vinegar sauce over the cooked cabbage. Add carrot, red pepper, and red cabbage and toss to blend. Serve immediately or chill and serve cold. Salt and pepper to taste.

Each serving:

 less than 1   **0 mg**   **2**   **Calories 75**

ORANGE AND OLIVE SALAD
Edward Giobbi

> *Serves 4*
>
> 4 navel oranges
> 3 tablespoons extra virgin olive oil
> 1 teaspoon safflower oil
> 1 clove garlic, finely chopped
> 12 dried black olives, pitted and sliced
> salt to taste (optional)
> freshly ground black pepper to taste

Wash the skins of the oranges thoroughly. Leaving the skin on, cut oranges in slices about 1/8 to 1/4 inch thick with a sharp knife.*

---

*Oranges may be sliced ahead of time, but do not blend with other ingredients until ready to serve (olives will stain oranges). Do not refrigerate.

Combine with the remaining ingredients and gently mix.† Serve as a salad.

Each serving:

 2   CH 0 mg   SF2 **less than 1**   **Calories 185**

†Sometimes hot pepper flakes are used in this recipe.

BROCCOLINI

Use any shape of pasta for this tasty salad.

> *Serves 6*

> no stick cooking spray
> 1 tablespoon extra virgin olive oil
> 2-1/2 cups fresh broccoli florets
> 4 green onions with tops, chopped
> 3 cloves garlic, minced
> 1/4 cup red wine vinegar
> 1 tablespoon chopped fresh basil (or 1 teaspoon dried basil)
> 1 tablespoon chopped fresh oregano (or 1 teaspoon dried oregano)
> 2 tablespoons chopped fresh parsley
> 1/8 teaspoon cayenne pepper
> 8 ounces whole wheat pasta elbows or spirals, cooked according to package directions
> 1/2 pound cherry tomatoes, halved
> 1/2 cup freshly grated Parmesan cheese
> salt to taste
> freshly ground pepper

Spray a large frying pan with no stick cooking spray. Add the olive oil and heat. Add the broccoli, green onions, and garlic. Sauté until the vegetables are crisply cooked, about 5 minutes.

Mix the vinegar with the basil, oregano, parsley, and cayenne pepper. Gently toss the pasta with the broccoli mixture, vinegar mixture, cherry tomatoes, and Parmesan cheese. Salt to taste. Top with freshly ground pepper. Refrigerate for 4 hours.

Each serving:

SF1 2   CH 7 mg   SF2 1   **Calories 137**

LOBSTER SALAD

Here's a reward for any job well done! Lobster is expensive, but it is also very low in saturated fat. The lobster in this salad can be fresh, frozen, or canned. Serve this salad on your finest china and you can proudly say, "This lobster salad is superb!"

Serves 2

1 cup cooked lobster, fresh, frozen, or canned
1 medium-sized red onion, chopped finely
2 ribs celery with leaves, chopped
1/3 cup green pepper, chopped into 1/4-inch pieces
3 tablespoons parsley, chopped coarsely
1 teaspoon chopped fresh tarragon
   (or 1/4 teaspoon dry tarragon)
1/4 cup Light Salad Dressing (page 101)
1 teaspoon lemon juice
1/8 teaspoon white pepper
2 medium-sized lettuce cups
parsley sprigs for garnish
lemon wedges for garnish

Combine the lobster with the red onion, celery, green pepper, parsley, and tarragon. Blend the salad dressing with the lemon juice and the white pepper. Mix with the lobster. Chill for 1 hour.

Divide lobster salad between two lettuce cups. Garnish with parsley sprigs and lemon wedges.

Each serving:

 less than 1   **53 mg**   **1**   **Calories 120**

CREAMY PRUNE MOLD

Smooth and sweet, this salad is also very high in calcium and soluble fiber.

Serves 6

1 can (15 ounces) prunes
2 tablespoons lemon juice
1 package (6 ounces) orange-flavored gelatin
1-1/2 cups 1% low-fat cottage cheese
lettuce leaves for garnish
orange slices for garnish

Salads (Clockwise, starting at upper left):

Marinated Vegetable Salad (Page 115)
Pasta Salad (Page 106)
Orange and Olive Salad (Page 116)

Drain the prunes, reserving liquid. Add water to make 1-1/3 cups prune liquid. Pit and chop prunes.

Heat the prune liquid to boiling. Remove from heat and add the lemon juice and the gelatin. Stir until dissolved.

Chill until gelatin is slightly set, about 1 to 1-1/2 hours. With an electric mixer, whip gelatin mixture until it is fluffy. Gently fold in prunes and cottage cheese.

Pour the mixture into a 4-cup mold that has been rinsed with water or into a 9-inch square glass dish. Chill until firm. To remove prune whip from the mold, immerse in warm water for 2 to 3 minutes. Invert onto a 9-inch plate that has been lined with lettuce leaves. Garnish with orange slices.

Each serving:

 less than 1   **3 mg**   **2**   **Calories 121**

7

SANDWICHES

BEAN BURRITO

Refried beans are a good way to add large amounts of soluble fiber to your diet. When you serve refried beans on corn tortillas, you add even more fiber. This portable treat is also tasty and quick to make.

Serves 4

no stick cooking spray
1 tablespoon vegetable oil
1 medium onion, chopped
1 clove garlic, minced
1 cup chili hot beans (or Mexican beans)
4 corn tortillas, warmed
1 cup tomato Salsa (page 35) or commercially prepared salsa
2 ounces shredded Monterey Jack cheese
2 ounces shredded extra sharp Cheddar cheese

Preheat oven to 350°F. Spray a baking pan with no stick cooking spray.

In a heavy skillet, heat the vegetable oil, then brown the onion and garlic. Add the beans, mashing them with a fork as they fry.

Spread each corn tortilla with 1/4 cup bean mixture, 1/4 cup salsa, and 1/4 of each cheese. Roll and carefully place into the prepared pan. Bake for 15 minutes. Burrito will be crispy and cheese melted.

Each serving:

 3   **15 mg**   **3**   **Calories 256**

HOT TURKEY DELIGHT

Just what's in that sliced turkey from the deli? If that question troubles you, then bake your own turkey breast for sandwiches. It's easy and makes good hot sandwiches like this one.

Serves 4

1 turkey breast, 5 pounds* (or 1 pound leftover baked turkey
   breast, sliced and reheated)
1 cup chicken stock (homemade or prepared)
2 tablespoons oat bran
4 slices oat bran bread, toasted
cranberry sauce for garnish
chopped parsley for garnish

Preheat oven to 350°F. Place turkey breast in a heavy pot or large dutch
oven. Bake, uncovered, for 1 hour 30 minutes or until a thermometer
placed in the thickest part of the meat registers 180°F. Remove turkey
from the pot and allow to cool slightly.

While turkey cools, heat chicken stock. Whisk oat bran into chicken
stock. Continue to whisk until mixture thickens. The gravy will be
slightly grainy. (For a smooth gravy, mill oat bran by placing 1-1/2 cups
oat bran in a blender or food processor and blending for 1 to 2 minutes).
Remove from heat.

Remove turkey skin and bone and slice turkey into 3-1/2-ounce portions. Place each on a slice of toast, and cover with 1/4 gravy. Sprinkle
parsley over gravy and garnish with cranberry sauce. Serve immediately.

Each serving:

 less than 1   **83 mg**   **1**   **Calories 184**

*A 5-pound breast will yield approximately 10 3-1/2-ounce turkey servings.

HAM AND BROCCOLI FIESTA

Here's a creamy blend of ham and vegetable in a delicate sauce. Pour
over an English muffin or bagel—delicious!

Serves 4

1 bunch broccoli
1 cup skim milk
3 tablespoons oat bran (for best results,
   use a coarsely milled oat bran)
2 ounces fat-free ham, shredded
1 jar (4 ounces) chopped pimiento, drained
1/2 cup shredded extra sharp Cheddar cheese
4 toasted bagels, or 4 toasted English muffins
salt to taste
freshly ground pepper

Ham and Broccoli Fiesta (*continued*)

Wash the broccoli, cut the stem off, and separate the top into small florets. Peel the stem and chop. Steam in a vegetable steamer for 4 minutes, until tender crisp.

In a medium-sized saucepan, heat the milk. With a wire whisk, blend in the oat bran, whisking until sauce is thickened, then add the ham, broccoli, pimiento, and cheese. Salt to taste. When the cheese is melted and other ingredients are hot, spoon 1/4 of mixture over each of 4 bagels or English muffins (8 halves). Sprinkle with freshly ground pepper.

Each serving:

 4   23 mg   2   **Calories 304**

REUBEN ROLLS

This sandwich takes a little effort, but it is well worth it! It's good hot or cold.

Makes 2 rolls, 12 servings

no stick cooking spray
1-1/2 cups all-purpose white flour
1/2 cup bread flour
1-1/2 cups rye flour
1/2 teaspoon salt
1 package (1/4 ounce) active dry yeast
2 tablespoons vegetable oil
1 tablespoon caraway seed
1-1/4 cups very warm water (115°F)
3 tablespoons Thousand Island dressing
1-1/2 cups sauerkraut, rinsed and drained
8 ounces fat-free ham slices
4 ounces part-skim mozzarella cheese, thinly sliced
2 ounces freshly grated Parmesan cheese

Spray a large bowl with no stick cooking spray.

In a second large mixing bowl blend 1 cup of the all-purpose white flour with the bread flour, rye flour, salt, and yeast. Stir thoroughly using a wooden spoon. Add the oil, caraway seed, and very warm water. Continue to stir until all ingredients are well blended. The dough will be stiff. Turn onto a floured board and knead in enough of the remaining flour until the dough is smooth and satiny. This will take about 10 minutes. (This dough may also be mixed and kneaded in a food processor or with an electric mixer that has a dough hook.)

Place the dough in the prepared bowl, turn to coat all sides with no stick cooking spray, cover with plastic wrap, and allow to rise in a warm, draft-free place for 60 minutes. The dough should be warm, light, and almost doubled in bulk.

Spray a large cookie sheet with no stick cooking spray.

Knead down the dough and divide it into 2 balls. On a well-floured surface, roll the first part into a 9×12-inch rectangle. Spread half the Thousand Island dressing on the rectangle, keeping it 1 inch away from all four sides. Then sprinkle half the sauerkraut on top of the Thousand Island dressing. Next, place half of the ham slices over the sauerkraut, half the mozzarella slices on top of the ham, and half the grated Parmesan cheese on top of all. Carefully roll sandwich up, keeping fillings in as tightly as possible. The roll should be 12 inches by approximately 3 inches. Carefully place on prepared cookie sheet seam side down. Repeat with second Reuben Roll.

Make sure all edges of the rolls are sealed and the ends of the rolls are folded under. Cover with plastic wrap and allow to rise in a warm, draft-free place for 30 more minutes. Preheat oven to 350°F. Brush with beaten egg white. Bake for 35 to 40 minutes or until roll is well browned. Serve hot, room temperature, or cold.

Each serving:

 2   **15 mg**   **1**   **Calories 225**

CALIFORNIA SLIM

Here's a magnificent combination of veggies. If you don't have a sandwich toaster, grill the sandwich on a griddle or in a large skillet.

Makes 1 sandwich

1/2 cup Brussels sprouts
1 cup water
1 tablespoon chopped celery
2 tablespoons shredded carrots
1/4 cup spicy sprouts
2 teaspoons Light Salad Dressing (page 101)
1/2 teaspoon Dijon mustard
1 slice (1 ounce) part-skim mozzarella cheese
salt to taste
freshly ground pepper
2 slices oat bran (or other) bread or 1 large pita
no stick cooking spray

Clean the Brussels sprouts. Make an X in the base of each to facilitate cooking. Heat the water in a small saucepan. Add Brussels sprouts and cook for 5 minutes. Add celery and carrots and cook until vegetables are tender, about 5 more minutes. Drain.

California Slim *(continued)*

Blend the cooked vegetables with the sprouts, salad dressing, and mustard. Salt and pepper to taste. Spread onto a slice of oat bran bread. Top with cheese and the second slice of bread.

Spray a sandwich toaster or griddle with no stick cooking spray. Grill the sandwich on both sides until hot, about 5 minutes. Or, stuff the mixture and cheese into the pita and bake for 10 minutes in a 350°F oven.

Each sandwich:

 3   18 mg   2   **Calories 255**

PITA PIZZAS

This sandwich is quick and easy. It can be made with prepared tomato sauce, or you can use your own freshly prepared sauce.

> *Serves 2*
>
> no stick cooking spray
> 2 Oat Bran Pitas (page 96) or regular pita bread
> 1/2 cup Tomato Sauce (page 194 or prepared)
> 1/4 cup corn, frozen, canned, or fresh, cooked and drained
> 1 small zucchini, scrubbed and grated with skin on
> 1/4 cup shredded part-skim mozzarella cheese
> 2 tablespoons freshly grated Parmesan cheese
> freshly ground pepper

Preheat broiler. Spray a cookie sheet with no stick cooking spray. Place the pitas on the cookie sheet and broil 4 inches from source of heat until both sides are crispy, about 5 minutes.

Reduce the oven temperature to 350°F.

Top each pita with half of the spaghetti sauce, corn, and zucchini. Sprinkle with mozzarella and Parmesan cheese. Bake for 20 minutes. The cheese should be melted and the vegetables hot. Pepper to taste.

Each serving (on a 7-inch pita bread):

 4   19 mg   2   **Calories 301**

QUESADILLA

Here's a favorite sandwich that's quick to make if you keep the ingredients on hand. Or you may use commercially prepared flour tortillas and salsa.

Serves 2

no stick cooking spray
4 Oat Bran Tortillas (page 88) or flour tortillas
1/2 cup fresh tomato Salsa (page 35)
1/2 cup cooked corn
1/4 cup shredded Monterey Jack cheese

Spray a griddle or large skillet with no stick cooking spray. Heat to hot.

Spread half of the salsa onto each tortilla. Sprinkle with half of the corn, then half of the cheese. Top with second tortilla.

Grill, turning one time, until tortillas are golden brown and filling is hot.

Each serving (made with Oat Bran Tortillas and homemade Salsa):

 less than 1   **20 mg**   **3**   **Calories 313**

VEGGIE PITAS

This sandwich is an all-time favorite at our house. We use a wide variety of veggies, but always onion, garlic, and tomato.

Serves 4

no stick cooking spray
1 tablespoon olive oil
1 medium-sized onion, sliced
1 clove garlic, minced
1 large tomato, chopped
1 stalk (1 cup) broccoli, separated into florets,
    stem peeled and sliced
1 large zucchini, scrubbed and shredded with skin on
1 large carrot, sliced
1 tablespoon chopped fresh basil (or 1 teaspoon dry basil)
1/2 teaspoon ground oregano
4 Oat Bran Pitas (page 96) or regular pita bread
1 tablespoon chopped parsley
1/4 cup grated Parmesan cheese
1/2 cup (4 ounces) shredded part-skim mozzarella cheese
salt to taste
freshly ground pepper

Preheat broiler. Spray a baking sheet with no stick cooking spray.

Heat olive oil in a medium-sized skillet. Add onion and garlic and cook until they are brown. Add tomato, broccoli, zucchini, carrot, basil,

Veggie Pitas (*continued*)

and oregano. Cover and sauté vegetables for about 6 minutes, until they are tender crisp.

Meanwhile, place the pita bread on the baking sheet and broil 4 inches from source of heat until the pita is crisp, about 5 minutes. With a slotted spoon, spoon 1/4 of veggie mixture onto each pita bread. Sprinkle with parsley. Blend cheeses, and top hot vegetables with cheese mixture. Broil, 4 inches from source of heat until cheese is melted and bubbly, about 5 minutes. Salt and pepper to taste.

Each serving (using a 7-inch pita bread):

 5   21 mg   2   **Calories 290**

FAMOUS VEGETABLE SANDWICH

Here's a good recipe for tofu. It has the flavor of egg salad with almost no cholesterol. This is a chilled sandwich that would be great for the executive lunch box! The filling will stay fresh for up to 1 week, refrigerated.

Makes filling for 8 sandwiches

3/4 to 1 pound firm tofu
1/4 cup Light Salad Dressing (page 101)
1 tablespoon Dijon mustard
1 tablespoon soy sauce (or 1 tablespoon Worcestershire sauce)
1 clove garlic, minced
1 rib celery, chopped
1/2 teaspoon tumeric
1 tablespoon chopped fresh dill weed (or 1 teaspoon dried dill)
1/2 cup grated carrot
3 minced scallions
salt to taste
freshly ground pepper

Drain tofu. In a medium-sized bowl, mash the tofu with a fork. Add salad dressing, mustard, and seasonings. Add vegetables and lightly mix again. Chill. Salt and pepper to taste.

Serve with lettuce and tomato on oat bran bread, whole-grain bread, or in large pita pockets.

Each sandwich (on 2 slices oat bran bread):

 1   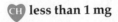 less than 1 mg   2   **Calories 207**

8

SEAFOOD ENTREES

FRESH PERCH FILLETS WITH VEGETABLES

Ocean perch is particularly good for this tasty meal, although any mild fish fillets will work. Attractive and colorful, this dish is also very low in fat and calories.

Serves 4

1 cup water
1 cup zucchini slices
1 medium-sized red pepper, sliced
1 cup snow peas, washed and stemmed
1 medium-sized onion, sliced
1 cup sliced celery
1 cup broccoli florets
no stick cooking spray
1 tablespoon olive oil
4 fresh ocean perch fillets, 6 ounces each
1 teaspoon chopped fresh basil (or 1/2 teaspoon dried basil)
1/2 teaspoon dried chervil
8 thin slices lemon for garnish
paprika for garnish
chopped parsley for garnish
salt to taste
freshly ground pepper

In a medium-sized saucepan, bring the water to a boil, then add the zucchini, red pepper, snow peas, onion, and celery. Cover saucepan and cook for 5 minutes. Add broccoli and cook until broccoli is bright green and tender crisp, another 5 minutes.

Meanwhile, spray a medium-sized skillet with no stick cooking spray, add the olive oil, and heat. When oil is hot, add the perch fillets. When one side of the fillets are browned, turn them over, reduce heat, cover

Fresh Perch Fillets with Vegetables (*continued*)

pan, and continue to cook. The perch will be cooked in about 10 minutes, when the fish is translucent and flakes when poked with the tines of a fork. Sprinkle on basil and chervil.

To serve, place the fish in the center of a platter and arrange the vegetables around the edges. Top with lemon slices, paprika, chopped parsley, and freshly grated pepper. Salt to taste.

Each serving:

 less than 1   **46 mg**   **3**   **Calories 188**

FILLETS OF SOLE PRIMAVERA
Edward Giobbi

This is a delightful, light, attractive-looking dish.

> *Serves 4*
>
> 4 cups sliced mushrooms
> 2 tablespoons safflower or peanut oil
> salt and freshly ground black pepper to taste
> 4 fillets of lemon sole, grey sole, or flounder
>   (about 6 ounces each)
> juice of 1 lime or lemon (I prefer lime)
> 4 teaspoons Pesto (page 195), optional
> 2 cups chopped whole scallions
> 4 cups fresh ripe tomatoes cut into 1/2-inch cubes
> olive oil
> 4 tablespoons minced Italian parsley or fresh coriander

Sauté the mushrooms in the oil until all moisture is cooked out, then season with salt and pepper.

Preheat the oven to 500°F.

Wash and pat the fish dry and place in a shallow baking dish. Squeeze lime juice or lemon juice over, add salt and pepper, and spread 1 teaspoon pesto over each fillet. Add a layer of mushrooms, a thick layer of scallions, and a layer of tomatoes so that the vegetables make a mound. Season with more salt and pepper and sprinkle with olive oil, then parsley.

Place baking dish, uncovered, in the oven and bake until fish separates when pricked with a fork—8 to 10 minutes. To serve, lift out each portion with a wide spatula so that the fish does not separate.

Each serving:

 1   **86 mg**   **2**   **Calories 319**

FILLET OF FISH GENOA STYLE
Edward Giobbi

Serves 3

1 fish fillet about 1-1/2 pounds, cut crosswise
    in pieces about 1-1/2 inches wide
flour for dredging
corn oil or vegetable oil for shallow-frying
salt and freshly ground black pepper to taste
3 tablespoons olive oil
1 tablespoon safflower oil
2 cloves garlic, minced
2 tablespoons chopped capers
juice of 2 lemons
4 tablespoons minced Italian parsley

Dredge the fish in the flour. Heat 3/4 inch oil in a medium skillet. When oil is hot, add the fish and cook about a minute on each side for thicker fillets—less for thin. Do not overcook or let fish get too brown. As soon as it is tender, remove from oil and blot on paper towels.

    In the meantime, heat the olive oil and safflower oil in a small pan, then add the garlic. As soon as garlic begins to turn golden, add the capers, lemon juice, and parsley; cook a minute or so, then pour over hot fish.

Each serving:

 3   113 mg   less than 1   **Calories 399**

SCROD FILLET WITH POTATOES
Edward Giobbi

Serves 4

4 medium potatoes, peeled and cut in half lengthwise
2 tablespoons olive oil
1 teaspoon safflower oil
1 medium onion, thinly sliced
4 tomatoes, coarsely chopped
12 dried black olives
2 tablespoons chopped fresh basil or 1 teaspoon dried
salt and hot pepper flakes or freshly ground black pepper
    to taste
2 pounds fresh scrod fillet in one piece, or cod,
    striped bass, or any large white-fleshed fish
1 tablespoon crushed rosemary
1 teaspoon chopped fresh mint for garnish

Scrod Fillet with Potatoes (*continued*)
Boil the potatoes about 5 minutes, then drain and reserve.

Heat the two oils in a medium skillet and add the onion, tomatoes, olives, basil, salt, and pepper (I prefer hot pepper flakes). Cover and simmer over moderate heat for 10 minutes.

Preheat oven to 450°F.

Put the fish on a baking tray and sprinkle with rosemary and salt and black pepper. Arrange the potatoes around fish and pour sauce over fish and potatoes. Cover with foil and bake for 15 minutes.

Garnish with mint.

Each serving:

 1   113 mg   2   **Calories 428**

CAJUN CRABMEAT STUFFED SNAPPER

Look for a good buy on snapper, then go for it! Crabmeat and snapper are both low in saturated fat. The preparation method here allows for maximum flavor with minimum saturated fat.

Serves 4

no stick cooking spray
2 tablespoons light margarine
1/4 cup minced onion
1/4 cup chopped celery
2 tablespoons chopped fresh parsley
1 clove garlic, minced
2 tablespoons cajun seasoning (for best results,
    use a cajun seasoning without added salt or MSG)
2 tablespoons all-purpose white flour
1 cup dry white wine
1/2 cup cooked crabmeat, fresh, frozen, or canned
4 red snapper fillets, about 7 ounces each (haddock, halibut,
    and other white-flesh fish can also be used)
lemon wedges for garnish
parsley sprigs for garnish
salt to taste
freshly ground pepper

Preheat the oven to 400°F. Spray a cookie sheet with no stick cooking spray.

In a medium-sized skillet, heat the margarine. Sauté the onion, celery, parsley, and garlic until the onion is translucent. Mix 1 tablespoon of the cajun seasoning and flour with the white wine. Whisk into the onion mixture, cooking until smooth and thick. Add the crabmeat.

Divide the crabmeat among the 4 fillets. Sprinkle with the remaining cajun seasoning. Place on cookie sheet and bake for 12 to 15 minutes; the snapper flesh should just flake. Serve on a platter garnished with lemon and parsley. Salt and pepper to taste.

Each serving:

 less than 1   **97 mg**   **less than 1**   **Cal. 292**

STUFFED TROUT

Here's entertaining made easy! Your guests will love this healthy meal. Make and chill the stuffing in advance, and the trout will be ready in 25 minutes!

Serves 4

4 whole small trout, 6 to 8 ounces each,* cleaned
2 tablespoons light margarine
1 medium-sized onion, finely chopped
1/2 cup chopped celery
1/2 cup chopped green peppers (1/4-inch pieces)
1 medium zucchini, scrubbed and grated with skin on
2 cloves garlic, minced
1 cup fresh bread crumbs
2 egg whites
2 tablespoons freshly grated Parmesan cheese
no stick cooking spray
chopped parsley
lemon wedges
salt to taste
freshly ground pepper

Wash the whole trout, removing any small bones. Pat dry.

Melt the margarine in a large skillet and add the onion, celery, peppers, zucchini, and garlic. Sauté for 3 minutes. Remove from heat. Add the bread crumbs and blend well. Mix the egg whites with the Parmesan cheese and add to the bread crumb mixture. Chill stuffing for at least 30 minutes or up to 24 hours.

Preheat the oven to 350°F. Spray a baking pan with no stick cooking spray. Open trout and lightly stuff each trout with 1/4 of the stuffing (1/2

*If whole trout are unavailable, use trout fillets. To stuff, divide the stuffing among the 4 fillets. Bake for 15 to 20 minutes, until fish just flakes.

Stuffed Trout (*continued*)

cup to 3/4 cup). Spread stuffing over interior surface of trout. Close trout and place on the baking pan. Bake for 25 minutes; the stuffing should be hot, and the fish should just flake when pricked with the tines of a fork.

Remove to a serving platter. Sprinkle with parsley and garnish platter with lemon wedges. Salt and pepper to taste.

Each serving:

 1   2 mg   1   **Calories 289**

FRESHWATER FISH STEW
Edward Giobbi

> *Serves 6*
>
> 2 pounds catfish (if large, cut in sections)*
> 2 pounds freshwater perch
> 3 tablespoons olive oil
> 1 tablespoon safflower oil
> 2 medium onions, finely sliced
> 2 cloves garlic, finely chopped
> 1/2 cup dry white wine
> 2 cups chopped tomatoes, fresh if possible (drain if canned)
> 1 teaspoon thyme
> 6 slices French or Italian bread, toasted
> chopped Italian parsley or fresh mint for garnish (optional)†

Gut the fish, scrape off scales, wash well, and set aside.

Heat the oils in a medium skillet, then add onions and cook until they wilt. Add garlic and cook several minutes. Add wine, cover, lower heat, and cook until half the wine cooks out. Add tomatoes and thyme, cover, and cook over low to medium heat for 10 minutes.

Place catfish in a shallow ovenproof dish, cover, and cook in a pre-heated 500°F oven about 10 minutes. Add perch, cover, and return to oven to cook about 5 to 8 minutes, depending on the size of the fish.

Serve hot over toast.

Each serving:

 2   62 mg   1   **Calories 341**

---

*You may find that the odor catfish expels while cooking is offensive (it is similar to dried stockfish), but the taste is delicate and most satisfying.
†I find chopped parsley or chopped fresh mint enhances this recipe, although it does not call for it.

BROILED SPLIT FISH WITH PESTO
Edward Giobbi

Any small to medium fish that can be split can be used in this recipe, but a white-fleshed fish is better here than a dark-fleshed fish.

Serves 2

> 2 white-fleshed fish, such as rock bass, small striped bass, small red snapper, etc., split
> salt and freshly ground black pepper to taste
> 2 tablespoons Pesto (page 195)
> juice of 1 to 2 limes or lemons

Place fish on a baking tray, salt and pepper it, and spoon about 1 tablespoon pesto on top of each portion.

Bake fish, uncovered, in a preheated 450°F oven until cooked, about 15 minutes. Squeeze lime or lemon juice over fish several minutes before serving.

Each serving:

 2   78 mg   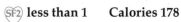 less than 1   **Calories 178**

STEAMED RED SNAPPERS
Edward Giobbi

Any white-fleshed whole fish can be cooked this way—whiting, black bass, weakfish, trout, porgy, and so forth.

Serves 2

> 2 small red snappers, cleaned, heads on
> 2 tablespoons chopped fresh coriander or Italian parsley
> 1 teaspoon minced garlic
> salt and freshly ground black pepper to taste
> about 10 large lettuce leaves from such lettuce
>   as Bibb, romaine, etc.

Wash fish. Stuff cavity with coriander and garlic. Salt and pepper outside of fish.

Blanch lettuce leaves in boiling water about 10 seconds. Run cold water in pot until lettuce leaves cool. Carefully wrap fish with lettuce leaves, leaving head exposed.

Place fish in a steamer, or on a straw or bamboo rack. Cover and steam about 15 minutes. Serve whole fish, still wrapped in lettuce leaves.

Each serving:

 less than 1   97 mg   1   **Calories 177**

SWORDFISH STEAK MARINER STYLE
Edward Giobbi

Serves 2

4 teaspoons olive oil
4 teaspoons safflower oil
1 medium onion, finely chopped
1 cup chopped tomatoes, fresh if possible (drain if canned)
6 dried black olives, pitted and sliced
hot pepper flakes to taste (optional)
1 tablespoon capers
1 tablespoon chopped fresh mint
salt and freshly ground black pepper to taste
1 swordfish steak, about 1 pound
flour for dredging
juice of 1 lemon
1 tablespoon finely chopped Italian parsley for garnish

Heat 1 teaspoon of the olive oil and 1 teaspoon of the safflower oil in a medium skillet, then add onion. When it begins to brown, add tomatoes, olives, hot pepper flakes, capers, and mint. Cover and simmer for 10 minutes, then remove from skillet and reserve. In the same skillet heat remaining 3 teaspoons olive oil and 3 teaspoons safflower oil.

Put salt and freshly ground black pepper on the swordfish, dust lightly with flour, and add to the hot oil. Lightly brown both sides of the fish. Add lemon juice, turn fish, and add sauce. Cover and cook over moderate heat about 5 minutes. Garnish with parsley.

Each serving:

 5   125 mg   1   **Calories 530**

BROILED MACKEREL
Edward Giobbi

Serves 3

2-pound whole mackerel, split, head on
juice of 1 lime
hot pepper flakes to taste (optional)
salt to taste

Garnish

juice of 1 lemon
2 tablespoons finely chopped Italian parsley
2 cloves garlic, finely chopped
2 tablespoons extra virgin olive oil

Seafood Entrées (Clockwise, starting at upper left):
Swordfish Mariner Style (Page 134)
Shrimp with Artichoke Hearts and Mushrooms (Page 136)
Broiled Split Fish with Pesto (Page 133)

Place the split mackerel on a plate and sprinkle the lime juice, pepper flakes, and a little salt on top. Refrigerate and marinate for at least 2 hours.

In a small bowl, mix the lemon juice, parsley, garlic, and olive oil. Put aside.

Broil the mackerel over hot coals about 3 to 4 minutes on each side. Garnish fish with lemon-juice-and-parsley mixture.

Variation

The fish can be served without sauce. In that case, garnish with lemon wedges.

Each serving:

 6   **CH 1 mg**   **SF2 less than 1**   **Calories 326**

FISH CAKES
Edward Giobbi

These fish cakes are very good with horseradish and tomato sauce and a green salad.

Serves 4

1 pound any white-fleshed fish fillets, including freshwater fish
3 medium potatoes, boiled, peeled, and mashed
1-1/2 teaspoons finely chopped Italian parsley
1 teaspoon minced garlic
2 egg whites, lightly beaten
salt and freshly ground black pepper to taste
1-1/2 cups fresh bread crumbs
corn oil or peanut oil for frying

Grind the fish and place in a mixing bowl with the mashed potatoes, parsley, garlic, 1 of the egg whites, salt, and pepper. Blend well, then form into 8 patties about the size of a medium-sized hamburger. Roll in the other egg white, dust with bread crumbs, then gently pat to make the bread crumbs adhere.

Pour about 3/4 inch oil into a medium skillet. When oil is hot, add patties, 3 or 4 at a time, until lightly brown on both sides. Blot on paper towels and serve immediately.

Each serving:

 less than 1   **CH 57 mg**   **1**   **Calories 252**

SHRIMP WITH ARTICHOKE HEARTS
Edward Giobbi

Serves 6

3 tablespoons olive oil
1 tablespoon safflower oil
2 cups sliced fresh mushrooms
salt and freshly ground black pepper to taste
3/4-ounce package dried boletus mushrooms,
    soaked in warm water for 15 minutes
2 cloves garlic, finely chopped
1 cup thinly sliced scallions
3/4 cup dry white wine
2 tablespoons finely chopped fresh mint
1 teaspoon crushed rosemary
9-ounce package frozen artichoke hearts
1 pound large shrimp, with shells on

Heat the oils in a large skillet, then add fresh mushrooms, salt, and pepper and cook over high heat, uncovered, stirring often until mushrooms begin to brown. Drain dried mushrooms, reserving 2 tablespoons liquid. Add dried mushrooms and reserved liquid, garlic, scallions, wine, mint, and rosemary to the cooked mushrooms. Cover and cook over medium heat for about 10 minutes.

In the meantime, blanch artichoke hearts in boiling water, drain when water returns to a boil, and add to mixture in skillet. Cover and cook about 10 minutes over low to medium heat. Taste for salt. Add shrimp, turn up heat, and cook until they turn pink. Do not overcook.

Remove shells from shrimp before serving.

Each serving:

 1   78 mg   1   **Calories 173**

SALT COD FLORENTINE STYLE
Edward Giobbi

Serves 4

3 tablespoons olive oil
1 tablespoon safflower oil
2 cups finely chopped onion
1 teaspoon minced garlic
3 tablespoons chopped Italian parsley
2 cups seeded, chopped tomatoes
2 pounds salt cod, presoaked, cut into pieces 2 × 2-1/2 inches

freshly ground black pepper to taste
flour for dredging
corn or vegetable oil for frying

Soak the codfish in a pot of cold water for 2 to 3 days, depending on the thickness of the fish, changing the water from time to time. Drain, wash, and pat dry.

Heat the 2 oils in a medium saucepan or skillet. Add the onion, and when it begins to brown, add the garlic and parsley. Sauté for a minute, then add the tomatoes, cover, and simmer for 20 minutes.

In the meantime, wash and blot dry the presoaked cod. Grind black pepper over the fish and dust with flour. Heat about 1/2 inch corn oil or vegetable oil in a medium skillet and when hot gently add floured pieces of salt cod and lightly brown on both sides. Remove from oil and blot on paper towels, then add to sauce. Cover and simmer over low heat for 25 minutes.

Each serving:

 3   185 mg   1   **Calories 536**

SEAFOOD VERACRUZ

This stew combines many flavors and textures. It is very low in saturated fat and a good source of fiber.

Serves 6

2 tablespoons extra virgin olive oil
1 large green pepper, seeded and cut into 1/2-inch chunks
1 large yellow onion, sliced
2 cloves garlic, minced
2 large ripe tomatoes, chopped
1 teaspoon dry chervil
1/2 teaspoon dried oregano
1 teaspoon cumin
1 teaspoon chili powder
1/2 pound uncooked shrimp, shelled, deveined, and cleaned
1/2 pound large (sea) scallops, cut in halves
1/2 pound fresh cod, cut into 1-inch pieces
1/2 cup dry white wine
2 tablespoons all-purpose flour
salt to taste
2 cups hot cooked rice
2 tablespoons freshly chopped parsley for garnish
6 lime twists for garnish
freshly ground pepper

Seafood Veracruz (*continued*)

Heat the oil in a large stock pot, then add the green pepper, onion, and garlic and sauté for 5 minutes. Add the tomatoes, chervil, oregano, cumin, and chili pepper.

Cover and cook for 10 minutes, until tomatoes are cooked and flavors developed.

Add the shrimp, scallops, and cod, cover, and cook until shrimps are cooked, about 3 minutes. In a small bowl, whisk wine and flour together, then whisk into the seafood mixture. Heat for an additional 2 minutes until sauce thickens and flour cooks. Salt to taste.

Divide rice among 6 large soup bowls, then top with the seafood and sauce. Garnish with chopped parsley, a twist of lime, and freshly ground pepper.

Each serving:

 less than 1   **88 mg**   **1**   **Calories 181**

TUNA LOAF
Edward Giobbi

The overly rich, dense texture of tuna is totally transformed in this light, airy dish—so much less compact than the usual meatloaf. It doesn't slice *perfectly*, but you can re-form each slice nicely on the plate when you serve it. It should be served at room temperature with a mixed green salad as an accompaniment. Use leftovers as a sandwich spread.

Serves 6

3 boiling potatoes, about 1 pound
2 tablespoons olive oil
1 teaspoon safflower oil
1 large onion, finely chopped
3 egg whites, lightly beaten
1/2 cup bread crumbs
2 tablespoons grated lemon rind
2-1/2 tablespoons finely chopped Italian parsley
salt and freshly ground black pepper to taste
1/2 tablespoon good mustard
2 cans (7 ounces each) tunafish
spinach sauce, or another sauce, such as hot pepper or red sauce

Boil the potatoes, peel, and mash in a mixing bowl. Heat the two oils in a medium skillet, add the onion, and cook until it begins to brown. Add to the mashed potatoes along with the rest of the ingredients, and mix well.

Place the mixture in the center of a piece of cheesecloth, roll up cheese-cloth around it, and form a sausage shape about 3 inches wide and 10 inches long. Tie ends of cheesecloth. Place tuna roll in a steamer and steam for 20 minutes, or poach for 20 minutes in water or broth.

Remove roll from heat and allow to cool. Take off cheesecloth, cut loaf in slices about 3/4 inch thick, and serve with one of the recommended sauces.

Each serving:

 4   37 mg   (SF2) 1   **Calories 408**

PIZZA WITH MIXED SEAFOOD

Here's a personal favorite. It's full of flavor and great nutrition.

Makes 1 14-inch pizza, 8 slices

> 1 tablespoon vegetable oil, preferably safflower or canola
> 2 stems broccoli, washed, separated into small florets
>   and peeled and sliced stems
> 1-1/2 cups sliced fresh mushrooms
> 1/2 cup chopped onion
> 2 teaspoons chopped fresh oregano
>   (or 3/4 teaspoon dried oregano)
> 1 tablespoon chopped fresh cilantro
> 1/3 cup low-fat milk
> 1 8-ounce package of reduced-fat cream cheese, softened
> 1 unbaked 14-inch oat bran Pizza Crust (page 98)
> 1 can (6-3/4 ounce) clams, drained and picked over
> 1 can (6-3/4 ounce) tiny shrimp, drained
> salt to taste
> freshly ground pepper

Preheat oven to 425°F. In a medium-sized frying pan, heat oil. Sauté broccoli, mushrooms, and onion for 5 minutes. Add oregano and cilantro. Remove from heat; stir in milk and cream cheese. Allow cream cheese to soften. Mash until a smooth sauce forms.

Arrange seafood on the 14-inch oat bran pizza shell. Spoon vegetable mixture over the top. Salt to taste.

Bake for 20 minutes. Sprinkle with freshly ground pepper. When cooked, pizza topping will be lightly browned and the underside of the crust will be deep brown. Cut into 8 slices.

Each slice:

 4   73 mg   (SF2) 3   **Calories 316**

STEAMED FISH BALLS
Edward Giobbi

Serves 3 as a main course

1 flounder, about 1-1/2 pounds, filleted,
    head and bones reserved*
1/4 pound fresh spinach, washed, blanched,
    drained, and chopped
1 teaspoon minced garlic
1 egg white, lightly beaten
1 teaspoon grated lemon zest (yellow part of rind)
salt to taste

The Sauce

1 tablespoon olive oil
1 tablespoon safflower oil
1 teaspoon minced garlic
2 anchovy fillets, chopped
fish head and bones
3 tablespoons dry white wine
1 cup chopped tomatoes, fresh if possible (drain if canned)
1 tablespoon chopped Italian parsley
hot pepper flakes to taste

First make the sauce: Heat the two oils in a medium skillet or saucepan, then add the minced garlic and chopped anchovy fillets. Cook until the garlic begins to take on color. Add fish head and bones and wine. Cover and simmer about 3 minutes. Add tomatoes and parsley, cover, and simmer for 20 minutes. Remove and discard bones and head. Strain sauce or blend in a food processor. Keep it warm while you prepare the fish.

Chop the fillets, add chopped cooked spinach, minced garlic, egg white, lemon zest, and salt and mix well. Form 6 balls about the size of golf balls.

Steam the fish balls in a steamer about 3 to 5 minutes.

Serve hot on a heated platter. Spoon sauce over balls and serve with steamed vegetables.

Each serving:

 1   40 mg   less than 1   **Calories 183**

*Any white fish will do, including freshwater fish.

9

POULTRY & MEAT ENTREES

BROILED CHICKEN
Edward Giobbi

Serves 6

2 chickens, split
salt and freshly ground black pepper to taste
1 tablespoon rosemary

The Basting Sauce

1 cup wine vinegar
1 teaspoon finely chopped garlic

Salt and pepper both sides of the chicken, then rub with rosemary leaves. Broil chicken over coals, about 20 minutes on each side, basting occasionally with the wine vinegar and garlic when the chicken begins to brown.

Each serving:

 1   **70 mg**   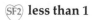 **less than 1**   **Calories 112**

CHICKEN COUNTRY STYLE
Edward Giobbi

Enjoy this dish during the winter months; it is both hardy and delicate. It is best when made with an older chicken—I use a full-grown rooster. If a tough chicken is used, then allow more cooking time and add vegetables later.

141

Chicken Country Style (*continued*)

> *Serves 8*
>
> 1 large chicken, about 4 pounds
> 1 bay leaf
> 3 stalks celery, cut into 3-inch lengths
> 2 cups carrots, scraped and cut into 2-inch lengths
> salt and freshly ground black pepper to taste
> 2 cups chopped tomatoes, fresh if possible (drain if canned)
> 1 pound Brussels sprouts, trimmed
> 1 tablespoon rosemary
> 12 small white onions, peeled
> 1/2 pound mushrooms (cut large mushrooms in half)
> 8 medium potatoes, peeled and cut into large chunks
> 2 cups fresh shelled peas or a 10-ounce package frozen peas,
>   blanched and drained
> 3 tablespoons chopped Italian parsley
> finely chopped Italian parsley for garnish

Cut up the chicken, cover with cold salted water, and soak about 2 hours. Wash and drain.

Place chicken in a wide pot about 3 inches deep, so that all the chicken fits in one layer.

Add 1 cup water, bay leaf, celery, carrots, salt, and pepper and bring to a boil. Add tomatoes, cover, and boil over medium heat about 20 minutes. Add Brussels sprouts, rosemary, and onions and continue cooking 20 minutes more. Add mushrooms, potatoes, peas, parsley, salt, and pepper and cook, partially covered, about 20 minutes more, until potatoes are tender.

Garnish with parsley.

Each serving:

 1   71 mg   4   **Calories 336**

CHICKEN BREASTS WITH SHRIMP AND ASPARAGUS
Edward Giobbi

> *Serves 4*
>
> 2 whole chicken breasts, skinned, boned,
>   and fat removed (about 1-1/2 pounds)
> juice of 1 lemon
> 2 cloves garlic, finely chopped
> 2-1/2 tablespoons safflower oil
> 1 tablespoon olive oil

2 cups asparagus cut into 2-inch lengths
salt and freshly ground black pepper to taste
flour for dredging
1 cup chicken stock
1-1/2 cups thinly sliced scallions
1 tablespoon finely chopped fresh mint
1/2 pound shrimp, shelled*
3 tablespoons freshly grated Parmesan cheese

Place chicken breasts in a bowl with lemon juice and garlic, and marinate at least 2 hours.

Heat the oils in a medium skillet, then add asparagus and cook, uncovered, over high heat, tossing, until tender. Remove asparagus with a slotted spoon and reserve.

Salt and pepper the chicken breasts and dust lightly with flour. Turn heat to high under skillet, add chicken breasts, and brown them, uncovered.

When both sides of the chicken breasts are lightly browned, add stock, scallions, and mint, cover, lower heat to medium, and simmer about 10 minutes. Add shrimp and asparagus. Cover, turn up heat, and cook until shrimp turn pink—do not overcook them. Sprinkle with Parmesan cheese. Turn off heat and let dish sit for several minutes. Serve on hot plates.

Each serving:

 2   12 mg   1   **Calories 318**

*Shucked fresh oysters can be used in place of shrimp.

BROILED CHICKEN WITH BEER SAUCE
Edward Giobbi

Serves 2

2-3/4- to 3-pound frying chicken, split*
salt and freshly ground black pepper to taste
1 cup tomatoes, peeled, seeded, chopped,
   and put through a food mill
1 cup light beer
1 tablespoon good mustard
1 tablespoon finely chopped Italian parsley
1 teaspoon crushed rosemary

*The average small fryer, or spring chicken as we called them, weighed from 2-1/2 to 2-3/4 pounds dressed. Unfortunately, it is rather difficult to find small fryers in the average supermarket today.

Broiled Chicken with Beer Sauce (*continued*)
Wash the split chicken and salt and pepper it.

Heat the broiler for at least 15 minutes. Place the chicken in a baking dish skin side down and broil close to the heat, about 8 minutes on each side. In the meantime, boil tomatoes and beer in a small saucepan, uncovered, over moderate heat until reduced by half. Stir the mustard, parsley, and rosemary in, then spoon sauce over chicken. Turn chicken over occasionally and baste with the sauce. Cook until chicken is tender and separates from bone—a 2-3/4-pound chicken takes about 45 minutes. Watch carefully or reduce heat if the broiler seems too high.

Garnish with remaining sauce. This sauce, by the way, can be used to baste any broiled meats.

Each serving:

 3   192 mg   less than 1 Calories 362

CHICKEN BREASTS WITH PEPPERS, ONIONS, MUSHROOMS, AND TOMATOES
Edward Giobbi

Serves 4 to 6

3 plump boned chicken breast halves, skin and fat removed,
    then cut into 1/2-inch strips
2 cloves garlic, chopped
juice of 1-1/2 to 2 lemons or limes
salt and freshly ground black pepper to taste
4 tablespoons safflower oil or 2 olive oil and 2 safflower
2 cups green peppers cut into 1/2-inch strips
2 medium onions, sliced
1 cup thinly sliced mushrooms
1 cup coarsely chopped tomatoes, fresh if possible
    (drain if canned)
pinch hot pepper flakes
2 tablespoons chopped Italian parsley

Put the chicken breasts in a deep bowl and marinate in garlic, lemon or lime juice, salt, and pepper for at least 2 hours. Heat 2 tablespoons of the safflower oil in a skillet, then add the vegetables, hot pepper flakes, and parsley. Quickly cook vegetables, stirring often—do not overcook. Remove from skillet when vegetables are *al dente*.

Drain the chicken and reserve the marinade. Add remaining 2 tablespoons oil to skillet and when hot add chicken. Cook over very high heat a couple of minutes, turning often, until chicken whitens; if the meat starts to stick to the pan, add a little marinade to loosen it. Add vegetables and cook together for several minutes.

Serve with rice.

Each serving:

 1   30 mg   SF2 1   **Calories 182**

CRISPY "FRIED" CHICKEN
Good Housekeeping

Here's a low-fat, high-soluble fiber answer to conventional fried chicken. We removed the skin, but added pungency with the spicy marinade. And a bonus is the crunch that comes from oat bran flakes.

> *Serves 4*
>
> 1/3 cup low-fat plain yogurt
> 2 tablespoons lemon juice
> 1 tablespoon minced peeled ginger root
> 1 garlic clove, minced
> 1/2 teaspoon ground cumin
> 1/4 teaspoon ground cayenne pepper
> 2 whole medium-sized chicken breasts, halved and skinned
> 1-1/4 cups oat bran flake cereal, crushed
> no stick cooking spray
> cherry tomatoes and parsley sprigs for garnish

In a medium-sized bowl, combine the yogurt, lemon juice, ginger root, garlic, cumin, and the cayenne pepper. Add the chicken to the marinade, turning the pieces to coat well. Cover and refrigerate at least 4 hours, turning the chicken occasionally.

Preheat oven to 400°F. On a sheet of waxed paper, place the crushed cereal. Remove the chicken from marinade with as much of the marinade as possible. Coat the flesh side of the chicken with the cereal. Spray a 12×8-inch baking dish with no stick cooking spray; arrange the chicken, flesh-side up, in a single layer. Bake about 50 minutes or until golden brown and fork-tender. To serve, arrange the chicken in a basket; garnish with tomatoes and parsley.

Each serving:

 1   70 mg   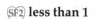 less than 1   **Calories 190**

QUICK AND EASY TURKEY TENDERS

Turkey is very low in saturated fat and cholesterol. This recipe features easy-to-use turkey tenderloin. We include the basic recipe with four variations.

Serves 6

1 package (1 to 1-1/4 pounds) fresh turkey tenderloin
   (or boneless chicken breast)
2 large egg whites
2 tablespoons low-fat evaporated milk
1-1/4 cups oat bran
1 teaspoon paprika
1/2 cup corn oil margarine
salt to taste
freshly ground pepper

Cut the turkey tenderloins into 6 thin slices by cutting across the turkey tenderloin, carefully, with a sharp knife. With a meat mallet or the back of a meat cleaver, pound turkey tenders to 1/4-inch thickness. Cut small slits around edges to keep from curling.

Whip egg whites lightly with the milk. Mix the oat bran with the paprika. Dip meat into egg whites, then into oat bran-paprika mixture. Place on baking rack and allow to dry for 5 minutes.

In a large skillet, heat 1/4 cup margarine. Sauté turkey tenders, 3 at a time, in the margarine. Turn one time. Add margarine as necessary. Total time should be about 12 to 15 minutes.

Each serving:

 3   63 mg   1   **Calories 315**

Variations

Turkey Tenders with Savory Dressing. Mix 1 cup low-fat yogurt with 1 teaspoon Dijon mustard and 1/4 cup scallions, finely chopped. Serve over the cooked turkey. Serves 6.

Each serving:

 2   33 mg   1   **Calories 338**

Turkey Italienne. In a small skillet, heat 2 tablespoons olive oil. Sauté 1 chopped tomato, 1 small sliced onion, and 1 tablespoon Italian seasoning for 5 minutes. Place 1/2 cold turkey tender on top of the mixture, cover, and heat an additional 5 minutes. Top with 1 thin slice skim mozzarella cheese and serve on a toasted Italian roll. Serves 1.

Each serving:

 3   **CH** 36 mg   **SF2** 2   **Calories 330**

Turkey Enchiladas Suisa. Place 1/4 cup prepared enchilada sauce on a corn tortilla. Top with 1/2 cold turkey tender and 1 thin slice Swiss cheese. Top with second corn tortilla. Grill until cheese melts and turkey is hot. Serves 1.

Each serving:

 3   **CH** 37 mg   **SF2** 3   **Calories 338**

Turkey Reuben. Coat 1 slice of rye bread with Thousand Island dressing. Top with 1/2 cold turkey tender, 1/4 cup sauerkraut, 1 thin slice Swiss cheese, and second slice of rye bread. Grill until cheese melts and turkey is heated through. Serves 1.

Each serving:

SFI 3   **CH** 37 mg   **SF2** 1   **Calories 275**

CREAMY CHICKEN PAPRIKASH

Here's a lean and light dish that is ready to eat in 30 minutes.

Serves 4

2 whole, boneless, skinless chicken breasts (1-1/2 pounds)
1/4 cup vegetable oil
1 large yellow onion, chopped
2 cloves garlic, minced
1 medium-sized green pepper, seeded and chopped
   into 1/4-inch pieces
2 tablespoons Hungarian paprika
   (available in specialty stores or use regular paprika)
1/4 teaspoon cayenne pepper
1/2 cup chicken stock (homemade or prepared)
1 cup low-fat yogurt
1 tablespoon all-purpose flour
chopped parsley
salt to taste
freshly ground pepper
2 cups hot cooked noodles

Rinse the chicken breasts, split into 4 pieces, and pat dry.

Heat the oil in a medium-sized skillet. Add chicken breasts and sauté until well browned. Remove chicken and add the onion, garlic, green

Creamy Chicken Paprikash (*continued*)
pepper, and spices. Sauté until vegetables are tender and blended with spices. Add chicken to skillet with chicken stock, cover, and cook for 10 minutes or until chicken breasts are tender.

Blend the yogurt with the flour. Reduce temperature of the chicken mixture and add yogurt, stirring through the mixture. Heat for 2 more minutes. Sprinkle with chopped parsley; salt and pepper to taste. Serve with hot noodles.

Each serving:

 less than 1   **36 mg**   **1**   **Calories 194**

ROAST CHICKEN WITH HONEY
Edward Giobbi

This chicken is excellent with potatoes. Peel enough potatoes—1/2 per person—then cut in half lengthwise. Add them to the roasting pan after chicken has browned and you've removed the water from the pan. Baste the potatoes with the honey mixture, adding more honey if needed.

> *Serves 4*
>
> 4-pound roasting chicken, all fat removed
> 2 cloves garlic, slivered
> freshly ground black pepper to taste
> about 2 tablespoons rosemary leaves
> salt to taste
> 1 cup orange juice
> 1 tablespoon good mustard
> 4 tablespoons honey

Force garlic under chicken skin over breast, and put some in the cavity of the chicken. Force some pepper and rosemary under skin over breast and put some in cavity. Truss chicken, then rub with remaining rosemary and pepper and salt.

Place chicken in a roasting pan in a preheated 400°F oven with about 3/4 inch water on the bottom. When chicken begins to brown, discard all liquid. Blend together the orange juice and mustard and add, lowering heat to 350°F. Cook about 1 hour and 20 minutes in all, basting chicken often until sauce thickens. Add honey to chicken, and continue roasting until honey thickens and glazes chicken, about 15 minutes. Remove skin before serving.

Each serving:

 2   **141 mg**   **less than 1**   **Calories 268**

GRILLED CHICKEN BREASTS
Edward Giobbi

Serves 8

4 whole chicken breasts, skinned and boned
juice of 2 limes
1 tablespoon soy sauce
1 teaspoon minced garlic
2 tablespoons peanut oil
2 bay leaves
salt and freshly ground black pepper to taste
lemon wedges for garnish

Put the chicken breasts in a mixing bowl and sprinkle the remaining ingredients over them. Refrigerate for several hours.

Grill breasts over hot coals about 3 minutes on each side, depending on thickness of breasts. Do not overcook.

Serve with lemon wedges.

Each serving:

 SFI 1   **CH** 61 mg 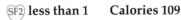 **SF2** less than 1   **Calories 109**

ROAST STUFFED CHICKEN
good
Edward Giobbi

This recipe has a holiday character. It makes roast chicken, which can be ordinary, into something rather festive.

Serves 6

1 tablespoon safflower oil or vegetable oil
1 small onion, chopped
3 large mushrooms, chopped
2 tablespoons finely chopped Italian parsley
3/4 cup fresh bread crumbs
1 teaspoon thyme
2 tablespoons yellow raisins, soaked in warm water
    for 10 minutes and drained
1 tablespoon sweet marsala or sweet sherry
1 egg white, lightly beaten
salt and freshly ground black pepper to taste
3-1/2 pound whole chicken
1 tablespoon rosemary
about 1 cup wine vinegar

Roast Stuffed Chicken (*continued*)

Heat the oil in a small skillet, then add onion and mushrooms, and cook until onion wilts. Combine the mushroom-and-onion mixture with the parsley, bread crumbs, thyme, raisins, marsala, egg white, salt, and pepper. Fill the chicken with the stuffing, sew it up, and truss. Rub salt and pepper and rosemary on chicken. Place a rack in a small baking pan just large enough to hold the chicken. Pour 1/2 cup vinegar and 1/2 cup water into the bottom of the baking pan.

Preheat oven to 500°F. Roast the chicken, basting occasionally, about 1 hour and 15 minutes, turning it as it begins to brown, and add more vinegar when pan juices dry. (I use about an additional 1/2 cup.)

Each serving:

 1   83 mg   **less than 1**   **Calories 194**

CHICKEN OR TURKEY CROQUETTES
Edward Giobbi

> *Serves 4*
>
> 2 medium potatoes
> 2 cups boiled boned chicken or turkey
> 2 tablespoons chopped Italian parsley
> 1 teaspoon grated lemon rind
> about 1/2 teaspoon grated nutmeg
> 2 egg whites, lightly whipped
> salt and freshly ground black pepper to taste
> corn oil for frying
> flour for dredging

Boil potatoes with skins on until just tender, then cool, peel, and mash. Grind chicken and put in a bowl with the potatoes and remaining ingredients, except oil and flour, mixing well. Form croquettes about 2 inches long and 1 inch wide. Don't refrigerate.*

Heat about 3/4 inch oil in a small skillet. Dust croquettes with flour, then gently place a few at a time in the hot oil. Fry until golden brown on both sides. Remove and blot on paper towels. Repeat until all are done.

Each serving:

 2   58 mg   1   **Calories 282**

*If croquettes are refrigerator-cold, they will cool off the oil so that more is absorbed in frying.

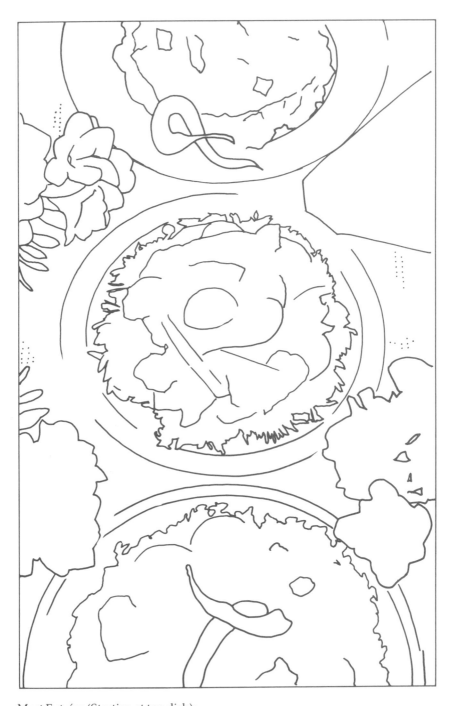

Meat Entrées (Starting at top dish):

Texas-style Beef Skillet (Page 160)
Chicken Breasts with Peppers, Onions, Mushrooms, and Tomatoes (Page 144)
Veal with White Beans (Page 154)

BROILED CHICKEN BREASTS
Edward Giobbi

Serves 3 to 6

3 whole boned chicken breasts, fat removed
4 tablespoons wine vinegar or juice of 3 lemons
3 cloves garlic, sliced
1 tablespoon rosemary
freshly ground black pepper to taste
2 tablespoons chopped Italian parsley or fresh coriander
3 tablespoons olive oil
1 teaspoon safflower oil
salt to taste
lemon wedges for garnish

Place chicken breasts in a bowl. Combine the remaining ingredients except salt, pour over chicken, and marinate at least 2 hours.

Preheat broiler for 10 minutes. Place breasts on baking dish or tray. Pour marinade over breasts and add salt. Broil close to heat about 3 to 5 minutes on each side. If breasts have skin on, broil skin side first. Do not overcook.

Serve with lemon wedges.

Each serving:

 1   61 mg   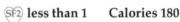 less than 1   Calories 180

CHICKEN CUTLETS
Edward Giobbi

These simple, delicious cutlets go well with fresh green vegetables or a green salad.

Serves 6

3 whole chicken breasts, split, skinned, boned, and fat removed
salt and freshly ground black pepper to taste
2 cloves garlic, sliced
2 lemons
2 egg whites, lightly whipped
bread crumbs
corn oil or vegetable oil (not olive oil)

Flatten chicken breasts between two sheets of waxed paper with a meat pounder or flat side of a heavy knife. Salt and pepper the breasts and lay

Chicken Cutlets (*continued*)

them in a deep bowl. Add garlic and juice of 1 of the lemons. Marinate in the refrigerator at least 2 hours.

Remove the breasts from the marinade and dip them in egg whites, then in bread crumbs. In the meantime, heat about 3/4 inch oil in a medium skillet.

When oil is hot (test by flipping bread crumbs in oil; if oil boils violently, it is ready), use tongs to place each breast, one at a time, gently into the oil. Turn over after 1 minute, cooking about 2 minutes in all—don't overcook. Blot on paper towels and repeat with remaining cutlets. Serve on hot plates immediately, using remaining lemon to make wedges as a garnish.

Each serving:

 1   61 mg   less than 1   **Calories 153**

CHICKEN WINGS WITH POTATOES AND BROCCOLI
Edward Giobbi

The ingredients in this recipe go very well together, and the dish is particularly good served with a hot pepper sauce or a tomato sauce.

Serves 6

18 chicken wings
4 cloves garlic, skins on
1-1/2 teaspoons rosemary
salt and freshly ground black pepper to taste
about 1/2 cup water
1 large onion, finely chopped
1 cup dry white wine
1 tablespoon dried oregano
5 medium potatoes, peeled, cut into 4 sections lengthwise, and blanched
1 bunch broccoli, cut into bite-sized pieces and blanched
2 tablespoons safflower oil or vegetable oil

Wash chicken wings. Fold tips of wings under the large wing bone so that wings remain flat. Put them in a baking dish so that they are in one layer, add garlic, rosemary, salt, and pepper, and pour the water around them. Bake wings in a 450°F preheated oven, uncovered, until they begin to brown, shaking pan occasionally so they don't stick. Drain off all fat. Add onion and continue to cook until it begins to brown, then add wine, oregano, and potatoes. Cover with foil and bake about 15 minutes more.

Add blanched broccoli, sprinkle with oil and salt, and continue to bake until potatoes are tender—about 20 minutes.

Each serving:

 6   83 mg   2   **Calories 488**

TURKEY WING STEW
Edward Giobbi

Here is an economical dish that is most satisfying during the winter months.

> *Serves 4*
>
> 4 turkey wings
> 1 large onion, cut into 4 sections
> 2 cups chopped tomatoes, fresh if possible (drain if canned)
> 1 tablespoon crushed rosemary
> 1 cup dry white wine
> 4 stalks tender celery, about 3 inches long
> 3 cloves garlic, skins on
> salt and freshly ground black pepper
>   or hot pepper flakes to taste
> 3 bay leaves
> 2 medium parsnips, peeled and cut in half
> 4 medium potatoes, peeled and cut in half
> 1 medium green pepper, cut into 1-inch-wide slices
> 1/3 cup water

Place turkey wings in a skillet or shallow saucepan with onion, tomatoes, rosemary, wine, celery, garlic, salt, pepper, and bay leaves. Cover and simmer over low heat about 1 hour. Add parsnips, potatoes, peppers, and water. Partially cover and cook about 1 more hour. Add more water if needed—sauce should be loose but not too much so.

Each serving:

 less than 1   27 mg   2   **Calories 173**

VEAL WITH ARTICHOKE HEARTS
Edward Giobbi

Serves 6

1-1/2 pounds veal cut into large chunks (shoulder or leg)
juice of 1 lemon
1 pound mushrooms
3 tablespoons olive oil mixed with 4 tablespoons safflower oil
2 medium onions, thinly sliced
9-ounce package frozen artichoke hearts
salt and freshly ground black pepper to taste
1/2 cup dry marsala or sherry
flour for dredging
3 tablespoons minced Italian parsley for garnish

Marinate veal with lemon juice for several hours.

Separate mushroom caps from stems and in a skillet sauté both over moderate heat in 1-1/2 tablespoons of the oil, stirring occasionally. When mushrooms begin to brown, add onions and cook, uncovered, until onions wilt. In the meantime, put the artichoke hearts in boiling water. Cook 1 minute, and drain. Add them to the skillet with salt and pepper and cook, covered, over low heat for 5 minutes. Add 1/4 cup of the marsala, salt, and pepper, cover, and simmer over low heat for 5 minutes.

Remove veal from lemon juice. Salt and pepper the pieces, then lightly dust with flour. Heat remaining 1-1/2 tablespoons oil in a skillet, then add veal. Cook over high heat, turning veal until it is lightly browned. Lower heat, add the remaining 1/4 cup marsala, cover, and simmer for 3 to 5 minutes, depending on the size of the veal pieces. Add mushroom-and-artichoke mixture to veal, cover, and simmer for several minutes. Garnish with parsley and serve hot.

Each serving:

 5   81 mg   1   **Calories 398**

VEAL WITH WHITE BEANS
Edward Giobbi

Serves 6

2 tablespoons olive oil
2 tablespoons safflower oil
1-1/2 pounds stewing veal, cut into 1- to 2-inch pieces,
    trimmed of fat
2 cloves garlic, skins on
1 medium onion, finely chopped

salt and freshly ground black pepper to taste
1/2 cup dry white wine
1 teaspoon rosemary
1 bay leaf
1/2 pound fresh mushrooms, cut in half
1 cup chopped tomatoes, fresh if possible (drain if canned)
2 cups cooked dried white beans
   or 2 cups canned cannellini beans
1/4 cup beef or chicken stock
chopped Italian parsley for garnish

Heat the oils in a heavy casserole, then add veal and cook over high heat, turning often. When meat begins to brown, add garlic and onion. When onion wilts, add salt, pepper, wine, rosemary, bay leaf, and mushrooms, lower heat, and simmer about 8 minutes. Add tomatoes, beans, and stock. (If canned beans are used, do not add them until veal has cooked about 45 minutes.) Cover and boil gently over low heat about 1-1/2 hours. Garnish with chopped parsley and serve hot, with rice.

Each serving:

 4   81 mg   2   **Calories 342**

VEAL WITH EGGPLANT AND PEAS
Edward Giobbi

This dish is good served with boiled potatoes, preferably new potatoes, or rice.

Serves 4

1 pound lean veal, cut into stewing-sized pieces,
   any gristle removed
salt and freshly ground black pepper to taste
flour for dredging
2 tablespoons olive oil
1 tablespoon safflower oil
1 medium onion, coarsely chopped
3/4 cup dry white wine
1 teaspoon crushed rosemary
1 cup chopped tomatoes, fresh if possible (drain if canned)
1 pound eggplant, cut into 1-inch squares about 1/4-inch thick
2 cups fresh or frozen peas, blanched and drained
1 pound eggplant, cut into 1/4-inch slices for garnish

Salt and pepper the veal and lightly dust with flour. Heat the oils in a large skillet, add veal, and brown over very high heat, stirring often.

Veal with Eggplant and Peas (*continued*)

When veal is golden brown, add onion. Cook until onion begins to brown, then add wine and rosemary, cover, and lower heat. Cook until wine cooks out. Add tomatoes, cover, and simmer over low heat, stirring often, about 45 minutes. Add cut-up eggplant and blanched peas, cover, and simmer about 30 minutes. Salt to taste.

In the meantime, place the sliced eggplant on a lightly oiled tray. Preheat oven to 500°F for at least 15 minutes. Sprinkle some olive oil and salt on eggplant slices and bake until lightly brown, then turn and brown the other side. Garnish each serving of veal stew with eggplant slices.

Each serving:

 4   81 mg   3   **Calories 384**

Variation

Use pork tenderloin instead of the veal, removing all the visible fat.

VEAL-STUFFED EGGPLANT WITH TOMATO SAUCE
Edward Giobbi

You can serve this very good dish with potatoes or rice, or simply a green vegetable.

Serves 6 to 9

The Sauce

2 tablespoons olive oil
1 tablespoon safflower oil
1 medium onion, chopped, about 3/4 cup
4 cups coarsely chopped tomatoes, fresh if possible
    (drained if canned)
2 tablespoons chopped fresh basil or 1 teaspoon dried
salt and freshly ground black pepper to taste

2 medium to large eggplants
corn or vegetable oil for frying
4 egg whites, lightly beaten
about 1-1/4 cups flour for dredging
1-1/2 pounds ground lean veal
1 tablespoon finely chopped Italian parsley
1 teaspoon minced garlic
1 teaspoon grated lemon rind
1/2 teaspoon grated nutmeg

To make the sauce: Heat olive oil and safflower oil in a medium skillet, add onion, and sauté until it begins to brown. Add tomatoes, cover, and simmer. Add basil, salt, and pepper, cover, and simmer about 20 minutes.

In the meantime, cut the eggplants in half, then slice them lengthwise about 1/4 inch thick. Spread the slices on a tray, sprinkle with salt, and let stand about 20 minutes. Blot the slices dry. Heat about 3/4 inch corn oil or vegetable oil in a medium skillet, then dip eggplant slices in 3 egg whites, dust with flour, and lightly brown in the oil, several pieces at a time, not crowding the pan. Blot cooked eggplant slices and continue cooking remaining pieces in the same way.

Mix the veal with the remaining 1 egg white, parsley, garlic, lemon rind, nutmeg, salt, and pepper.

Put the tomato sauce through a food mill or food processor and blend. Preheat oven to 450°F.

In a deep baking dish 9 or 10 inches square, place a layer of eggplant, some sauce, another layer of eggplant and sauce. Spread all the veal mixture over eggplant, pour some sauce over veal, then a layer of eggplant. Repeat layers of eggplant and sauce until eggplant is used up, finishing with sauce. Cover and bake about 30 minutes. Let stand about 30 minutes before serving.

Each serving (for 9):

 3   54 mg   2   **Calories 316**

SAVORY STUFFED CABBAGES

Mini stuffed cabbages were always a family favorite as an appetizer. Here's an adaptation of that recipe, but in an entrée size.

Serves 6

no stick cooking spray
1/2 pound lean ground pork
2 large egg whites
1/4 cup onion, finely chopped
1 teaspoon white Worcestershire sauce
1/2 pound fat-free ham, ground
1 cup oat bran (for best results, use a coarsely milled oat bran)
1 teaspoon caraway seed
2 tablespoons chopped parsley
12 medium-sized cabbage leaves
2 cups sauerkraut, rinsed and drained
1 can (16 ounces) tomatoes with liquid

Savory Stuffed Cabbage (*continued*)

Preheat the oven to 350°F. Spray a 9×13-inch decorative baking dish with no stick cooking spray.

In a small frying pan, brown the pork. Drain all fat from cooked pork. Add to the pork the egg whites, onion, Worcestershire sauce, ham, oat bran, caraway, and parsley. Mix well.

Meanwhile, immerse the cabbage leaves in boiling water for 3 minutes until they become limp. Place 2 tablespoons sauerkraut and 1/4 cup meat mixture on each cabbage leaf. Roll up each leaf, making sure meat mixture is enclosed.

Arrange the rolls in the baking dish. Put the tomatoes, their liquid, and remaining sauerkraut on top of the cabbage rolls. Bake, uncovered, for 35 minutes. Serve immediately.

Each serving:

 1 12 mg 2 **Calories 157**

STUFFED CABBAGE WITH TOMATOES
Edward Giobbi

Serve these cabbage rolls with boiled potatoes or rice, preferably plain rice.

Serves 5 to 6

1 medium cabbage

The Stuffing

1 pound ground lean veal
1 teaspoon minced garlic
2 tablespoons yellow raisins
2 tablespoons chopped pine nuts
1 cup fresh bread crumbs
2 egg whites, lightly beaten
2 tablespoons finely chopped Italian parsley
salt and freshly ground black pepper to taste
1 teaspoon dried oregano

1 tablespoon olive oil
1 tablespoon safflower oil
1 medium onion, finely chopped
1 cup chopped tomatoes, fresh if possible (drain if canned)
1 cup chicken or beef broth
chopped Italian parsley or fresh coriander for garnish

Carefully remove cabbage leaves, blanch in boiling water, drain, and let cool. If leaves are difficult to separate, drop the whole head into boiling water first. Boil about 5 minutes, drain, and then remove leaves.

Mix the stuffing ingredients in a bowl and set aside.

Heat the oils in a medium skillet, then add onion. When onion begins to brown, add tomatoes, cover, and simmer for 5 minutes. Add broth and cook for several minutes. Reserve.

Spread out cabbage leaves. For each leaf, make a ball about the size of a golf ball from the stuffing, flatten it a bit and place it in the middle of the leaf. Fold one end of the leaf over the stuffing and roll it up. Place filled rolls seam side down on a medium baking tray so that they fit snugly. Repeat until all the meat is used up. Pour the reserved tomato-and-broth sauce over the stuffed cabbage. Cover with foil and bake in a preheated 450°F oven about 1 hour.

To serve, garnish with chopped Italian parsley or fresh coriander.

Each serving:

 2   54 mg   1   **Calories 223**

RAINBOW PEPPERS AND BEEF

With so many beautiful and colorful sweet peppers available, you'll be able to create a masterpiece of color with this recipe. It is also delicious!

Serves 6

> 6 large sweet peppers (green, red, yellow)
> 1 pound lean ground beef
> 1/2 cup chopped onion
> 2 cloves garlic, minced
> 2 large tomatoes, chopped
> 1 teaspoon ground oregano
> 1 teaspoon hot sauce
> 2 teaspoons white Worcestershire sauce
> 1 cup oat bran
> no stick cooking spray
> 1/2 cup shredded mozzarella cheese
> salt to taste
> freshly ground pepper

Cut the tops from the peppers. Discard the seeds and membranes from the interior of the peppers. Chop enough of the tops to make 1/2 cup. Set aside. Cook the peppers in boiling water for 3 minutes until they are tender. Drain well.

Rainbow Peppers and Beef (*continued*)

In a large-sized skillet, brown the ground beef, onion, garlic, and chopped pepper until meat is brown and vegetables are tender. Drain fat from pan. Add the tomatoes, oregano, hot sauce, and Worcestershire. Simmer for 15 minutes until flavors are well blended. Remove from heat and add oat bran.

Preheat the oven to 350°F. Spray a 9×13-inch baking dish with no stick cooking spray.

Stuff peppers with meat mixture. Place in the baking dish and sprinkle peppers with cheese. Bake, uncovered, for 30 minutes. Serve immediately. Salt and pepper to taste.

Each serving:

 2 75 mg 1 **Calories 263**

TEXAS-STYLE BEEF SKILLET

In this recipe, lean strips of meat are carefully simmered with vegetables and seasonings and then served with warm corn tortillas. This recipe will serve 8 hungry people and is good when reheated. It is also delicious when made with boneless, skinless chicken breast or fresh shrimp.

Serves 8

> 1 tablespoon peanut oil
> 1 pound lean round steak, cut into very thin slivers, 2×1/4 inch
> 3/4 cup chopped onion
> 2 large fresh tomatoes, chopped coarsely
> 1 can (22 ounces) chili hot beans
> 1 cup oat bran
> 3 tablespoons chopped green pepper
> 1-1/2 teaspoons chili powder
> 2 cloves garlic, minced
> 1 cup water
> 1/2 cup shredded Monterey Jack cheese
> 8 corn tortillas (page 92) or buy prepared

In a heavy pot or dutch oven, heat the peanut oil until hot, then quickly sauté the round steak pieces until they are no longer pink. Add the onion, tomatoes, the beans with their liquid, the oat bran, green pepper, chili powder, garlic, and water. Simmer for 20 minutes, stirring occasionally.

Top with cheese. Cover and allow the cheese to melt. Serve with warm tortillas.

Each serving:

 1   CH 54 mg   SF2 2   **Calories 327**

Variation: 1 pound boneless, skinless chicken breast cut into very thin slivers, 2×1/4 inches.

SF1 1   CH 51 mg   SF2 2   **Calories 283**

10

VEGETARIAN ENTREES

VEGETABLE CURRY

What's the perfect vegetarian food? Curry. This particular dish is hot, spicy, and full of nutrients.

Serves 4

8 ounces dry small white beans
1/4 cup light margarine
3 medium-sized onions, chopped
5 tablespoons chopped jalapeño peppers (optional)
2 green peppers, seeded and chopped into 1/4-inch pieces
1 red pepper, seeded and chopped into 1/4-inch pieces
1/4 teaspoon cayenne pepper
1/2 teaspoon white pepper
1 to 3 tablespoons curry powder
3 large, very ripe tomatoes, chopped
    (or 3 cups canned tomatoes with liquid)
1/2 cup frozen corn, thawed and drained
1/2 cup frozen peas, thawed and drained
1 stalk broccoli, separated into florets,
    stems peeled and sliced, steamed
salt to taste
freshly ground pepper

For Accompaniment

cooked rice
chopped apple
chopped green onions
raisins
toasted sesame seeds

In a medium-sized saucepan, cover the beans with water. Bring to a boil, cover, reduce heat, and simmer until beans are tender but not mushy, about 1-1/2 hours.

In a large dutch oven or heavy pot, heat the margarine. Sauté the onions and peppers with the cayenne pepper, white pepper, and curry powder for 10 minutes. Add tomatoes to the mixture in the dutch oven. Simmer uncovered for 10 minutes. Add the hot beans with any cooking liquid, corn, and peas and heat for 5 minutes until vegetables are hot. Add broccoli, and salt and pepper to taste.

Serve curry with the cooked rice and bowls of chopped apple, green onions, raisins, and sesame seeds.

Each serving (not including condiments):

 2   **0 mg**   **3**   **Calories 265**

VEGETARIAN SHEPHERD'S PIE

Here's the perfect way to utilize leftover veggies. If you have leftover bean or lentil soup, use it to replace or add to the kidney beans!

Serves 8

no stick cooking spray
2 tablespoons light margarine
1 medium onion, chopped
2 cloves garlic, minced
1 bunch broccoli
1 green pepper, seeded and chopped into 1/2-inch pieces
4 medium-sized carrots, diced
1 cup frozen corn, drained
2 large tomatoes, chopped
1 bay leaf
1 can (14 ounces) kidney beans with liquid
1 teaspoon hot sauce
1 teaspoon Worcestershire sauce
3 large potatoes, peeled, cooked, and mashed with skim milk
salt to taste
freshly ground pepper

Preheat oven to 450°F. Spray a 9×13-inch baking dish with no stick cooking spray.

In a large saucepan, heat the margarine. Sauté onion and garlic for 5 minutes.

Meanwhile, wash broccoli. Separate into florets and peel and slice the stem. Add broccoli, green pepper, carrots, corn, tomatoes, bay leaf, kidney beans with liquid, hot sauce, and Worcestershire sauce to skillet.

Vegetarian Shepherd's Pie *(continued)*

Heat thoroughly. Pour into prepared baking dish. Cover and bake for 30 minutes until vegetables are steamed and flavors blended. Remove bay leaf.

Uncover and top with mashed potatoes. Bake for an additional 15 minutes until potatoes are lightly browned. Serve immediately. Salt and pepper to taste.

Each serving:

 less than 1   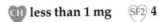 **less than 1 mg**   **4**   **Calories 211**

CORN PUDDING

This dish gives you the nutrition of cornmeal and the flavor of Tex-Mex cooking.

Serves 4

no stick cooking spray
3 tablespoons light margarine
1 small onion, minced
3 ribs celery, chopped
1 cup grated carrots
1 cup vegetable stock (homemade or prepared)
1/4 cup all-purpose white flour
1 cup skim milk
1 small can (4 ounces) chopped green chilis (hot or mild), drained
6 egg whites, room temperature
1-1/2 cups white or yellow cornmeal
1 teaspoon cumin
1/4 teaspoon cayenne
1/4 cup shredded Monterey Jack cheese
freshly ground pepper
salt to taste

Preheat the oven to 375°F. Spray a 3-quart casserole dish with no stick cooking spray.

Heat 1 tablespoon margarine in a medium-sized skillet. Brown the onion in the margarine. Add the celery, carrots, and 1/2 cup vegetable stock.

In a 3-quart saucepan, heat remaining margarine. Whisk in flour, remaining stock, and milk for a thick and smooth sauce. Continue to heat while adding vegetable mixture and chilis. Stir to make a smooth sauce. Remove from heat.

Place egg whites in a very clean mixing bowl. With electric mixer, whip egg whites until soft peaks form. Sprinkle cornmeal, cumin, and cayenne over eggs and gently fold in.

Fold egg mixture into vegetable mixture. Pour into casserole dish and top with cheese. Bake for 40 minutes. Sprinkle with freshly ground pepper and serve immediately. Salt to taste.

Each serving:

 2   **1 mg**   **2**   **Calories 435**

STUFFED POTATOES

What could be easier than putting a few baking potatoes in the oven? This is an appetizing recipe that makes good use of the nutritious potato and other veggies.

Serves 4

4 large baking potatoes, well scrubbed
2 tablespoons light margarine
1 medium-sized onion, minced
2 cloves garlic, minced
1/4 cup all-purpose flour
2 cups skim milk
1 cup frozen corn, thawed
1 cup frozen peas, thawed
1/4 cup freshly grated Parmesan cheese
1/4 cup shredded mozzarella cheese
salt to taste
freshly ground pepper

Preheat oven to 400°F. Prick potatoes and bake until cooked, about 1 hour, 15 minutes.

Meanwhile, heat margarine in a medium-sized saucepan. Brown onion and garlic. Whisk in flour, then milk, to form a thin, smooth sauce. Add corn, peas, and cheeses, allowing cheese to melt. Salt to taste.

Make a cross in the top of each potato. Split open. Place in a large, shallow soup bowl and ladle cheese and vegetable sauce over tops. Salt and pepper to taste.

Each serving:

 4   **15 mg**   **5**   **Calories 468**

VEGETABLE NOODLE BAKE

A hearty dish, Vegetable Noodle Bake is also delicious and economical. It is very rich in soluble fiber.

Serves 8

3 cups water
1 package (10 ounces) frozen black-eyed peas
1 to 1-1/2 cups chicken stock
no stick cooking spray
1/4 cup vegetable oil
1 medium-sized onion, chopped
3 ribs celery, chopped
2 grated carrots
1 potato, grated with skin on
1 cup frozen corn, thawed
4 chopped tomatoes
1/4 teaspoon cayenne pepper
1 teaspoon chili powder
1/2 teaspoon dry mustard
1 tablespoon chopped fresh sage (or 1/2 teaspoon ground sage)
2 tablespoons chopped fresh basil (or 2 teaspoons dry basil)
5 tablespoons all-purpose flour
salt to taste
12 ounces whole wheat noodles,
   cooked according to package directions
2 ounces finely grated extra sharp Cheddar cheese
1/2 cup chopped fresh parsley
1 large ripe tomato, sliced
freshly ground pepper

In a medium-sized saucepan, bring the water to a boil. Add black-eyed peas, return to a boil, reduce heat, cover, and simmer until tender, about 30 minutes. Drain, saving cooking liquid. Add stock to make 3 cups liquid.

Preheat oven to 350°F. Spray a 10×15-inch baking pan with no stick cooking spray.

In a large heavy pot or dutch oven, heat the vegetable oil. Sauté the onion until translucent. Add the celery, carrots, potato, corn, tomatoes, cayenne pepper, chili powder, dry mustard, sage, and basil. Cook until the vegetables are tender crisp. Sprinkle with the flour. Blend in the 3 cups black-eyed pea liquid and stock, heating and stirring to form a thick gravy. Salt to taste.

Place half the noodles in the bottom of the baking pan. Top with half of the vegetable mixture. Add remaining noodles, then top with remaining vegetable mixture. Bake for 40 minutes. to serve, top with grated cheese and chopped parsley. Cut tomato slices into halves and use to garnish sides of pan.

Each serving:

(SF1) 2   (CH) 19 mg   (SF2) 6   **Calories 292**

VEGETABLE ENCHILADAS

Here's an authentic Tex-Mex recipe. For best results, use "chili hot beans" or "Mexican-style kidney beans."

Makes 6 2-tortilla servings

no stick cooking spray
2 tablespoons vegetable oil
1 medium-sized onion, minced
1 medium-sized green pepper, chopped into 1/2-inch pieces
1/4 cup chopped fresh cilantro
2 cups frozen corn, thawed
2 cups zucchini, scrubbed and grated with skin on
1 can (15 ounces) chili hot beans
    (or Mexican-style kidney beans) with liquid
1 teaspoon cumin
1 teaspoon chili powder
12 Corn Tortillas (page 92) or buy prepared
2 cups Tomato Salsa (page 35) or buy prepared
1/3 cup shredded extra sharp Cheddar cheese
1/3 cup shredded Monterey Jack cheese
salt to taste
freshly ground pepper

Preheat oven to 350°F. Spray a 9×13-inch baking dish with no stick cooking spray.

In a large skillet, heat the vegetable oil. Sauté the onion and green pepper until vegetables are just tender. Add the cilantro, corn, and zucchini and heat until zucchini is tender, about 5 minutes. Pour the beans into a small bowl. With the back of a fork, mash the beans in their liquid. Add to vegetables with cumin and chili powder. Stir thoroughly.

Soften the tortillas, if necessary, by wrapping in foil and placing in the preheated oven.

Place 1/3 cup filling in each tortilla. Roll tortillas up and place in baking dish. Cover with salsa and cheeses. Bake until sauce bubbles and cheese melts, about 20 minutes. Salt and pepper to taste.

Each serving:

(SF1) 2   (CH) 5 mg   (SF2) 5   **Calories 352**

HEARTY CABBAGE STEW

This stew is hearty enough to be a main dish, and delicious enough to become a favorite.

Serves 8

2 tablespoons light margarine
2 medium onions, sliced
2 ribs celery, sliced
12 ounces pearled barley
7 cups vegetable stock (homemade or prepared)
1 medium-sized cabbage, shredded
2 sliced carrots
2 large all-purpose potatoes, scrubbed and cubed with skins on
3 chopped tomatoes
chopped parsley for garnish
salt to taste
freshly ground pepper

In a large stock pot, heat the margarine. Cook onions and celery until just translucent. Add barley and brown. Stir in stock, cabbage, carrots, potatoes, and tomatoes. Bring to a boil, reduce heat, cover, and simmer until barley is tender, about 45 minutes to 1 hour.

Ladle into soup bowls. Sprinkle with parsley. Salt and pepper to taste.

Each serving:

 1   1 mg   3   **Calories 306**

BARLEY CASSEROLE

Barley is one grain that does not need to presoak. You can make this casserole ahead of time and put it on a timer.

Serves 6

12-ounce package medium pearled barley
3 cups vegetable stock (homemade or prepared)
no stick cooking spray
2 tablespoons light margarine
1 cup chopped celery
2 medium red onions, chopped
1 medium-sized red pepper, seeded and chopped
1/2 pound sliced mushrooms
1 large carrot, coarsely grated
1 tablespoon chopped fresh basil (or 1 teaspoon dry basil)
1 tablespoon Worcestershire sauce

1/3 cup freshly grated Parmesan cheese
2 tablespoons chopped fresh parsley
salt to taste
freshly ground pepper

Put the barley in a medium-sized saucepan and cover with stock. Bring to a boil, cover, lower heat, and simmer for 20 to 30 minutes until barley is tender. Watch barley carefully so that it does not dry out. Add a little water, if necessary.

Preheat the oven to 350°F. Spray a 3-quart casserole with no stick cooking spray.

In a large-sized skillet, heat the margarine. Sauté celery, onions, and pepper until translucent, about 10 minutes. Add mushrooms, carrot, basil, and Worcestershire. Cover skillet and simmer until vegetables are tender. Add cooked barley, stir thoroughly, and pour into the prepared casserole. Top with cheese and chopped parsley.

Bake for 30 minutes. Serve immediately. Salt and pepper to taste.

Each serving:

 2   5 mg   4   **Calories 297**

FALAFEL

A classic Middle Eastern dish, Falafel combines potato and garbanzo beans—two excellent sources of soluble fiber. Serve 3 or 4 hot Falafel in a warmed pita with shredded lettuce, sliced radishes, and Hummus (page 34).

Serves 6

2 tablespoons olive oil
2 cloves garlic, minced
1 medium-sized onion, chopped
3 cups canned garbanzo (or cici) beans, drained
1 large potato, cooked and mashed with skim milk
1/2 cup chopped cilantro (or parsley)
1/4 cup low-fat yogurt
1/4 teaspoon cayenne pepper
1 teaspoon paprika
juice of 1 lemon
no stick cooking spray
salt to taste
freshly ground pepper

In a medium-sized skillet, heat the olive oil. Brown the garlic and onion in oil. Mash the garbanzo beans with a fork or purée in a food processor.

Falafel *(continued)*

Add to browned vegetables. Add the potato, cilantro, yogurt, cayenne pepper, paprika, and lemon and blend thoroughly. Salt and pepper to taste. Chill for at least 1 hour.

Preheat the oven to 350°F. Spray a cookie sheet with no stick cooking spray.

Scoop up about 2 to 2-1/2 tablespoons of the mixture and repeat to make 24 balls in all. Place them on the cookie sheet and bake for 15 minutes.

Serve hot in pita pockets with shredded lettuce and tomato.

Each serving:

 1 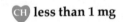 **less than 1 mg** 3 **Calories 286**

SOUTHERN-STYLE CORN PONE

This southern-style corn pone is mild-flavored and hearty, and includes nutrients that make a complete protein.

Serves 6

2 cups dry pinto beans
no stick cooking spray
1 can (4 ounces) chopped green chilis, mild or hot
1/4 teaspoon cayenne powder
1 teaspoon chili powder
1-1/2 cups white or yellow cornmeal
1/2 cup all-purpose flour
2 teaspoons baking soda
1 teaspoon salt
1 quart low-fat buttermilk
4 egg whites, slightly beaten
2 tablespoons light margarine, melted
1/4 cup chopped cilantro (use parsley if cilantro is not available)

Cover pinto beans with water and soak overnight.

Preheat oven to 400°F. Spray a 9×13-inch baking dish with no stick cooking spray.

In a large saucepan, combine pinto beans, undrained chilis, cayenne powder, and chili powder. Cover with water. Heat to a boil, lower heat, cover pan, and simmer for 1 hour or until pinto beans are tender. Drain pintos, reserving 1 cup liquid (if liquid is not quite a cup, add water). Pour pintos with 1 cup liquid into the baking dish.

In a medium-sized mixing bowl, mix cornmeal, flour, baking soda, and salt. In another medium-sized bowl, blend the buttermilk with the egg whites, melted margarine, and cilantro. Stir the wet ingredients into the dry ingredients. Pour over hot beans.

Bake until corn pone is rich golden brown and pulls away from the baking dish, about 30 to 35 minutes.

Each serving:

 1   6 mg   (SF2) 3   **Calories 386**

CARIBBEAN-STYLE BLACK BEANS AND RICE

This dish has authentic Caribbean flavor. Ladle into large bowls; each serving should be half rice, half beans.

Serves 6

12 ounces black beans
5 cups vegetable stock (homemade or prepared)
2 tablespoons olive oil
1 large onion, chopped
2 green peppers, seeded and chopped into 1/2-inch chunks
2 cloves garlic, minced
1/4 teaspoon ground oregano
1 bay leaf
1 teaspoon ground cumin
1/4 cup lime juice
salt to taste
3 cups hot cooked rice
6 lime wedges for garnish
freshly ground pepper

In a large bowl, cover beans with water and soak overnight. Drain beans and place in a large soup pot. Cover with vegetable stock. Bring to a boil.

Meanwhile, in a large skillet, heat olive oil and sauté the onion, green peppers, and garlic. Carefully, add the vegetables to the hot beans along with the oregano, bay leaf, and cumin. Cover, lower heat to a simmer, and cook until beans are tender and the liquid is thick, about 1 hour.

Just before serving, add lime juice and salt to taste. Place 1/2 cup rice in each large soup bowl. Add beans and their liquid and garnish with a lime wedge and freshly ground pepper.

Each serving:

 1   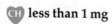 less than 1 mg   (SF2) 2   **Calories 353**

VEGETABLE TURNOVERS WITH SPINACH-CHEESE FILLING

These little packages are delightful. Make the whole receipe and freeze any leftovers for great lunchbox treats!

Makes 6 2-turnover servings

no stick cooking spray
1 package (1/4 ounce) active dry yeast
1-1/4 cups oat bran (for best results,
    use a coarsely milled oat bran)
2 to 2-1/2 cups all-purpose flour
1/2 teaspoon granulated sugar
1 teaspoon salt
2 egg whites
3 tablespoons vegetable oil
3/4 cup very warm water (115°F)
1 small onion, chopped
2 cloves garlic, minced
2 ribs celery, sliced
1 pound spinach, with tough stems removed
    and leaves rinsed three times to remove sand
2 tablespoons freshly grated Parmesan cheese
1/4 cup crumbled feta cheese
1/2 cup 1% low-fat cottage cheese
salt to taste
freshly ground pepper
1 egg white, beaten to blend
Dijon mustard

Spray a bowl with no stick cooking spray.

In a medium-sized mixing bowl, blend the yeast with 1 cup of the oat bran, 2 cups flour, sugar, and salt. With a wooden spoon, blend in 2 egg whites, 2 tablespoons oil, and the very warm water. Stir thoroughly and continue to stir until all ingredients are well blended. Turn onto a floured board and knead to incorporate the remaining 1/2 cup flour. Knead until dough is smooth and satiny, about 10 minutes. (The dough may be mixed and kneaded in a food processor or in an electric mixer fitted with dough hooks.)

Place dough in the prepared bowl, cover, and allow to rise in a warm, draft-free place for 30 minutes.

Meanwhile, prepare the filling: In a large skillet, heat the remaining 1 tablespoon of oil. Sauté onion and garlic until translucent. Add celery and spinach, a little at a time. Cover skillet, adding more spinach as it cooks down. Remove cover, and cook until all liquid has been absorbed.

Sprinkle with the remaining oat bran and stir to blend. Add cheeses and mix to blend and heat. Cool slightly and salt and pepper to taste.

Preheat oven to 400°F. Spray a cookie sheet with no stick cooking spray.

Divide dough into 12 portions. On a floured board, roll each portion into a 5-inch round, about 1/8 inch thick. Fill half of the circle with 1/3 cup filling. Fold over and seal edges with the tines of a fork. Brush with egg white.

Bake for 15 to 20 minutes until turnovers are browned. Serve with Dijon mustard on the side.

Each serving:

 3   11 mg   (SF2) 2   **Calories 379**

RED BEANS AND RICE, CAJUN STYLE

This is a hearty dish and completely vegetarian. Blending beans and rice will also make a complete protein.

Serves 8

1/2 pound dry red beans (kidney beans)
7 cups vegetable stock (page 51 or prepared)
1 large yellow onion, chopped
1 large green pepper, chopped
1-1/2 cups chopped celery
2 cloves garlic, minced
2 bay leaves
1 tablespoon cajun seasoning
salt to taste
4 cups hot cooked rice
freshly ground pepper

Cover beans with cold water and soak overnight.

Drain the beans. In a large soup pot, heat vegetable stock. Add the beans, onion, green pepper, celery, garlic, bay leaves, and cajun seasoning. Bring to a boil, reduce heat, cover, and simmer for 1 hour.

Continue cooking the beans until they become tender. Watch the pot carefully to prevent scorching of beans. Add more water to the pot as needed. When beans are tender, remove bay leaves, salt to taste, and serve by ladling a portion of red beans over 1/2 cup hot cooked rice in a large bowl. Pepper to taste.

Each serving:

 less than 1   1 mg   (SF2) 4   **Calories 281**

MEATLESS CHILI

If you are in a hurry, try this recipe. It is easy, delicious, and an excellent source of soluble fiber.

Serves 4

1 can (14 ounces) kidney beans
2 cups Salsa (page 35)
1 cup frozen corn

Blend all ingredients in a medium-sized saucepan. Heat to a boil, reduce heat, cover, and cook for 6 to 10 minutes, until corn kernels are heated through.

Each serving:

 less than 1   0 mg   5 **Calories 169**

VEGETABLE CASSEROLE WITH THREE CHEESES

This is a casserole that everyone will love—it is colorful and cheesy, and it tastes great.

Serves 6

no stick cooking spray
1/4 cup soft margarine
4 cups thinly sliced celery
2 tablespoons chopped green pepper
2 cups sliced fresh mushrooms
2 cups frozen peas, thawed
2 cups frozen corn, thawed
1/4 cup flour
1 cup skim milk
1 cup 1% low-fat cottage cheese
2 tablespoons chopped pimiento
salt to taste
1/4 cup shredded extra sharp Cheddar cheese
1/4 cup freshly grated Parmesan cheese
freshly ground pepper

Spray a 9 × 13-inch decorative baking dish with no stick cooking spray.

Heat the margarine in a heavy pot or dutch oven, add the celery and green pepper, and sauté until tender for 5 minutes. Add the mushrooms and sauté for an additional 5 minutes. Add the peas and corn. Cover and cook for 7 minutes until vegetables are tender.

In a small bowl, whisk flour with milk. Add this to the vegetables, continuing to cook and stirring constantly to keep sauce smooth. Next, stir in cottage cheese and pimiento. Salt to taste.

Preheat oven to broil.

Pour vegetables into the prepared casserole. Top mixture with cheeses. Broil until cheese melts. Top with freshly grated pepper.

Each serving:

 3   **11 mg**   **3**   **Calories 198**

PIZZA PRIMAVERA

Here's a dish with plenty of quality fiber, calcium, and vitamins. Be creative in adding your own veggies!

Makes 1 14-inch pizza; 8 slices

1 tablespoon extra virgin olive oil
1 medium-sized onion, sliced
2 cloves garlic, minced
1 cup broccoli florets and stems
1 large red pepper, seeded and cut into strips
1 large tomato, chopped
1/2 cup sliced celery
1 medium-sized zucchini, sliced
2 tablespoons chopped fresh oregano
   (or 1 teaspoon dried oregano)
1/4 cup chopped fresh basil leaves (or 1 tablespoon dried basil)
1 unbaked, 14-inch oat bran Pizza Shell (page 98)
1 cup plain low-fat yogurt
1/2 cup freshly grated Parmesan cheese

Preheat the oven to 425°F. In a large frying pan, heat the olive oil until medium hot. Add the onion and the garlic and sauté until lightly browned. Add broccoli, red pepper, tomato, celery, zucchini, oregano, basil, and salt. Cover and sauté until the vegetables are tender, about 10 minutes. Remove cover and continue to cook until all juices have been absorbed, about 5 more minutes.

Spread the vegetables on the 14-inch oat bran pizza shell. Blend the yogurt with the Parmesan cheese and spread over vegetables. Bake at 425°F for 20 minutes. When cooked, the pizza topping will be lightly browned and the underside of the crust will be deep brown.

Each slice:

 3   **7 mg**   **2**   **Calories 256**

SPINACH LASAGNA

Try this recipe for flavor and appearance.

Serves 6

Ok

no stick cooking spray
2 tablespoons olive oil
1 large onion, chopped
2 cloves garlic, minced
1 pound spinach, washed 3 times to remove sand
1 teaspoon dried oregano leaves
1 tablespoon chopped fresh basil (or 1 teaspoon dry basil)
3 cups tomato sauce (homemade or prepared)
8 ounces whole wheat lasagna noodles,
    cooked according to package directions and drained
1/2 cup shredded part-skim mozarella cheese
1/4 cup grated Parmesan cheese
1 cup 1% low-fat cottage cheese

Preheat the oven to 375°F. Spray an 8×8-inch *deep* baking dish with no stick cooking spray.

In a large saucepan, heat the oil. Add onion and garlic and sauté until vegetables are translucent. Add spinach 1/3 at a time. Cover. As spinach cooks down, add more. With last batch of spinach, add oregano, basil, and tomato sauce. Blend thoroughly and remove from heat.

In the bottom of the baking dish, place 1 cup sauce. Place 1/3 noodles on top. Cover with 1 cup sauce, and 1/3 of cheeses. Repeat 2 times, ending with cheese attractively sprinkled on top of the sauce.

Bake for 40 minutes or until cheeses are well browned.

Each serving:

SF1 3   CH 10 mg   SF2 1   **Calories 252**

II

PASTA

PASTA WITH BEANS
Edward Giobbi

Serves 6

> 4 cups fresh shelled cranberry beans (shell beans) or 2 cups
>   dried cannellini, cranberry, or Great Northern beans*
> 1 small carrot
> 2 3-inch stalks celery
> 1 bay leaf
> salt and freshly ground black pepper to taste
> 3 tablespoons olive oil
> 1 tablespoon safflower oil
> 1 teaspoon or more finely chopped garlic (I prefer more)
> juice of 1 lemon
> 1 teaspoon marjoram
> 2 cups chicken or beef broth
> 2 tablespoons finely chopped Italian parsley
> 1 pound pasta, such as bows, penne, or ziti
> finely chopped Italian parsley for garnish

If using dried beans, soak overnight in water to cover.

Place beans in a saucepan, cover with water about 1 inch above beans, add carrot, celery, bay leaf, salt, and pepper to taste. Cover and boil gently until tender—about 2 hours for dried beans, 1 hour for fresh ones. Drain beans after they are cooked. Discard liquid, vegetables, and bay leaf.

In a medium skillet or saucepan heat the two oils. Add garlic and as soon as it takes on color, add lemon juice, then the beans, marjoram, broth, and parsley. Cover and simmer over low heat about 5 minutes.

*Two 1-pound 4-ounce cans cannellini beans may be substituted, in which case skip the first two steps of the recipe—preparing the beans. Add them when you pour in the broth.

177

Pasta with Beans (*continued*)

Purée beans and liquid in a food processor or food mill to a creamy sauce—the consistency of an average tomato sauce. Add more stock if needed.

Cook pasta in boiling salted water. Drain when *al dente*. Toss in sauce and serve. Garnish each portion with finely chopped parsley.

Each serving:

 1 0 mg 4 **Calories 569**

CUT PASTA WITH SPINACH
Edward Giobbi

This simple sauce, which you can practically make while the pasta boils, has a lovely creamy consistency when combined with the almost cooked pasta. It is good to make when spinach is abundant. We tend to identify green sauces with basil and summer, but this one can bring a touch of summer to the colder months.

Serves 6

1 pound fresh spinach, washed
3 tablespoons good olive oil*
1 teaspoon safflower oil
2 medium onions, coarsely chopped
3 anchovy fillets, coarsely chopped
1-1/2 cups chicken or beef stock
salt and freshly ground black pepper to taste
1 pound cut pasta such as penne, ziti, bows, etc.

Boil the spinach in a pot of boiling water for 1 minute; drain and let cool. When spinach is cool, squeeze out liquid.

In the meantime, heat the oils in a large skillet or shallow sauce-pan, add onions, and sauté uncovered until they begin to brown. Add chopped anchovy fillets and cook a minute or so. Add spinach, stock, salt, and pepper. Cover and simmer 10 minutes. In the meantime, cook pasta in boiling salted water. Put the spinach sauce in a food processor and purée to a creamy consistency.

Drain pasta and toss in sauce. Serve on heated plates immediately.

Each serving:

 1 2 mg 2 **Calories 391**

*If cheese is desired, use 1-1/2 tablespoons safflower oil and 2 tablespoons olive oil in the sauce. These will compensate for 6 tablespoons grated Parmesan cheese to be served on pasta.

CUT PASTA WITH ASPARAGUS AND MUSHROOMS
From Edward Giobbi

Serves 6

2 tablespoons olive oil
1 tablespoon safflower oil
1 pound asparagus cut into 1-1/2-inch pieces,
    tough ends removed
salt and freshly ground black pepper to taste
2 cups sliced mushrooms (not too thin)
4 cups Tomato Sauce (page 194)
1 pound cut tubular pasta, such as penne, macaroni, ziti,
    rigatoni
chopped Italian parsley for garnish

Heat the two oils in a skillet and sauté the asparagus. Add salt and pepper and cook over medium heat, stirring often, about 5 minutes—do not overcook. Remove with a slotted spoon and set aside.

Add the mushrooms to the oil, salt and pepper again to taste, and sauté over high heat. When mushrooms begin to brown, remove and add to the tomato sauce. Simmer in sauce 5 minutes, then add asparagus and simmer another 5 minutes.

Meanwhile, cook the pasta until *al dente*. Drain well and mix with the sauce, then garnish with parsley.

Each serving:

 2   **0 mg**   **2**   **Calories 488**

PASTA PRIMAVERA
Edward Giobbi

This recipe is an authentic Italian pasta primavera and should be made only when fresh tomatoes and basil are in season.

Serves 4 to 6

1 pound spaghettini, imported if possible
4 cups chopped fresh garden-ripe tomatoes,
    at room temperature
2 cloves garlic, finely chopped
3 tablespoons superior olive oil
1 tablespoon safflower oil
2 tablespoons slivered fresh basil
2 tablespoons chopped Italian parsley
salt and freshly ground black pepper to taste

Pasta Primavera (*continued*)

Boil pasta in rapidly boiling water. In the meantime, place the rest of the ingredients in a food processor or food mill and purée.

When pasta is cooked *al dente,* drain well by shaking the pasta in a colander so that all the water drains off. Toss with the raw tomato sauce and serve immediately.

Each serving:

 1   0 mg   2   **Calories 394**

VERMICELLI WITH MUSHROOMS AND WINE
Edward Giobbi

Serves 4 to 6

5 tablespoons olive oil mixed with 1 tablespoon safflower oil
2 medium onions, finely chopped
4 cups sliced mushrooms
5 tablespoons dry white wine
2 tablespoons minced Italian parsley
1 teaspoon dried oregano
3 cloves garlic, minced
salt and freshly ground black pepper to taste
2 cups fresh bread crumbs
1 pound vermicelli or spaghettini

Garnish

finely chopped Italian parsley
toasted bread crumbs

Heat 3 tablespoons of the oil in a medium skillet and add onions. When onions become translucent, add mushrooms and cook over high heat until liquid cooks out. Add wine, parsley, oregano, and garlic, cover, and simmer for 5 minutes. Add salt and pepper.

Put bread crumbs on a tray and sprinkle over them the remaining oil, salt, and pepper; then mix well. Place under broiler and brown.

Cook pasta in boiling water until *al dente,* then drain. Place equal portions of pasta on each plate, then ladle the mushroom-and-onion mixture in a mound on top. Garnish with parsley and a generous amount of toasted bread crumbs.

Each serving:

 2   0 mg   2   **Calories 479**

PASTA WITH WALNUT SAUCE
Edward Giobbi

Nuts are a wonderful substitute for cream. I have also tested this recipe
with pecans and pine nuts, with equally excellent results.

Serves 4

2 tablespoons olive oil
1 teaspoon plus 1 tablespoon safflower oil
1-3/4 cups chopped onion
2 cloves garlic, minced
2 cups tomatoes, fresh if possible,
   run through a food mill and drained
1 teaspoon dried oregano
salt and freshly ground black pepper to taste
1 tablespoon butter
4 cups thinly sliced mushrooms
3/4 pound pasta, any cut
10 walnuts, about 1/2 cup shelled

Heat the olive oil and 1 teaspoon of the safflower oil in a medium
saucepan; then add onion and cook over moderate heat until onion
begins to brown. Add garlic, simmer about 1 minute; then add tomatoes,
oregano, salt, and pepper, cover, and simmer for 20 minutes over low
heat.

In the meantime, heat butter and remaining 1 tablespoon safflower oil
in a medium skillet and add mushrooms, salt, and pepper. Cook, uncovered, over high heat, stirring often, until mushrooms begin to brown.
Set aside and keep warm.

In the meantime, cook pasta in rapidly boiling salted water until *al
dente*. While pasta is cooking, blend sauce and walnuts in food processor
until the sauce reaches a creamy consistency. Drain pasta, toss in sauce,
and garnish each portion with the cooked mushrooms.

Each serving (without mushrooms):

SF1 4   CH 8 mg   SF2 1   **Calories 384**

Each serving (with mushrooms):

SF1 4   CH 8 mg   SF2 2   **Calories 402**

PASTA WITH CHICKEN STRIPS

Here's a light and refreshing meal. Use fresh chicken breast and trim all visible fat.

Serves 6

2 tablespoons extra virgin olive oil
1 pound fresh skinless, boneless chicken breast,
    cut into 1-1/2 × 1/2-inch strips
2 large tomatoes, chopped
6 green onions, sliced
1-1/2 cups sliced mushrooms
1/4 cup chopped fresh parsley
3 tablespoons chopped fresh basil (or 2 teaspoons dried basil)
1/2 cup dry white wine
1/4 cup oat bran (for best results, use a coarsely milled oat bran)
16 ounces any style pasta, cooked according to package
    directions
1/2 cup freshly grated Parmesan cheese
salt to taste
freshly ground pepper

Heat the olive oil in a large frying pan. If you're using fresh chicken, quickly sauté the strips. Add tomatoes, onions, mushrooms, parsley, basil, and wine. (If you're using cooked chicken, add it here.) Cover and cook for 10 minutes, until the vegetables are tender and the flavors are blended. Add the oat bran, cover, and simmer for an additional 5 minutes.

Reheat the pasta by immersing in very hot water for 1 minute. Drain. Arrange the pasta on a serving platter. Top with the chicken-vegetable mixture and Parmesan cheese. Salt and pepper to taste.

Each serving:

 4   55 mg   1   **Calories 352**

PASTA WITH CHICKEN BREASTS, POTATOES, BROCCOLI, AND PESTO
Edward Giobbi

Serves 6 to 8

1 whole chicken breast, cut into strips about 1/2 inch wide
    and 3 inches long
1 teaspoon minced garlic
1 tablespoon soy sauce

Vegetarian Entrées and Pasta Entrées (Clockwise, starting at upper left):
Corn Pudding (Page 164)
Pasta with Broccoli and Tuna (Page 190)
Rigatoni with Shellfish and Brandy (Page 184)

freshly ground black pepper to taste
juice of 1/2 lemon
3 tablespoons olive oil
1 tablespoon safflower oil
salt to taste
3 medium potatoes, peeled and cut into bite-sized pieces
1 pound tubular pasta, such as ziti, rigatoni, or penne
6 cups broccoli cut into bite-sized pieces
3 tablespoons Pesto (page 195)

Marinate cut-up chicken breasts with garlic, soy sauce, pepper, and lemon juice for several hours.

Heat the oils in a saucepan. Remove chicken from marinade and cook for several minutes over high heat. Add marinade and cook, tossing, for 10 seconds or more. Turn off heat and set aside.

Bring a large pot of water to a rolling boil and add salt and potatoes. When water returns to a boil, add pasta. Stir, cook about 4 minutes, then add broccoli and cook until pasta is done *al dente*. Drain. Reserve some of the water—1/2 to 3/4 cup—and mix with the pesto until it has a thin saucelike consistency. Add to pasta and vegetables in a large serving bowl. Add chicken and juices and toss.

Each serving:

 1   15 mg   3   **Calories 369**

ZITI RATATOUILLE
Good Housekeeping

This recipe is so low in fat (only 2 tablespoons of oil), you can splurge with some Parmesan cheese.

Serves 4

8 ounces ziti macaroni
2 tablespoons olive or salad oil
2 garlic cloves, minced
1 medium-sized onion, diced
3 medium-sized zucchini, cut into bite-sized pieces
1 medium-sized unpeeled eggplant, cut into bite-sized pieces
1 green pepper, cut into pieces
2 teaspoons dried oregano leaves
1 teaspoon salt
1/4 cup water
2 large tomatoes, cut into wedges
1/4 cup grated Parmesan cheese
freshly ground pepper

Ziti Ratatouille (*continued*)

Prepare the macaroni as the label directs; drain. Meanwhile, heat the olive oil in a 6-quart saucepan over medium heat. Add the garlic and the onion and cook for 5 minutes, stirring occasionally. Add the zucchini, eggplant, green pepper, oregano, salt, and water; heat to boiling. Reduce the heat to low, cover, and cook until vegetables are tender, about 20 minutes, stirring occasionally. Stir in the tomatoes; heat through.

To serve, spoon the vegetable mixture over the ziti. Sprinkle with the Paramesan cheese and pepper.

Each serving:

 2   4 mg   2   **Calories 385**

RIGATONI WITH SHELLFISH AND BRANDY
Edward Giobbi

This recipe uses mussels, cherrystone clams, and scallops, but any combination of shellfish is fine—try oysters, for instance.

Serves 8

2 tablespoons olive oil
1 tablespoon safflower oil
1 medium onion, finely chopped
4 tablespoons finely chopped Italian parsley
3/4 pound sliced mushrooms, or 1/2 pound sliced mushrooms
   and 3/4-ounce package dried boletus mushrooms,
   soaked in warm water 15 to 20 minutes
salt and freshly ground black pepper to taste
hot pepper flakes to taste (optional)
2 teaspoons or less minced garlic
4 cups chopped tomatoes, fresh if possible,
   run through a food mill and drained
2 tablespoons finely chopped fresh mint or 1 teaspoon dried
1 dozen mussels, scrubbed and washed
1 dozen cherrystone clams
1 pound rigatoni
1/4 cup brandy
1/2 pound sea or bay scallops

Heat the oils in a saucepan, then add onion, 2 tablespoons of the parsley, fresh mushrooms, and drained dried mushrooms. Cook, uncovered, over moderate heat. Add salt, pepper, and optional hot pepper flakes.

Cook until liquid evaporates, then add garlic and cook several more minutes. Add tomatoes and mint. Cover and simmer 20 minutes.

Add mussels to the sauce, cover, and cook until they open. Remove mussels, and let cool. Meanwhile, add clams; while they are cooking, remove mussel flesh and discard shells. When clams open, remove, cool, and scrape out flesh, discarding shells. Cut clams in slices, discard tough mussel connections, and mix the two together.

Preheat oven to 450°F.

Boil pasta for 5 minutes in rapidly boiling salted water. Drain and place in deep ovenproof dish. Add sauce, clams, mussels, brandy, and the remaining 2 tablespoons parsley. Cover tightly and bake, stirring often, for about 20 minutes, until pasta is *al dente*. The scallops should be added about 10 minutes before end of cooking.

Serve immediately in hot bowls.

Each serving:

 1   38 mg   2   **Calories 361**

LINGUINE WITH BROCCOLI
Edward Giobbi

Serves 3 to 4

1 bunch fresh broccoli, or 1 pound broccoli di rape
6 tablespoons olive oil
2 tablespoons safflower oil
2 tablespoons coarsely chopped garlic
hot pepper flakes to taste (optional)
about 2-1/2 cups water
1/2 pound linguine or spaghettini, imported if possible,
    broken into 2-inch lengths
salt and freshly ground black pepper to taste

Cut off broccoli florets and peel the stems. Cut florets into 2-inch lengths, slicing large ones in halves or quarters. Wash and set aside.

Put oils, garlic, and hot pepper in a large skillet. Turn up heat. When oil gets hot, add broccoli, 1 cup of the water, and the uncooked pasta. Stir thoroughly to combine ingredients—if the pasta is not mixed well at the beginning it will stick together. Add salt and pepper and stir, then cover. Cook over moderate heat, stirring often and taking care that the pasta does not stick together and to the bottom of the pot. Add more water if needed. Cook about 10 minutes, until *al dente*. Serve hot.

Each serving:

 3   0 mg   3   **Calories 475**

PASTA FISHERMAN STYLE
Edward Giobbi

Serves 6

2 tablespoons olive oil
1 tablespoon safflower oil
2 teaspoons chopped shallots
1 teaspoon chopped garlic
hot pepper flakes to taste
3 cups peeled, chopped tomatoes,
    fresh if possible (drain if canned)
1 teaspoon dried oregano
1 cup fresh peas, cooked 3 or 4 minutes
2 teaspoons chopped fresh basil or 1 teaspoon dried
salt to taste
1 pound white fish fillet such as scrod, striped bass,
    red snapper, cut into 1-inch cubes
1 pound any tubular cut pasta, such as elbows, shells, etc.
2 teaspoons brandy or good bourbon (optional)
finely chopped Italian parsley for garnish

Heat the oils in a medium to large skillet or saucepan and add shallots. When shallots begin to get translucent, add garlic and hot pepper. When garlic begins to brown, add tomatoes, oregano, peas, basil, and salt. Cover and simmer for 15 minutes. Add fish and continue cooking, uncovered, for several minutes.

In the meantime, cook pasta a little less than *al dente*; then drain well. Add to sauce, turn up heat, add brandy, and cook over high heat a minute or two.

Garnish with parsley.

Each serving:

 1   42 mg   2   **Calories 454**

PASTA WITH OYSTERS AND HAM

This recipe offers an unusual combination, but the flavor of oysters and ham together is excellent.

Serves 4

2 tablespoons light margarine
8 ounces 95% fat-free ham, cut into 1/2-inch squares
1-1/2 cups green onions, finely chopped
2 cups evaporated skim milk
3 dozen medium-sized shucked oysters with liquor

salt to taste
freshly ground pepper
16 ounces whole wheat pasta bows,
 cooked according to package directions
lemon wedges
chopped parsley

Melt margarine in a medium-sized saucepan. Add the ham and onions and sauté for 5 minutes. Whisk in the milk and heat to a boil. Add oysters with liquor and stir until edges of oysters curl, about 2 minutes. Add the salt and pepper to taste.

Meanwhile, reheat the pasta by immersing in very hot water for 1 minute. Place 1/4 of pasta on each of 4 heated plates. Top with oyster/ham mixture and garnish with lemon wedges and parsley.

Each serving

 2 83 mg 1 **Calories 340**

PASTA WITH SHRIMP AND PESTO
Edward Giobbi

Serves 6

2 cups firmly packed fresh basil
3 tablespoons coarsely chopped Italian parsley
6 tablespoons extra virgin olive oil
4 teaspoons safflower oil
1 tablespoon coarsely chopped garlic
4 tablespoons pine nuts
4 tablespoons freshly grated Parmesan cheese*
salt and freshly ground black pepper to taste
1 pound cut pasta, such as penne, bows, medium-sized shells
2 cups peeled, sliced potatoes
3/4 pound fresh mushrooms, sliced
hot pepper flakes to taste (optional)
3/4 pound shrimp, shelled

Put in a food processor or blend with a mortar and pestle the basil, parsley, 3 tablespoons of the olive oil, 3 teaspoons of the safflower oil, garlic, pine nuts, Parmesan cheese, salt, and pepper. Blend to a creamy consistency.

Bring a large pot of salted water to a boil and add pasta and potatoes. In the meantime, heat 2 tablespoons olive oil and remaining 1 teaspoon safflower oil in a medium skillet, then add mushrooms, salt, and pepper.

*In the original pesto recipes, Pecorino cheese was used instead of Parmesan.

Pasta with Shrimp and Pesto (*continued*)

Cook over high heat, stirring often. When mushrooms begin to brown, remove with a slotted spoon and set aside.

Heat the remaining 1 tablespoon olive oil in the skillet, add the optional hot pepper flakes and shrimp, and cook over high heat until shrimp turns pink.

When pasta is done *al dente*, drain, reserving about 4 tablespoons of the cooking water to mix with the pesto so the sauce has the consistency of heavy cream. Add pesto to the pasta, mixing well. Serve pasta and potatoes in soup plates, sprinkle some cooked mushrooms on each portion, then top each portion with some shrimp.

Serve immediately.

Each serving:

 2   88 mg   3   **Calories 549**

LINGUINE WITH CLAM SAUCE

This dish is light, healthful, and delicious! It is best when made with fresh clams.

> *Serves 6*
>
> 4 dozen top neck clams, 6 pounds mussels,
>   or 2 cans minced clams (6-1/2 ounces each),
>   rinsed and drained, reserving 1/2 cup liquid
> 2 tablespoons cornmeal (if using fresh clams or mussels)
> 2 tablespoons extra virgin olive oil
> 1 medium onion, chopped
> 1 clove garlic, minced
> 2 large tomatoes, chopped
> 1 tablespoon chopped fresh basil (or 1 teaspoon dried basil)
> 1 bay leaf
> 1/2 cup dry white wine
> 16 ounces linguine, cooked according to package directions
> salt to taste
> freshly ground pepper

To prepare the fresh clams or mussels: Scrub clams and mussels, removing beards from mussels and discarding any clams or mussels that have opened. Soak for 1 hour in a solution of 1 gallon water with 2 tablespoons cornmeal to remove any excess sand. Rinse well.

Heat the olive oil in a large frying pan until hot. Add onion and garlic, and sauté for 5 minutes. Add tomatoes, basil, and bay leaf. Cover, reduce heat, and simmer for 10 minutes to blend flavors. Add the wine, then place the fresh clams or mussels on top; cover and cook over moderate heat until the shells open—5 minutes or more for clams, 3 to 4 minutes for mussels. If using canned clams, add reserved liquid at this time. Remove bay leaf. Salt and pepper to taste.

Meanwhile, reheat the pasta by immersing in very hot water for 1 minute. Arrange the pasta on a large serving platter and top with the sauce.*

Each serving:

 less than 1   **38 mg**   **1**   **Calories 243**

*You can serve the fresh clams and mussels in the shell, or you may remove from shell before serving.

PASTA WITH SHRIMP
Edward Giobbi

If this dish is to be served as a main course, we like the fresh asparagus cut in 2-inch lengths and sautéed in vegetable oil as a garnish on top of each portion of pasta.

Serves 6

1 tablespoon olive oil
3 tablespoons safflower oil
1 medium onion, coarsely chopped
1 teaspoon or more minced garlic
2 tablespoons finely chopped Italian parsley
hot pepper flakes to taste (optional)
2 cups coarsely chopped tomatoes,
    fresh if possible (drain if canned)
1 teaspoon dried oregano
salt to taste
1 pound pasta, preferably spaghettini or linguine
1 pound fresh medium shrimp, shells removed
4 tablespoons brandy or good bourbon
chopped Italian parsley for garnish

Heat the oils in a medium saucepan; then add onion and cook, uncovered, over moderate heat. When onion begins to brown, add garlic, parsley, and optional hot pepper. Simmer about 1 minute. Add tomatoes and oregano, cover, and lower heat. Add salt to taste and simmer for 20 minutes.

In the meantime, add pasta to rapidly boiling water. Add shrimp to sauce and cover and cook for 5 minutes.

Pasta with Shrimp (*continued*)

When pasta is almost cooked—about 1 minute before desired done-ness—drain pasta, add to sauce with shrimp, and add brandy. Turn up heat and cook 1 minute, mixing often.

Top with the asparagus, if you like, and garnish with chopped Italian parsley.

Each serving:

 1   114 mg   2 **Calories 494**

PASTA WITH BROCCOLI AND TUNA
Edward Giobbi

Here is a pasta recipe that can be made ahead of time and served at room temperature as a main course.

Serves 6

3/4 pound cut pasta, such as rigatoni, penne, ziti, etc.
4 tablespoons olive oil
4 cups fresh broccoli cut into bite-sized pieces
1 tablespoon safflower oil
1 teaspoon minced garlic
salt and freshly ground black pepper to taste
2 tablespoons Pesto (page 195)
1 cup thinly sliced whole scallions
2 9-ounce cans tunafish
2 cups sliced fresh, ripe tomatoes
12 dried black olives, pitted and sliced (optional)
2 tablespoons finely chopped Italian parsley
thinly sliced whole scallions for garnish

Cook pasta *al dente* in boiling salted water. Drain, add 3 tablespoons of the olive oil, toss, and let cool.

Cook broccoli in boiling salted water until almost cooked. Heat saf-flower oil and remaining tablespoon olive oil; then add broccoli, garlic, salt, and pepper. Cook until broccoli is tender. Toss with pasta, add pesto and mix well; then add scallions, tuna, tomatoes, remaining oil, and olives. Gently toss, add parsley. Do not refrigerate. Serve at room temperature.

Garnish with thinly sliced scallions.

Each serving:

 3   55 mg   3 **Calories 537**

PASTA BAKED WITH EGGPLANT AND WALNUTS
Edward Giobbi

Serves 6 to 8

2 tablespoons olive oil
1 tablespoon safflower oil
1 eggplant, about 1-1/2 pounds, cut into 1/2-inch-thick slices,
    then cut into manageable pieces (about 7 or 8 cups)
salt and freshly ground black pepper to taste
2 cups Tomato Sauce (page 194)
22 to 25 walnuts, shelled and chopped
1 pound cut pasta, such as penne, shells, ziti, etc.
2 tablespoons finely chopped Italian parsley
about 3/4 cup bread crumbs (mix with 1 tablespoon safflower oil)

Heat the two oils in a large skillet, then add eggplant, salt, and pepper. Cook over medium heat, tossing occasionally, until eggplant begins to brown. Turn off heat and set aside.

Blend the tomato sauce in a food processor or run through a food mill. Pour sauce into a food processor with walnut meats and blend. Or blend some of the sauce with walnuts using a mortar and pestle, then combine crushed walnut meats with the rest of sauce.

Preheat oven to 450°F. Cook pasta in a large pot of boiling water until almost done, draining about 5 minutes before cooking is completed. Put drained pasta in an ovenproof dish with sauce, mixing well. Add cooked eggplant and mix; then add parsley, top with bread crumbs, cover, and bake about 15 to 20 minutes.

Remove dish from oven, broil under high heat a minute or two to brown bread crumbs.

Each serving:

 2   0 mg   2   **Calories 455**

Variation

An alternative to baking is to cook pasta until done *al dente*, then toss with sauce and eggplant, cover with bread crumbs, and toast crumbs under broiler.

VEGETABLE LASAGNA
Edward Giobbi

This is a most satisfying lasagna recipe, which is excellent as a main luncheon course or dinner course. It is perhaps one of the lightest lasagna recipes you will have the pleasure to serve.

The original recipe calls for cream or beciamella sauce, for which I have substituted walnuts. The result is a creamy sauce without saturated fats.

If the recipe is served as a main course a mixed green salad would make a good accompaniment.

Baked slices of eggplant or zucchini can be used instead of fried eggplant and fresh peas can be used instead of artichoke hearts, but do not use too many varieties of vegetables or one will cancel the other out.

Serves 12, as a first course

2-1/4 to 2-1/2 pounds eggplant in slices 1/4 to 1/2 inch thick
9-ounce package frozen artichokes
4 tablespoons olive oil
2 tablespoons safflower oil
2 cups coarsely chopped onion
1 cup sliced carrots
2 cloves garlic, chopped
4 cups chopped tomatoes, fresh if possible (drain if canned)
1 teaspoon dried oregano
1 tablespoon dried basil
4 cloves
salt and freshly ground black pepper to taste
1 pound sliced mushrooms
corn or vegetable oil for shallow-frying
flour for dredging
1 pound lasagna pasta, preferably imported Italian
22 walnuts, shelled, 1 cup

Sprinkle eggplant slices with salt and let them drain for 1 hour; then wash and pat dry. Blanch frozen artichokes in boiling water, then drain.

Heat 2 tablespoons of the olive oil and 1 tablespoon of the safflower oil in a medium saucepan. Add onion and carrots. When onion wilts, add garlic and cook for several minutes. Add tomatoes, oregano, basil, clove, and salt and pepper to taste. Cover and simmer for 30 minutes, stirring occasionally. Pour into a food processor and blend. Return to pan, add artichokes, and cook 15 minutes more.

In the meantime, heat the remaining 2 tablespoons olive oil and 1 tablespoon safflower oil in a large skillet. Add the sliced mushrooms, salt, and pepper. Cook over high heat until mushrooms begin to brown. Remove from skillet and set aside.

Heat about 3/4 inch corn oil in a medium skillet. Dust eggplant slices with flour a few at a time, then shake off excess. When oil is hot, add some of the eggplant slices and cook until lightly brown. Blot dry on paper towels and repeat process until all slices are browned.

Cook pasta in rapidly boiling salted water for 5 or 6 minutes. Drain, rinse in cold water. On a baking tray about 12×12 inches and about 3 inches deep, lay one layer of pasta, then one layer of eggplant.

Spoon off about 2 cups sauce (without artichokes) and place in food processor. Add 1 cup warm water and the walnuts. Blend to a creamy consistency. Pour some of this sauce and artichoke hearts on top of the eggplant, add another layer of pasta, spread cooked mushrooms over, add another layer of pasta, a layer of eggplant and sauce. Repeat with another layer of eggplant, sauce, and pasta until all ingredients are used up. Top with a layer of pasta with sauce. Add some water if too dense. Cover with foil and bake 30 minutes in a preheated 400°F oven.

Each serving:

 1   0 mg   3   **Calories 337**

LASAGNA ROLL-UPS

This is a beautiful dish and quite easy to assemble in advance. It has less cheese than a typical lasagna with quite a good pasta flavor.

Makes 8 roll-ups

8 ounces whole wheat lasagna noodles
non stick cooking spray
2 tablespoons extra virgin olive oil
1 medium onion, chopped
2 cloves garlic, minced
1/2 cup chopped fresh mushrooms
3 tablespoons dry white wine
1 pound spinach, tough stems removed
   and washed 3 times to remove sand
1 teaspoon thyme
1-1/4 cups low-fat ricotta cheese
1/2 cup shredded part-skim mozarella cheese
1/4 cup freshly grated Parmesan cheese
2 tablespoons chopped fresh basil
   (or 2 teaspoons dry basil leaves)
1 quart Tomato Sauce (page 194 or prepared)
1/4 cup freshly grated Paramesan cheese for garnish
freshly ground pepper
basil leaves for garnish (optional)
salt to taste

Lasagna Roll-Ups *(continued)*

Cook lasagna noodles according to package directions. Drain.

Preheat the oven to 325°F. Spray an 8×8×2-inch square baking dish with no stick cooking spray.

Heat the olive oil in a heavy pot or dutch oven, add the onion and garlic, and sauté until translucent. Add the mushrooms and white wine. Add spinach (in batches, if necessary). Continue to cook, uncovered, until all cooking liquid has been absorbed. Add thyme.

In a separate bowl, combine the cottage cheese with the other cheeses and the basil.

To assemble, spread 1/4 cup cheese mixture on each lasagna noodle. Next, spread 1/4 cup spinach mixture on each lasagna noodle and roll up, jellyroll-style. Place 8 roll-ups in baking dish, seam side down. Top each roll with 2 tablespoons tomato sauce. Cover and bake for 30 minutes until each roll-up is warmed through.

Meanwhile, heat the remaining tomato sauce. To serve, garnish lasagna roll-ups with Parmesan cheese, basil leaves, and freshly ground pepper. Serve with additional tomato sauce on the side.

Each roll-up:

 5   **42 mg**   **1**   **Calories 281**

TOMATO OR MARINARA SAUCE
Edward Giobbi

Makes about 4 cups, enough for about 1-1/2 pounds pasta. Serves 6

3 tablespoons olive oil
1 teaspoon safflower oil
1-1/2 cups sliced carrots
2 cups coarsely chopped onion
salt and freshly ground black pepper to taste
2 cloves garlic, chopped
4 cups chopped tomatoes, fresh if possible (drain if canned)
2 tablespoons chopped fresh basil or 1 tablespoon dried
about 1/4 cup water or chicken or beef broth
finely chopped Italian parsley for garnish

Heat the oils in a large, shallow pan, then add carrots, onion, salt, and pepper. Sauté, uncovered, over moderate heat until onion begins to brown, then add garlic and cook about 1 minute. Add tomatoes and basil, cover, and simmer over low to medium heat for 20 minutes, stirring occasionally.

Pour sauce in a food processor and purée to a creamy consistency or force sauce through a food mill.

Return sauce to pan and add enough water or broth to make the sauce the consistency of heavy cream. Cover and simmer over low heat an additional 10 minutes.

Serve on pasta.

Each serving:

 1   0 mg   1   **Calories 116**

PESTO
Edward Giobbi

I have not used grated cheese in this recipe, as is traditional in pesto, but I have added more nuts to compensate, and I have found it to be completely satisfactory. It is important to use a fine olive oil, preferably extra virgin olive oil.

Yields about 3/4 pint (enough for about 2 pounds pasta or 3 cups rice)

2 tablespoons safflower oil
4 tablespoons good olive oil
2 cloves peeled garlic
1 cup walnut meats
4 cups tightly packed fresh basil
3 tablespoons chopped Italian parsley
salt and freshly ground black pepper to taste

Place all the ingredients in a food processor and blend. Put in a jar, add 1 inch oil (1/2 olive oil, 1/2 safflower oil) on top of pesto, and refrigerate. It will last all winter.

Each serving:

 1   0 mg   less than 1   **Calories 133**

12

SIDE DISHES

STUFFED REDSKIN POTATOES

We don't often bake redskin potatoes, but in this recipe they work well, adding color and a nice texture to the other ingredients.

Serves 6

6 large redskin potatoes, 4 inches in diameter, 2-1/2 to 3 pounds
1/2 cup 1% low-fat cottage cheese
1/4 cup chopped parsley
1 tablespoon margarine
1 tablespoon cajun seasoning
1/2 cup fat-free ham, finely chopped
1/2 cup green onions or scallions, sliced,
    including tender green tops
1 large green pepper, chopped into 1/4-inch pieces
no stick cooking spray
chives for garnish
salt to taste
freshly ground pepper

Preheat the oven to 350°F.

Wash the redskin potatoes and prick skins. Bake for 1 hour, or until potatoes are tender. Cool. Slice off the tops of the potatoes and scoop out the interior into a medium-sized bowl.

With an electric mixer, beat the interior of the potatoes with the cottage cheese and parsley. Set aside.

Heat the margarine in a medium-sized saucepan. Add cajun seasoning and ham and sauté until ham is crisp and blended with seasoning. Add green onions and green pepper, cover, and cook until vegetables are tender and covered with seasoning.

Spray a medium-sized baking pan with no stick cooking spray.

Blend ham mixture with potatoes. Divide filling among potato shells. Bake for 20 minutes or until potatoes are hot and lightly browned. Garnish with chopped chives. Salt and pepper to taste.

Each serving:

 less than 1   **4 mg**   **2**   **Calories 274**

BRUSSELS SPROUTS WITH LIGHT CHEESE SAUCE

Brussels sprouts are especially tasty with a nice cheese sauce. This one is light and flavorful.

> *Serves 6*
>
> 1 pound fresh Brussels sprouts
> 2 cups water
> 1 tablespoon light margarine
> 1 small onion, minced
> 2 cloves garlic, minced
> 2 tablespoons flour
> 1 cup skim milk
> 1/4 cup shredded extra sharp Cheddar cheese
> 1 tablespoon chopped chives
> 2 teaspoons freshly squeezed lemon juice
> freshly ground pepper
> salt to taste

Wash and clean the Brussels sprouts. Remove outer leaves and make a small X with a knife in the stem end of the Brussels sprout. This will enable sprouts to cook more evenly. In a medium-sized saucepan, bring the water to a boil, add the Brussels sprouts, cover, and cook for 7 to 9 minutes—until they have bright green color and are tender.

In a small saucepan, heat the margarine, then add the onion and garlic and sauté until translucent. Whisk flour with milk and add to onion mixture, whisking while the sauce heats. Add cheese to sauce, and stir to melt.

Drain hot Brussels sprouts and pour into a serving bowl. Top with lemon juice, cheese sauce, and freshly ground pepper. Salt to taste.

Each serving:

 1   **6 mg**   **1**   **Calories 85**

TINY PEAS AND ONIONS, CAESAR STYLE

This side dish has a delicious garlic flavor and the homemade croutons add zest.

Serves 4

2 tablespoons olive oil
2 cloves garlic, minced
1 cup Italian bread cubes
1 cup water
1 package (10 ounces) tiny peas with onions
1/4 cup freshly grated Parmesan cheese
freshly ground pepper
salt to taste

Heat the oil in a medium-sized skillet. Add the garlic and bread cubes and sauté, stirring, until they are toasted and well flavored.

Bring the water to a boil in a small saucepan, then add the peas and onions, cover tightly, and cook for 5 minutes. Drain.

Toss the hot peas and onions with Parmesan cheese. Just before serving, add croutons and freshly ground black pepper. Salt to taste.

Each serving:

 2   5 mg   1   **Calories 133**

HOT 'n SPICY GLAZED CARROTS

Cayenne pepper perks up flavors in this tasty vegetable side dish, which will brighten up any meal.

Serves 6

6 large carrots
1 cup water
2 tablespoons light margarine
2 tablespoons honey
1/4 teaspoon cayenne pepper
1/2 teaspoon cinnamon
salt to taste
freshly ground pepper

Julienne the carrots by peeling them, then cutting them into very thin strips.

Bring the water to a boil in a medium-sized saucepan, then add carrots and cook until tender crisp, about 5 minutes. Drain and add margarine,

honey, cayenne pepper, and cinnamon. Toss carrots to coat. Serve immediately. Salt and pepper to taste.

Each serving:

 less than 1   **0 mg**   **1**   **Calories 80**

CONTINENTAL ZUCCHINI BAKE

This is delicious—tender vegetables with a wonderful cheese topping
and lots of good nutrition.

Serves 6

1 cup water
4 medium-sized zucchini, scrubbed and sliced
no stick cooking spray
2 tablespoons vegetable oil, preferably safflower or canola
8 green onions or scallions with tender green tops, chopped
1 medium-sized yellow onion, chopped
2 cloves garlic, minced
1 medium green pepper, chopped into 1/2-inch chunks
1 tablespoon freshly chopped basil, or 1 teaspoon dried basil
1 cup freshly grated Parmesan cheese
1/2 cup fresh bread crumbs
2 tablespoons chopped fresh parsley
chopped chives for garnish
paprika for garnish
salt to taste
freshly ground pepper

Bring the water to a boil in a large saucepan. Add the zucchini, cover,
return to a boil, and cook until zucchini is tender crisp, about 2 minutes.
Drain.

Preheat oven to 350°F. Spray a 2-quart casserole with no stick cooking
spray.

Heat oil in a small skillet. Add the onions, garlic, and green pepper
and sauté until vegetables are tender. Stir in the cooked squash and the
basil.

Place the vegetables in the prepared dish. Top with Parmesan cheese,
bread crumbs, and chopped parsley. Bake for 30 minutes, until topping
is browned and crunchy.

Sprinkle with chopped chives and paprika. Serve immediately. Salt
and pepper to taste.

Each serving:

 4   **13 mg**   **2**   **Calories 218**

PEARLS AND PEAS
WITH CREMINI MUSHROOMS

The firm, dark-fleshed cremini mushrooms are particularly good in this dish, but if they are not available, use any fresh mushroom.

Serves 6

1 cup water
1 cup pearl onions (use canned if fresh are not available)
2 tablespoons olive oil
1 clove garlic, minced
1 cup cremini mushrooms, washed and sliced very thin*
1 package (10 ounces) frozen tiny peas
1/4 cup chopped mint
1/2 teaspoon white pepper
1/8 teaspoon allspice

Bring the water to a boil in a small saucepan, then add the onions and cook until they are tender, about 10 minutes.

Drain the pearl onions and cool. Cut the stem end of each onion and slip off its tough skin.

Heat the olive oil in a medium-sized skillet. Add the garlic and mushrooms and sauté until vegetables are brown. Add the peas, cover, and cook until peas are tender, about 5 minutes.

Add the onions to the mushroom mixture with mint, pepper, and allspice. Heat to blend flavors. Serve hot.

Each serving:

 less than 1   **0 mg**   **1**   **Calories 68**

*If cremini mushrooms are not available, use any type of firm, white mushroom.

RED CABBAGE, PENNSYLVANIA STYLE

Here's tender cabbage in a tangy, sweet and spicy sauce. This is a most attractive side dish and one with plenty of good nutrition.

Serves 6

2 tablespoons olive oil
1/4 cup brown sugar, packed
2 tablespoons red or white wine vinegar
1 teaspoon caraway seed
1 teaspoon paprika
4 cups shredded red cabbage (1 small head)
2 large Granny Smith apples, cored, seeded, and cubed

In a large skillet, heat the oil with the sugar, vinegar, caraway seed, and paprika. When mixture boils, stir to blend. Add cabbage. Cover and cook for 15 minutes. Add apples and cook 15 minutes longer until cabbage is very tender. Uncover and cook, stirring occasionally, until cabbage absorbs sauce and has an attractive glaze. Serve immediately.

Each serving:

 less than 1   0 mg   2   **Calories 118**

POTATOES WITH CELERY, TOMATOES, AND ONIONS
Edward Giobbi

This simple recipe goes well with grilled meats and fish.

Serves 5 to 6

5 medium potatoes, peeled and cut in thick slices
10 pieces of celery, about 4 inches long each
2 medium onions, sliced
2 cups chopped tomatoes, fresh if possible (drain if canned)
3 tablespoons vegetable oil
1 teaspoon dried oregano
salt and freshly ground black pepper to taste
2 tablespoons finely chopped Italian parsley

Distribute all the vegetables in a shallow baking dish. Pour oil and seasonings over them and mix in. Cover and bake in a preheated 450°F oven about 30 minutes, or until potatoes are tender.

Each serving (for 6):

 1   0 mg   2   **Calories 238**

HOT CAJUN FRIES

This is a simple recipe, but these potatoes will brown and crisp beautifully. What could be easier?

Serves 4

no stick cooking spray
4 baking potatoes
1 lemon
1 to 2 teaspoons cajun seasoning

Hot Cajun Fries *(continued)*

Preheat the oven to 425°F. Spray a cookie sheet with no stick cooking spray. Cut the unpeeled potatoes into thin, long strips. Place in a bowl of ice water with the juice of 1 lemon to prevent potatoes from browning.

Drain the potatoes. Distribute evenly over the cookie sheet and sprinkle with cajun seasoning. Bake for 20 to 25 minutes, turning potatoes several times. Potatoes will be cooked and lightly browned. Serve immediately.

Each serving:

 0   0 mg   2   **Calories 125**

STUFFED ZUCCHINI

Here's the healthful zucchini dressed up in a side dish. We've used low-fat ham to add just a hint of flavor and color to this tasty recipe.

> *Serves 8*
>
> 4 medium zucchini, about 2 pounds
> 4 ounces fat-free ham, chopped
> no stick cooking spray
> 2 tablespoons margarine
> 1 small onion, minced
> 2 cloves garlic, minced
> 2 tablespoons chopped pimiento or sweet red pepper
> 2 tablespoons chopped parsley
> 1 cup fresh bread crumbs (preferably made from oat bran bread)
> 1/4 cup freshly grated Parmesan cheese
> salt to taste
> freshly ground pepper
> parsley sprigs for garnish

Heat water in a large soup pot. Cook whole zucchini in boiling water until just tender, about 15 minutes. Allow to cool slightly. Cut zucchini into halves and scoop out the pulp. Be careful to keep the shells intact. Reserve the shells.

Mash the zucchini pulp and blend with chopped ham.

Preheat oven to 325°F. Spray a cookie sheet with no stick cooking spray.

Melt the margarine in a heavy skillet, add the onion, garlic, and chopped pimiento and sauté slowly for 2 minutes. Add the parsley, bread crumbs, and zucchini pulp and sauté 5 minutes.

Place the 8 zucchini halves on the cookie sheet. Divide the filling among the halves. Sprinkle the filled squash with the Parmesan cheese.

Bake for 20 minutes or until filling is browned and cheese melts. Salt and pepper to taste. Garnish with parsley sprigs.

Each serving (made with oat bran bread crumbs):

 1   7 mg   2   **Calories 86**

FRIED CAULIFLOWER
Edward Giobbi

The batter in this recipe can be used on a variety of vegetables, such as blanched broccoli, mushrooms, peppers, and asparagus.

> *Serves 4*
>
> 1 cup flour
> salt and freshly ground black pepper to taste
> 2/3 cup dry white wine
> 1 egg white, lightly beaten
> 1/2 a medium cauliflower
> corn oil or vegetable oil

In a mixing bowl, stir together the flour, salt, pepper, wine, and egg white, then cover and let sit for 1 hour.

Boil cauliflower florets about 5 minutes, then drain. Heat 3/4 inch oil in a small skillet. When oil is hot, dip the florets one at a time into the batter with a pair of tongs, then gently place them in the hot oil and cook, turning occasionally, until they are a golden brown. Don't crowd them. Repeat the process, blotting finished florets on paper towels. Serve hot.

Each serving:

 less than 1   0 mg   (SF2) 2   **Calories 184**

DANDELION GREENS WITH POTATOES
Edward Giobbi

> *Serves 6*
>
> 12 cups cleaned dandelion greens
> 2 cups diced potatoes
> 4 tablespoons olive oil
> 1 tablespoon safflower oil
> 3 cloves garlic, chopped
> hot pepper flakes to taste (optional)
> salt to taste

Dandelion Greens with Potatoes (*continued*)

Boil dandelion greens with potatoes about 5 minutes. Drain, saving 1 cup liquid.

Heat the oils in a skillet, then add garlic and hot pepper. As soon as garlic takes on color, add dandelion greens, potatoes, reserved liquid, and salt; then cover and cook over low heat for 20 to 30 minutes. Mash potatoes with a fork and add more oil if desired.

Each serving:

 2   **0 mg**   **1**   **Calories 211**

CAJUN POTATO PANCAKES

Here's an unusually colorful potato pancake. It has a crispy exterior and a colorful interior.

> *Makes 8 potato pancakes*
>
> 1 cup water
> 1/2 cup finely shredded cabbage
> 1/4 cup finely chopped green pepper
> 1 small onion, minced
> 1 tablespoon chopped pimiento
> 1-1/2 cups mashed potatoes (prepared with skim milk)
> 1 egg white
> 1 tablespoon cajun seasoning
> salt to taste
> 1/4 cup soft margarine
> freshly ground pepper

In a heavy skillet, heat the water. Add the cabbage, green pepper, onion, and pimiento and simmer until vegetables are tender, about 8 minutes. Drain vegetables.

In a large mixing bowl, combine the cooked vegetables with the mashed potatoes. Then, beat the egg white, lightly, with cajun seasoning. Add this mixture to the potato mixture. Salt to taste. Form into 16 balls and chill thoroughly.

When ready to cook, heat the margarine in a large, heavy skillet. Flatten each potato pancake and sauté, several at a time, adding more margarine as necessary. Carefully turn the pancake to brown both sides. Hold cooked potato pancakes in 250°F oven until all are cooked. Sprinkle with freshly ground pepper and serve hot.

Each potato pancake:

 less than 1   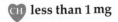 **less than 1 mg**   **1**   **Calories 188**

POTATO BALLS
Edward Giobbi

Serves 6 to 8

4 medium Idaho baking potatoes
1 tablespoon olive oil
4 tablespoons chopped pine nuts
2 tablespoons chopped Italian parsley
1 teaspoon marjoram
salt and freshly ground black pepper to taste
1 egg white, lightly beaten
fresh bread crumbs
corn oil for frying

Wash potatoes, then peel and mash them. Mix thoroughly with olive oil, pine nuts, parsley, marjoram, salt, and pepper.

Form balls with the mixture about the size of a walnut (about 1 heaping tablespoon), roll in egg white, then in bread crumbs.

Heat about 3/4 inch corn oil in a 9- or 10-inch skillet until hot but not smoking (oil should boil quickly when balls are added). Place balls gently in the pan with tongs, not too many at a time—the pan should not be crowded. Cook until golden brown, then remove and blot on paper towels. Repeat. Serve hot.

Each serving (for 8):

 less than 1   **0 mg**   **1**   **Calories 140**

BAKED RISOTTO
Edward Giobbi

Serves 8

9-ounce package frozen artichoke hearts
1 medium onion, minced
3 tablespoons safflower oil
1 cup peas, fresh if possible
1 cup sliced mushrooms
about 4 cups beef or chicken broth
salt and freshly ground black pepper to taste
2 cups Arborio or Carolina long-grain rice
2 tablespoons butter or olive oil

Cook the artichoke hearts in boiling water 1 minute; drain, coarsely chop them, and set aside.

Sauté onion in safflower oil in a medium casserole. When onion begins to brown, add peas, artichoke hearts, mushrooms, 1 cup of the

Baked Risotto (*continued*)

stock, salt and pepper. Cover and cook gently for 20 minutes. In the meantime, in a separate pot boil 4 cups water, stir in the rice, and boil for 5 minutes. Drain and add rice to vegetable mixture. Add butter and 2 more cups stock. Cover and place in preheated 400°F oven, stirring occasionally and adding more stock as is needed (at least 1 more cup). Taste for salt. The dish should be done in 10 minutes or so, depending on the rice.

Each serving:

 2   8 mg   1   **Calories 276**

BROCCOLETTI DI RAPE WITH BEANS
Edward Giobbi

Broccoletti di rape, sometimes called broccoli rab, is seen more frequently today in farmers' market, and many gardeners are growing their own. To prepare it, cut the florets off about 3 inches from the top. Cut the tender stems into 3-inch lengths and peel them. Remove and discard any tough or discolored leaves. This dish is an excellent vegetable accompaniment with broiled meats and fish.

> *Serves 4*
>
> 1 cup dried cannellini or Great Northern beans
> 5 cups water
> 1 tablespoon olive oil
> 1 tablespoon safflower oil
> salt and freshly ground black pepper
>   or hot pepper flakes to taste
> 1 tablespoon crushed rosemary
> 1 cup finely chopped onion
> 1 teaspoon finely chopped garlic
> 6 cups broccoletti di rape, cut up

Put dried beans in a small bowl, add 2 cups water, and soak overnight. Beans will triple in bulk after soaking.

Pick out and discard any discolored beans. Pour beans in a medium stock pot, preferably terracotta. Add 3 cups water and all the other ingredients except the rape, bring to a boil, cover, and boil gently about 1-1/4 hours until beans are tender. Add rape and cook about 10 more minutes, then turn off heat and let stand about 10 to 15 minutes.

Each serving:

 1   0 mg   6   **Calories 252**

LIMA BEANS, BROCCOLI, AND RICE
Edward Giobbi

This recipe makes a delicious complete lunch dish.

Serves 6 to 8

2 cups dried lima beans, soaked in cold water about 2 hours
6 cups water
1 tablespoon crushed rosemary
1 bay leaf
hot pepper flakes to taste (optional)
1 medium onion, coarsely chopped
salt and freshly ground black pepper to taste
3 cups broccoli cut into bite-sized pieces

The Sauce

3 tablespoons vegetable oil (I prefer 1 tablespoon olive
    and 2 tablespoons safflower)
1 medium onion, coarsely chopped
2 cups chopped tomatoes, fresh if possible (drain if canned)
1/4 cup diced celery
3 tablespoons chopped fresh basil or 1 tablespoon dried
salt and freshly ground black pepper to taste

1 cup Carolina long-grain rice

Drain lima beans, then put in a saucepan with 4 cups of the water, the rosemary, bay leaf, hot pepper, onion, salt, and freshly ground black pepper. Cover and boil gently for about 1-1/2 hours. Add broccoli. Cook another 20 minutes. Keep warm.

To make the sauce, heat the oils in a skillet, then add onion and sauté until brown. Add the rest of the ingredients. Cover and simmer over medium heat about 20 minutes.

Cook 1 cup rice in 2 cups water. When rice is cooked, mix in the tomato sauce.

Put a serving of cooked rice on each plate. Make a well on each rice mound, pour lima-bean-and-broccoli mixture over, and serve.

Each serving (for 8):

 less than 1   **0 mg**   **3**   **Calories 337**

RICE WITH TOMATOES
Edward Giobbi

Good as is, this rice dish also makes a wonderful stuffing for tomatoes and peppers.

> *Serves 6*
>
> 3 tablespoons vegetable oil—safflower oil will do, or peanut oil
> 2 medium onions, finely chopped
> 4 cups chopped tomatoes, fresh if possible (drain if canned)
> 3 tablespoons chopped fresh basil or Italian parsley
> salt and freshly ground black pepper to taste
> 2 cups Carolina long-grain rice

Heat the oil in a medium skillet, then add onions. Cook over medium to high heat, and when onions begin to brown, add tomatoes, basil, salt and pepper. Cover, lower heat, and simmer about 10 minutes.

In the meantime, add 2 cups good-quality rice to 4 cups water. When water boils, cover pot tightly and turn heat down as low as possible. Cook rice until it absorbs the water. Mix in sauce and serve in bowls as a first course or as a starch in a main course.

Each serving:

 1   0 mg   1   **Calories 33**

CORN BREAD STUFFING WITH OYSTERS

Some stuffings are bland to look at, tasteless, and full of calories and fat. This moist stuffing is colorful, flavorful, and tasty.

> *Serves 6*
>
> 2 tablespoons light margarine
> 1 medium onion, chopped coarsely
> 1 cup sliced celery
> 8 ounces shucked oysters with liquor
> 6 cups Corn Bread, crumbled (page 93 or prepared)
> 1/4 cup chopped fresh parsley
> 2 egg whites, beaten to blend
> salt to taste
> freshly ground pepper

In a large skillet, melt the margarine over medium-high heat. Add the onion and celery, cover, and cook for 7 minutes. Add the oysters and their liquor. Reduce heat to a simmer and cook until oysters curl, about 5 minutes.

Remove from the heat and add the corn bread, parsley, and egg whites, mixing well. If stuffing seems dry, add just a little water. Return to the heat and cook for 2 minutes to heat and blend flavors. Serve hot.

Each serving:

 less than 1   **21 mg**   **2**   **Calories 179**

OAT BRAN STUFFING

This is a moist stuffing that works well for stuffing poultry. It has an excellent flavor, and it also makes a good side dish.

> *Serves 6*
>
> 2 tablespoons soft margarine
> 1 cup chopped celery
> 1/2 cup chopped onion
> 4 cups oat bran bread, cubed (about 6 to 7 slices)
> 1/4 cup chopped parsley
> 1 teaspoon sage
> 1/2 to 3/4 cup chicken stock (freshly made or prepared)
> salt to taste
> freshly ground pepper

In a medium-sized skillet, heat the margarine, then sauté the celery and onion until tender and juicy.

Toss the bread cubes with the parsley and sage. Add the celery mixture and toss. Add just enough chicken stock to moisten the stuffing.

Use the stuffing to stuff a large (4 pound) chicken or other poultry. Or place in a 2-quart casserole dish that has been sprayed with no stick cooking spray. Cover and bake at 325°F for 30 minutes.

Each serving:

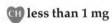 **less than 1**   **less than 1 mg**   **1**   **Calories 100**

13

DESSERTS

CARROT CAKE

Years ago, carrot cakes were laden with fat and sugar, but this one is light, moist, and delicious!

Makes 1 9×13-inch cake; 15 servings

no stick cooking spray
1 cup oat bran (for best results,
  use an oat bran that is coarsely milled)
1 cup all-purpose flour
1 cup granulated sugar
1 teaspoon baking powder
1 teaspoon baking soda
1 teaspoon salt
1 teaspoon ground cinnamon
1/2 teaspoon cloves
1 cup apple juice
3 cups finely shredded carrot
1/3 cup vegetable oil, preferably safflower or canola
4 large egg whites
1 package (8 ounces) reduced-fat cream cheese, softened
2 tablespoons corn syrup
1 teaspoon vanilla
1 cup sifted confectioners' sugar

Preheat oven to 325°F. Spray a 13×9×2-inch baking pan with no stick cooking spray.

In a mixing bowl, combine oat bran and flour with the sugar, baking powder, baking soda, salt, cinnamon, and cloves. Add the apple juice, carrot, oil, and egg whites. Beat at low speed with an electric mixer until the ingredients are combined. Beat on medium speed for 2 minutes.

Pour into the prepared pan, pushing the batter a little higher around the edges than in the middle. Bake for 60 minutes until the center of the cake is firm to touch. Cool.

Combine the cream cheese with corn syrup and vanilla. Gradually add the confectioners' sugar and beat until it is smooth. Spread the cooled cake with the cream cheese frosting.

Each serving:

 3 13 mg 1 **Calories 230**

APPLESAUCE CAKE

A delicious, moist cake that retains good flavor after standing a day or two.

Makes 12 servings

no stick cooking spray
3/4 cup raisins
2-1/4 cups all-purpose flour
1 teaspoon salt
1-1/2 teaspoons baking soda
1 teaspoon cinnamon
1/2 teaspoon ground cloves
1/3 cup walnuts, chopped
1 cup brown sugar, packed
1/2 cup light margarine
2 tablespoons white sugar
1/2 teaspoon grated lemon peel
1 egg, beaten
1-1/2 cups natural apple sauce

Preheat oven to 325°F. Spray a 10×10×2-inch baking pan with no stick cooking spray.

Plump raisins by steaming them over boiling water for 5 minutes.

Meanwhile, sift flour, then measure. Sift with salt, soda, cinnamon, and cloves. Blend 1/4 cup flour mixture with raisins and walnuts.

Cream margarine. Add brown sugar and white sugar and cream until well blended. Add lemon and egg.

Add flour to creamed mixture alternately with apple sauce. When well blended, add raisins-nut mixture.

Pour into prepared pan, pushing the batter a little higher around the edges than in the middle. Bake for 40 minutes, until cake tests done. Cool in the pan for 10 minutes before removing from pan.

Each serving:

 1 23 mg 1 **Calories 252**

STARS AND STRIPES SHORTCAKE

This dessert is best when made with fresh berries. We like to serve it on patriotic holidays using strawberries and blueberries.

Serves 8

6 cups fresh berries (raspberries, strawberries, blueberries),
    washed
1/2 cup plus 1 tablespoon granulated sugar
no stick cooking spray
1-1/2 cups oat bran (for best results,
    use an oat bran that is coarsely milled)
2 cups all-purpose flour
1 tablespoon baking powder
1/2 teaspoon salt
1/2 cup vegetable oil, preferably safflower or canola
2 large egg whites
2/3 cup skim milk

Combine the berries with 1/4 cup sugar and allow to cure for 30 minutes at room temperature.

Preheat oven to 450°F. Spray a cookie sheet with no stick cooking spray.

Meanwhile, mix the oat bran and flour with 1/4 cup sugar, the baking powder, and salt. Cut the oil into the oat bran mixture with a pastry blender or with a fork until the mixture resembles coarse crumbs. Combine the egg whites with milk and add to oat bran, stirring until just moistened.

Sprinkle a cutting board with a little flour. With a rolling pin, roll the shortcake dough to a 1/2-inch thickness. With a medium-sized star-shaped cookie cutter, cut the dough into medium-sized stars (or other shapes you desire). Try to keep dough scraps to a mimimum and reroll dough only 1 time so that it does not toughen. Place stars on cookie sheet (there should be 16 medium-sized stars). Sprinkle with remaining 1 tablespoon sugar.

Bake the stars for 10 minutes or until they are lightly browned and firm to touch. Remove shortcake stars from cookie sheet and cool for 10 minutes on a wire rack. Place two stars in each serving bowl and cover with fruit.

Each serving:

 2   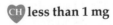 less than 1 mg   2   **Calories 295**

WHOLE-GRAIN ANGEL CAKE

Here's a delicate whole-grain cake. Tender, with rich mellow flavor, this cake has almost no fat, and is low in calories. For a special treat, serve it with Fruit Sauce (page 68).

Makes 1 10-inch cake; 12 servings

no stick cooking spray
1/2 cup whole wheat pastry flour (if pastry flour is unavailable, use whole wheat graham flour)
1/2 cup cake flour, sifted
3/4 cup confectioners' sugar, sifted
12 large egg whites, room temperature
1-1/2 teaspoons cream of tartar
1/4 teaspoon salt
1/2 cup granulated sugar
1-1/2 teaspoons vanilla
1/2 teaspoon almond extract

Preheat the oven to 375°F. Prepare a 10-inch tube pan by cleaning it well. Spray with no stick cooking spray.

Mix the whole wheat pastry flour (or graham flour) with the sifted cake flour and sifted confectioners' sugar. Set aside.

In a large mixing bowl, whip the egg whites with the cream of tartar and salt until the mixture is foamy. Sift the granulated sugar, 2 tablespoons at a time, over egg whites, continuing to whip on high speed until stiff peaks form. Make sure all sugar has been incorporated into the egg whites. (You can tell this by pinching a bit of the whipped egg white between your fingers. If sugar has been incorporated, you will feel no grains.) Fold in the vanilla and almond extract.

Spoon the whole wheat mixture, 1/4 at a time, over the whipped egg whites. Fold in gently until just blended.

Pour batter into the tube pan. Cut gently through the batter with a knife to remove any large bubbles. Bake for 45 minutes or until the crust is golden brown and cracks are very dry. Remove the cake from the oven and invert to cool for 1 hour. Loosen sides and bottom of cake from cake pan. Carefully remove cooled cake from pan.

Each serving:

 less than 1   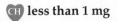 **less than 1 mg**   **less than 1**   **Cal. 138**

BROWN SUGAR SANDIES

These cookies are attractive as well as tasty. You can roll them into your favorite shape and glaze with confectioners' icing if you like.

Makes 36 cookies

no stick cooking spray
1-1/2 cups brown sugar
1/2 cup soft margarine
2 egg whites
2-1/2 cups all-purpose flour
1 teaspoon baking soda
1 teaspoon baking powder
1 teaspoon allspice
1 tablespoon cinnamon
granulated sugar for sprinkling

Preheat oven to 375°F. Spray a cookie sheet with no stick cooking spray.

With an electric mixer, cream the brown sugar with the margarine and the egg whites. Mix the flour with baking soda, baking powder, allspice, and cinnamon.

Add the dry ingredients to the brown sugar mixture a little at a time. The mixture should be very firm.

Roll out the dough on a floured board, about 1/2 inch thick. Cut into rounds or other shapes with a floured cookie cutter.

Place the rounds on a greased cookie sheet, sprinkle with sugar, and bake for 10 to 12 minutes, or until edges are lightly browned.

Each cookie:

 less than 1   **0 mg**   **less than 1**   **Cal. 76**

RUM RAISIN BARS

Here's a nutritious cookie bar.

Makes 24 bars

no stick cooking spray
1 cup raisins
2/3 cup freshly brewed, hot coffee
    (preferably a blend of French roast and chicory)
2 tablespoons rum
1/2 teaspoon cinnamon
1/2 cup light margarine
3/4 cup sugar
2 egg whites

Desserts (Clockwise, starting at upper left):

Strawberry Pie (Page 226)
Hot and Spicy Raspberry Flambé (Page 222)
Stars and Stripes Shortcake (Page 212)

1-1/2 cups flour
1/2 teaspoon baking powder
1/2 teaspoon baking soda
1/4 teaspoon salt
1/2 cup sifted confectioners' sugar
1 to 2 teaspoons cool coffee

Preheat oven to 350°F. Spray a 9×13-inch baking pan with no stick cooking spray.

Mix the raisins with the hot coffee, rum, and cinnamon. Allow the raisins about 20 minutes time to absorb the liquid.

Meanwhile, cream the margarine with the sugar and the egg whites. Mix the flour with the baking powder, baking soda, and salt. Blend the raisin mixture into the creamed mixture and the dry ingredients into all.

Pour raisin bar mixture into the prepared pan. Bake for 25 to 30 minutes until mixture is browned and firm.

Mix the confectioners' sugar with just enough coffee for easy spreading. Glaze the hot Rum Raisin Bars immediately. Allow to cool thoroughly before cutting.

Each serving:

 less than 1   **0 mg**   **less than 1**   **Cal. 95**

CHOCOLATE BANANA BROWNIES

This brownie is packed with nutrition and flavor.

Makes 16 brownies

no stick cooking spray
4 tablespoons cocoa powder
3/4 cup water
1 very ripe banana
1 cup white sugar
2 large egg whites
1 teaspoon vanilla extract
1 teaspoon baking powder
1/4 teaspoon salt
1 cup all-purpose flour
1/2 cup oat bran (for best results,
    use an oat bran that is coarsely milled)

Preheat the oven to 350°F. Spray an 8-inch round or square cake pan with no stick cooking spray.

Place the cocoa, 1/4 cup water, and the banana, into a large blender cup or into the bowl of a food processor that has been fitted with a steel

Chocolate Banana Brownies (*continued*)
blade. Blend until it is smooth. Add the sugar, egg whites, vanilla extract, baking powder, and salt and blend until the mixture is smooth. Add the flour, oat bran, and 1/2 cup water a little at a time and blend again until smooth.

Pour the chocolate mixture into the prepared pan. Bake at 350°F for 20 to 25 minutes. Wait until the brownies have cooled to cut into servings. Store brownies in the refrigerator.

Each brownie:

 1   0 mg   less than 1   **Cal. 123**

OATMEAL RAISIN DROP COOKIES

This moist cookie has old-time spicy flavor. They are soft, easy to eat, and they keep well.

Makes 36 cookies

no stick cooking spray
1 cup raisins
1-1/2 cups all-purpose flour
1 teaspoon baking soda
1/4 teaspoon salt
1 teaspoon cinnamon
1/2 teaspoon nutmeg
1/2 cup light margarine
1 cup sugar
1 egg
2/3 cup buttermilk
1 cup oatmeal
1/2 cup oat bran (for best results use a coarsely milled oat bran)
1/4 cup finely chopped walnuts

Preheat oven to 375°F. Spray baking sheets with no stick cooking spray.
Plump raisins by steaming over boiling water for 5 minutes.
Sift flour. Measure then sift with soda, salt, cinnamon, and nutmeg.
Cream margarine with sugar and egg until mixture is smooth and fluffy. Add flour mixture and buttermilk, alternately, to the egg mixture. Blend until very smooth. Add oatmeal, oat bran, raisins, and nuts. Stir to blend.

Drop heaping teaspoonfuls onto the prepared sheets. Bake for 10 to 12 minutes. Cookies will be evenly browned.

Each cookie:

 less than 1   37 mg   1   **Calories 157**

QUICK AND EASY BROWN SUGAR COOKIES

Bake these cookies in a flash. They keep beautifully and are a great way to add dietary fiber during snack time.

Makes 30 cookies

no stick cooking spray
1-1/2 cups oat bran (for best results,
   use an oat bran that is coarsely milled)
1 cup all-purpose flour
1/2 teaspoon baking soda
1/2 teaspoon salt
1/4 cup light margarine
1/4 cup vegetable oil, preferably safflower or canola
1/4 cup apple juice
1/3 cup light brown sugar, packed
2 egg whites
1 teaspoon vanilla

Preheat oven to 400°F. Spray a cookie sheet with no stick cooking spray.

Combine the oat bran and flour with the soda and salt. With an electric mixer, blend the margarine with the oil. Add the apple juice, the brown sugar, the egg whites, and the vanilla and beat well. Add the dry ingredients to wet ingredients and mix to blend well.

Drop the dough by teaspoonfuls, 2 inches apart, onto the prepared cookie sheet. Bake for 8 to 10 minutes. Cookies will be lightly browned and firm to touch. Remove carefully and cool thoroughly before storing.

Each cookie:

 less than 1   **0 mg**   **1**   **Calories 62**

HOME-STYLE ALMOND CUSTARD

This is a smooth dessert made from egg white custard. It's a good way to add calcium to your diet without extra fat.

Serves 4

no stick cooking spray
2 cups skim milk
4 egg whites
1/4 cup sugar
1 teaspoon almond extract
1/4 teaspoon ground cinnamon
2 tablespoons slivered almonds, toasted

Home-style Almond Custard (*continued*)

Preheat oven to 325°F. Spray 4 1-cup glass custard cups with no stick cooking spray. Place custard cups in a pan of very hot water.

Pour the milk into a 1-quart saucepan. Heat until milk is scalded but not boiled.

With an electric mixer or with a wire whisk, whip the eggs until frothy. Add the sugar and the almond extract, beating well. Slowly, pour in the hot milk and whisk until just blended. Pour about 3/4 cup of the custard mixture into each of the 4 glass custard cups.

Carefully place pan with custards into the oven. Bake for 35 minutes or until custard is set.

Sprinkle with the cinnamon and the slivered almonds. Allow custards to rest for 30 minutes before serving.

Each serving:

 less than 1   **2 mg**   **less than 1**   **Cal. 126**

PRALINE SOUFFLÉ

This is a light and flavorful dessert that may be mixed up to 2 hours ahead of time. Bake just before serving.

Serves 6

Praline

3/4 cup sugar
1/4 cup pecans, very finely chopped

no stick cooking spray

Soufflé

8 egg whites
1 whole egg
1-1/2 cups milk
1-1/2 cups sugar
1/3 cup cornstarch
2 teaspoons vanilla
1 tablespoon dark rum

To prepare the praline: In a small saucepan over hot heat, melt and stir the sugar until it turns a deep caramel color. Add the pecans and stir until they are well coated. Carefully, pour the mixture onto a piece of aluminum foil and let it cool. When it cools, crush praline finely with a hammer or with a food processor.

To make the soufflé: Preheat the oven to 400°F. Spray a large straight-sided 12-inch soufflé baker with no stick cooking spray. In a heavy saucepan, whisk 2 egg whites, the whole egg, the milk, 1/2 cup of the sugar, the cornstarch, and the vanilla, stirring constantly. Cook over moderate heat to make a smooth, very thick custard. Remove from heat and stir in the rum.

Beat the remaining egg whites until frothy. Continue beating until stiff peaks form, gradually adding the remaining 1/2 cup of sugar, 1 tablespoon at a time. Stir 1/3 of the egg white mixture into the custard to lighten it; then fold remaining whites into the custard.

Pour the custard into the prepared soufflé baker. Top with praline. Bake for 30 to 35 minutes or until soufflé is puffed and lightly browned on top. Serve immediately.

Each serving:

 less than 1   **47 mg**   **0**   **Calories 296**

CAJUN-STYLE HONEY OAT BREAD PUDDING

Full of low-fat protein and calcium, bread pudding is a satisfying dessert and a great way to use up stale bread.

> *Serves 8*
>
> no stick cooking spray
> 1/2 loaf Honey Wheat Bread (page 95)
>   or 5 cups stale French or Italian bread cubes
> 6 egg whites
> 1-1/2 cups sugar
> 1 teaspoon vanilla extract
> 1 tablespoon allspice
> 1/4 cup margarine, melted
> 2 cups skim milk
> 1/2 cup raisins
> Chantilly Cream (page 227)

Preheat the oven to 350°F. Spray a 9×5-inch loaf pan with no stick cooking spray.

Cut the honey bread into cubes. Place in the loaf pan.

Beat the egg whites until frothy. Add the sugar, vanilla extract, allspice, margarine, milk, and raisins. Pour over the bread cubes, stirring to mix eggs evenly with bread cubes. Allow moisture to infuse and soak bread for 45 minutes.

Bake for 40 to 45 minutes until the loaf is browned and firm. Serve warm with Chantilly Cream.

Each serving:

 less than 1   **1 mg**   **less than 1**   **Cal. 271**

FRESH APPLESAUCE

This applesauce is ready in a flash. The skins are left on for optimum nutrition and soluble fiber content. You may adjust the sweetener to your taste and to the flavor of available apples.

Serves 4

4 large apples, quartered (use apples with red skins
    such as Jonathan or Rome)
3/4 cup water
1/3 cup granulated sugar
1 teaspoon cinnamon

Place apples, water, and sugar into a blender cup or food processor. Blend until smooth. Pour into a bowl, sprinkle with cinnamon, and serve immediately.

Each serving:

 less than 1   0 mg   1   **Calories 142**

OLD-FASHIONED BAKED APPLES

Here's an old-fashioned recipe that is made modern by using the micro-wave. We've also included directions for cooking in a conventional oven.

Serves 6

6 large baking apples, such as Rome, Jonathan, or Granny Smith
no stick cooking spray
3/4 cup raisins
1/2 cup brown sugar, packed
1 tablespoon light margarine
1-1/2 teaspoons ground cinnamon
1/4 teaspoon ground nutmeg
1/4 teaspoon ground cloves
1/2 cup water
1 cup skim milk

Core the apples with a wide core. Make a collar around each apple by cutting a strip of peel from around the top of the apple.

Spray a large microwave dish with no stick cooking spray. Place the apples in the dish. Fill the apples with raisins.

In a 1-quart microwave bowl, put the brown sugar, margarine, cinnamon, nutmeg, and cloves with 1/2 cup water. Cover and microwave on high for 1 minute. Stir. Cook another 30 seconds. The sugar should be melted, and the mixture should be very hot.

Carefully, pour the hot sugar mixture over and around the apples. Cover the apples with waxed paper and microwave on high for 10 to 12 minutes, turning every 3 minutes. Baste throughout so that fallen spices can penetrate apples. Apples will be hot and very tender.

Remove the apples to individual serving dishes. Serve with milk or Creamy Dressing, page 225.

In a Conventional Oven

Preheat oven to 350°F. Spray a large ovenproof baking dish with no stick cooking spray. Prepare apples as directed above. To prepare brown sugar sauce, place the sugar, margarine, cinnamon, nutmeg, and cloves in a small saucepan with water. Heat until mixture boils and sugar is dissolved. Pour over apples, cover, and bake for 45 minutes until apples are tender.

Each serving (without dressing):

 less than 1   **54 mg**   **1**   **Calories 232**

BANANAS FOSTER

We like to serve this dessert in the old-style, wide-mouthed champagne glasses. And it's so easy, you can serve it practically anytime.

Serves 4

1 pint vanilla ice milk
4 small bananas, firm but ripe
1 tablespoon light margarine
2 tablespoons light brown sugar, firmly packed
1/4 teaspoon cinnamon
1 tablespoon banana (or other) liqueur
1/2 cup dark rum

In advance, place 1 scoop ice milk into each of 4 wide-mouthed champagne or other goblets. Freeze until serving time.

Peel and slice the bananas. Melt the margarine in a saucepan or hot chafing dish and sauté bananas until golden. Sprinkle with the brown sugar and the cinnamon. When ready to serve, add the liqueur and rum to the banana mixture. Heat until liqueurs are just warm. Light carefully. When aflame, ladle over the frozen ice milk.

Each serving:

 2   **6 mg**   **1**   **Calories 351**

HOT AND SPICY RASPBERRY FLAMBÉ

Here's the perfect combination—raspberries and Frangelica liqueur. And, when you heat the liquor and ignite it, you burn off all the alcohol, leaving flavor without calories.

Serves 4

1 pint vanilla ice milk or frozen yogurt
1/2 cup sugar
1 tablespoon arrowroot
1/4 teaspoon cinnamon
1/4 teaspoon nutmeg
1/4 teaspoon allspice
1/2 cup water
juice of 1 lemon (2 tablespoons)
2 cups raspberries (fresh or dry pack frozen)
1/2 cup Frangelica liqueur

Scoop ice milk or frozen yogurt into 4 heatproof sherbet glasses. Freeze.

Combine the sugar with the arrowroot, cinnamon, nutmeg, and all-spice in a 1-quart saucepan. Whisk in water and lemon juice. Heat until mixture comes to a boil. Continue to cook until sugar is dissolved and sauce thickens. Remove hot sauce from heat.

Rinse and drain raspberries. Stir into hot sauce until raspberries are just warmed.

When ready to serve, pour the Frangelica into a small saucepan and heat until liquor is just warm. Add to raspberry sauce, ignite, and ladle over ice milk or frozen yogurt.

Each serving:

 1   6 mg   less than 1   Calories 298

TROPICAL FRUIT FLAMBÉ

Quick and easy to make, this sauce is best when served in dessert glasses and flamed. It also makes an elegant dessert when spooned over ice milk.

Serves 6

1 can (8 ounces) crushed pineapple, drained and juice reserved
1 tablespoon brown sugar
2 teaspoons arrowroot
2 tablespoons water
3 large, firm bananas
1 tablespoon lemon juice

2 tablespoons chopped pecans
2 tablespoons Cointreau (or other fruit liqueur)
4 tablespoons dark rum

Combine the pineapple juice with the brown sugar in a 1-quart sauce-pan. Cover and heat to a boil. Cook until sugar dissolves. The juice should be boiling.

Combine the arrowroot with the water. Whisk this into the pineapple juice and continue cooking and whisking until sauce is thick and smooth.

Peel and slice the bananas. Add bananas, pineapple, and pecans to pineapple juice mixture, cover, and cook just to heat through.

Pour the Cointreau and dark rum into a small pan and heat until liquors are just warm.

Place hot fruit into decorative heatproof glasses or goblets. Carefully ignite the liquors and ladle onto the fruit.

Each serving:

 less than 1   **0 mg**   **1**   **Calories 144**

BLUEBERRY COBBLER

Blueberries work best for this cobbler. And with blueberries in season so often, Blueberry Cobbler will become a family favorite.

Serves 6

no stick cooking spray
1 quart fresh blueberries, washed and drained
2/3 cup granulated sugar
1 tablespoon lemon juice
1 cup oat bran (for best results,
    use an oat bran that is coarsely milled)
1 teaspoon baking powder
1/4 teaspoon salt
1/4 teaspoon allspice
1 teaspoon cinnamon
1/4 cup vegetable oil
1/2 teaspoon vanilla
1/2 cup low-fat milk
1 tablespoon sugar for sprinkling

Preheat the oven to 400°F. Spray a 2-quart baking dish with no stick cooking spray. Spread the blueberries in the baking dish. Sprinkle them evenly with 1/3 cup of sugar and the lemon juice.

Mix the oat bran with the baking powder, salt, allspice, and cinnamon.

Blueberry Cobbler (*continued*)

Blend the oil with the remaining 1/3 cup sugar and vanilla. Add the oat bran mixture to the oil mixture alternately with the milk. Beat until smooth. Spread over the berries. Sprinkle the top with 1 tablespoon sugar.

Bake for 40 minutes until topping is well browned and is firm in the center. Serve warm.

Each serving:

 1   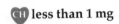 less than 1 mg   1   **Calories 279**

ALL-AMERICAN PEACH PIE

Pie is one of America's favorite desserts. If you use an oat bran pastry shell, you'll enjoy great taste and good nutrition. This pastry recipe can be used for any pie. For this particular pie, leave the skins on the peaches for even more fiber.

Serves 8

Pastry for 8-Inch Double Crust Pie

1-1/4 cups oat bran (for best results,
     use an oat bran that is coarsely milled)
1 cup all-purpose flour
2 teaspoons baking powder
1/2 teaspoon salt
1/3 cup vegetable oil
1/3 to 1/2 cup skim milk

For Peach Filling

5 cups pitted, sliced fresh peaches with skins
     (or a 20-ounce package of frozen peaches, not in syrup)
2 teaspoons lemon juice
3/4 cup granulated sugar
1/4 cup oat bran (for best results,
     use an oat bran that is coarsely milled)
1/2 teaspoon cinnamon
2 tablespoons margarine

In mixing bowl, combine the oat bran, all-purpose flour, baking powder, and salt. Mix thoroughly. Using a pastry blender, cut in the oil until the mixture has a coarse texture. Sprinkle the milk over the dough and blend until the mixture holds together well. Divide the pastry into 2 equal-sized balls and allow it to rest for 5 minutes.

Wet the surface of a counter and place a piece of plastic wrap on the wet counter. Sprinkle the plastic wrap with all-purpose flour. Place 1 ball of pastry on the plastic wrap and sprinkle the pastry with more all-purpose flour. Top the sprinkled pastry with a second piece of plastic wrap. Roll with rolling pin until the pastry is slightly larger than an 8-inch pie pan. Remove one side of the plastic wrap and fit pastry into pie pan, pastry side down. Pat pastry into place and remove second piece of plastic wrap. Repeat rolling procedure for other ball of pastry dough.

Preheat the oven to 425°F. In a large bowl, combine the peaches with the lemon juice. Add the sugar, oat bran, and cinnamon. Toss lightly to mix. Turn into the prepared pie pan. Dot the peach mixture with margarine. Remove the plastic wrap from the second piece of pastry dough and place it, pastry side down, onto the peaches. Remove second piece of plastic wrap. Flute edges of the pie and cut slits into top crust for steam to escape.

Place the pie on a large pan to catch any drips from baking. Bake the pie for 40 minutes or until the juice begins to bubble through the slits in the crust.

Each serving:

 2   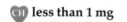 less than 1 mg   1   **Calories 331**

SUMMER FRUIT WITH CREAMY DRESSING
Good Housekeeping

To make the dressing for this dessert, we took low-fat cottage cheese, put it in the blender, and ended up with such a lovely topping we promise you won't miss the cream.

Serves 6

2 medium-sized peaches
2 kiwi fruit
1 cup strawberries
1 cup blueberries

Creamy Dressing

1 cup low-fat cottage cheese
1/2 cup orange juice
1 tablespoon lemon juice
1 tablespoon light brown sugar
1/8 teaspoon salt

Cut the unpeeled peaches into wedges. Peel and slice the kiwi fruit. Hull the strawberries; cut into halves. In a medium-sized bowl, combine the blueberries with the cut-up fruit.

Summer Fruit with Cream Dressing (*continued*)

To make the Creamy Dressing, blend in a blender at high speed the low-fat cottage cheese, the orange juice, lemon juice, light brown sugar, and the salt until smooth.

To serve, spoon the fruit into dessert dishes and top with the Creamy Dressing.

Each serving:

 0   2 mg   1   **Calories 100**

STRAWBERRY PIE

This is a very attractive dessert and with only 5 ingredients, it's simple to make.

Serves 8

1 quart strawberries
3/4 cup sugar
1 envelope unflavored gelatin
1/4 cup water
1 baked, 9-inch Pie Crust (1/2 of recipe, page 224, or prepared
   shell)

Wash and hull the strawberries. Remove 1 cup of the smallest berries for purée. Purée these berries in a food processor or blender until smooth.

In a saucepan, bring the strawberry purée and sugar to a boil. Boil for 3 minutes until all sugar is dissolved. Remove from heat.

Soften the gelatin in the water. When the gelatin is softened, combine it with the hot strawberry purée. Beat with electric mixer or with a whisk until the gelatin and strawberry purée mixture is smooth and thick.

Place the whole strawberries in the baked pie shell, displaying their most attractive sides and turning down tops where caps were removed. Carefully, pour hot purée over strawberries, coating all fresh berries.

Refrigerate for 4 hours before serving.

Each serving (on oat bran crust):

 less than 1   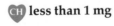 less than 1 mg   1   **Calories 188**

CHANTILLY CREAM

This is delicious with cakes, pies, puddings, or by itself.

Serves 8

1/4 cup brandy
1/2 vanilla bean
1 cup evaporated skim milk
2 cups cold water
1 teaspoon Grand Marnier
1/2 cup sugar
1/4 cup yogurt

Heat the brandy to almost a boil. Soak the vanilla bean in the brandy for 30 minutes. Remove vanilla bean, split, and scoop out seeds.

With the electric mixer, beat together 1 teaspoon of the brandy with the vanilla seeds, the milk, water, and the Grand Marnier. When the mixture is frothy, sprinkle the sugar over the surface and continue to beat. Blend in the yogurt. The Chantilly Cream will be about the consistency of whipping cream. Store in a closed container in the refrigerator for up to 1 week.

Use Chantilly Cream over mousses, cakes, and pies, or serve in 1/2-cup stemmed dessert glasses.

Each serving:

 2   15 mg   0   **Calories 106**

APPENDIX A

UNDERSTANDING CHOLESTEROL

Cholesterol is a waxy, odorless substance found only in foods of animal origin, including beef, poultry, fish, cheese, eggs, and dairy products. The human body—specifically, the liver—also manufactures cholesterol.

The body actually requires cholesterol to maintain good health. It is needed to build cell membranes throughout the body and to manufacture essential substances such as vitamin D and hormones. But the body produces all the cholesterol it needs for these purposes, and when excess cholesterol is consumed in the diet, it can cause problems, including the formation of plaques that obstruct the flow of blood through the coronary arteries. A number of studies have shown that individuals with high blood cholesterol levels have a much higher incidence of heart attacks than those with lower levels.

How high is too high? The risk of developing heart disease begins to rise after the blood cholesterol level exceeds 140 to 150, but initially this increase in risk is slight. The higher the cholesterol rises, the more rapidly the cardiovascular risk increases. A cholesterol level of 200 raises the heart-attack risk about 50 percent over a level of 150. But the next 50 points have a much more dramatic effect: A cholesterol level of 250 increases the heart attack risk by about three times over the 150 figure.

Research shows that by lowering your blood cholesterol level, you can reverse the risk and slow the buildup of plaques in your arteries—perhaps even reverse that process. Most people are able to lower their blood cholesterol to desirable levels with dietary changes alone.

The National Cholesterol Education Program has established the following guidelines for adults 20 years of age and over:

TOTAL BLOOD CHOLESTEROL

Less than 200 mg/dl = desirable blood cholesterol
200–239 mg/dl = borderline-high blood cholesterol
240 mg/dl or more = high blood cholesterol
Source: National Cholesterol Education Program

APPENDIX B

THE SF SYSTEM

*I*n the companion book to this title, *Count Out Cholesterol*, the American Medical Association introduced the "SF system"—a program for keeping track of your saturated fat (SF1) and soluble fiber (SF2) intake. For complete details of how this system works, refer to a copy of *Count Out Cholesterol*, available in bookstores or libraries.

So you can get started with the SF system immediately, however, here are the basic steps needed to find your personal SF1 and SF2 numbers.

As the first step toward calculating your own SF1 number, turn to the charts on pages 232 (men) and 233 (women). With these charts, you can determine the desirable weight for your sex and height. This is the weight you *should* be for your height and bone structure, not necessarily what you weigh right now.

Next, turn to the charts on pages 234 (men) and 235 (women). Using your "desirable weight" figure, follow the instructions at the bottom of the chart to ascertain your personal SF1 number. This number corresponds to the maximum number of grams of saturated fat you should eat per day. Each recipe in this book has been assigned an SF1 value that approximates the grams of fat in each serving size of that dish. During the course of the day, the *cumulative* SF1 value of all your meals and snacks should not exceed your SF1 number. If you can keep your intake of saturated fat at or below that level, your blood cholesterol measurement should begin to decline.

You also need to find your SF2 number—a figure that corresponds to the amount of soluble fiber you should eat each day. To do this, turn to pages 236 (men) and 236 (women), and use the same "desirable weight" and "activity level" rankings to determine your personal SF2 number, which corresponds to the number of grams of soluble fiber you should eat each day. Each recipe in this book has an assigned SF2 value that approximates the grams of soluble fiber in each serving size of that dish.

Now, what about dietary cholesterol? In general, you need to keep your cholesterol intake under 300 milligrams per day. If you're careful about monitoring your saturated fat consumption, your cholesterol intake will tend to take care of itself, since most foods high in saturated fat are also rich in dietary cholesterol.

When using the SF system, you don't need to limit yourself to only the recipes in this book. To calculate the SF1 and SF2 values of any dish, refer to the numerous charts in *Count Out Cholesterol*. Using your personal SF1 and SF2 numbers as a guide, you should see some rapid improvements in your blood cholesterol level.

DESIRABLE WEIGHTS[1] FOR MEN
(AGES 25 AND OVER)

Height[2]				
Feet	*Inches*	*Small Frame*	*Medium Frame*	*Large Frame*
5	2	112–120	118–129	126–141
5	3	115–123	121–133	129–144
5	4	118–126	124–136	132–148
5	5	121–129	127–139	135–152
5	6	124–133	130–143	138–156
5	7	128–137	134–147	142–161
5	8	132–141	138–152	147–166
5	9	136–145	142–156	151–170
5	10	140–150	146–160	155–174
5	11	144–154	150–165	159–179
6	0	148–158	154–170	164–184
6	1	152–162	158–175	168–189
6	2	156–167	162–180	173–194
6	3	160–171	167–185	178–199
6	4	164–175	172–190	182–204

To determine your ideal weight, find your height in the left-hand column. Then move across the page to the body frame that best describes you. For the purposes of this table, your body frame is "small" if you can wrap your left thumb and middle finger around your right wrist and have these two digits overlap. If the thumb and finger barely touch, then you have a "medium" body frame. If they don't touch at all, you have a "large" build.

[1]Weight in pounds according to frame (indoor clothing).
[2]With 1-inch heel shoes on.

SOURCE: *Metropolitan Life Insurance Company Actuarial Tables, 1959.*

DESIRABLE WEIGHTS[1] FOR WOMEN
(AGES 25 AND OVER)

| Height[2] | | | | |
Feet	Inches	Small Frame	Medium Frame	Large Frame
4	10	92–98	96–107	104–119
4	11	94–101	98–110	106–122
5	0	96–104	101–113	109–125
5	1	99–107	104–116	112–128
5	2	102–110	107–119	115–131
5	3	105–113	110–122	118–134
5	4	108–116	113–126	121–138
5	5	111–119	116–130	125–142
5	6	114–123	120–135	129–146
5	7	118–127	124–139	133–150
5	8	122–131	128–143	137–154
5	9	126–135	132–147	141–158
5	10	130–140	136–151	145–163
5	11	134–144	140–155	149–168
6	0	138–148	144–159	153–173

To determine your ideal weight, find your height in the left-hand column. Then move across the page to the body frame that best describes you. For the purposes of this table, your body frame is ''small'' if you can wrap your left thumb and middle finger around your right wrist and have these two digits overlap. If the thumb and finger barely touch, then you have a ''medium'' body frame. If they don't touch at all, you have a ''large'' build.

[1]Weight in pounds according to frame (indoor clothing).
[2]With 2-inch heel shoes on.

SOURCE: *Metropolitan Life Insurance Company Actuarial Tables, 1959.*

PERSONAL SF1 NUMBERS: MEN

Desirable Weight	Activity Level		
	Inactive	Moderately Active	Very Active
90	14	15	16
100	16	17	18
110	17	18	20
120	19	20	21
130	20	22	23
140	22	23	25
150	23	25	27
160	25	27	28
170	26	28	30
180	28	30	32
190	30	32	34
200	31	33	36
210	33	35	37
220	34	37	39

Find the figure in the left-hand column that most closely corresponds to the desirable weight you identified in Step 1. Then move across the chart to the vertical column that corresponds to your physical activity level. At the point where your ideal weight and activity level intersect, you will find *your* personal SF1 number. This number represents the maximum amount of saturated fat (in grams) that you should consume each day.

PERSONAL SF1 NUMBERS: WOMEN

Desirable Weight	Activity Level		
	Inactive	Moderately Active	Very Active
90	13	14	14
100	14	15	16
110	15	17	18
120	17	18	19
130	18	20	21
140	20	21	22
150	21	23	24
160	22	24	26
170	24	26	27
180	25	27	29
190	27	29	30
200	28	30	32
210	29	32	34
220	31	33	35

Find the figure in the left-hand column that most closely corresponds to the desirable weight you identified in Step 1. Then move across the chart to the vertical column that corresponds to your physical activity level. At the point where your ideal weight and activity level intersect, you will find *your* personal SF1 number. This number represents the maximum amount of saturated fat (in grams) that you should consume each day.

PERSONAL SF2 NUMBERS: MEN

Desirable Weight	Activity Level		
	Inactive	Moderately Active	Very Active
90	9	9	10
100	9	10	11
110	10	11	12
120	11	12	13
130	12	13	14
140	13	14	15
150	14	15	16
160	15	16	17
170	16	17	18
180	17	18	18
190	18	18	18
200	18	18	18
210	18	18	18
220	18	18	18

For instructions, see the next chart (below).

Note: A maximum of 18 grams of soluble fiber per day is recommended

PERSONAL SF2 NUMBERS: WOMEN

Desirable Weight	Activity Level		
	Inactive	Moderately Active	Very Active
90	8	8	9
100	9	9	10
110	9	10	11
120	10	11	12
130	11	12	13
140	12	13	14
150	13	14	15
160	14	15	16
170	14	15	17
180	15	16	17
190	16	17	18
200	17	18	18
210	18	18	18
220	18	18	18

Locate your ideal weight on the chart, and then your activity level. At the point where these columns intersect, you will find a number that represents the amount of soluble fiber (in grams) that you should eat each day. This is your SF2 number.

Note: A maximum of 18 grams of soluble fiber per day is recommended

INDEX

A NOTE ON THE TYPE

The text of this book was composed in a film version of Palatino, a type face designed by the noted German typographer Hermann Zapf. Named after Giovanbattista Palatino, a writing master of Renaissance Italy, Palatino was the first of Zapf's type faces to be introduced in America. The first designs for the face were made in 1948, and the fonts for the complete face were issued between 1950 and 1952. Like all Zapf-designed type faces, Palatino is beautifully balanced and exceedingly readable.

Composed by G&H SOHO
New York, New York

Printed and bound by R.R. Donnelley & Sons
Crawfordsville, Indiana

Color Separations by C.C.S.
Clearwater, Florida

Color inserts printed by Coral Graphics, Inc.
Plain View, N.Y.